About the

Born in the East End of London in 1943, Dick Kirby joined the Metropolitan Police in 1967. He saw the toughest slice of police-work, spending over half of his service with the Serious Crime Squad and the Flying Squad and was described by a Judge at the Old Bailey as being, 'one of the best detectives at Scotland Yard'. Kirby was commended for catching criminals by Commissioners, Directors of Public Prosecutions, Trial Judges and Magistrates on forty occasions for courage, determination and detective ability.

Dick Kirby is the author of *Rough Justice – Memoirs of a Flying Squad Detective* (Merlin Unwin Books, 2001), *The Real Sweeney* (Constable & Robinson, 2005) and *You're Nicked!* (Constable & Robinson, 2007). He has contributed to six other books, as well as magazines and national newspapers; he reviews books, and has appeared on radio and television. He is an international member of The American Police Writers, a member of The Crime Writers' Association and a former member of The Special Forces Club.

From his village home in Suffolk, Dick Kirby now lives life at a somewhat more leisurely pace with his family, writing, corresponding with friends all over the world, listening to music and tending his garden.

VILLAINS

Wild stories of blaggers and hijackers,
dodgy deals and fit-ups,
conmen and crooked cops

Dick Kirby

ROBINSON
London

**MORAY COUNCIL
LIBRARIES &
INFO.SERVICES**

20 24 67 02

Askews	
364.109224	

Constable & Robinson
3 The Lanchesters
162 Fulham Palace Road
London W6 9ER
www.constablerobinson.com

First published in the UK by Robinson,
an imprint of Constable & Robinson Ltd, 2008

Copyright © Dick Kirby, 2008

All rights reserved. This book is sold subject to the condition
that it shall not, by way of trade or otherwise, be lent, re-sold,
hired out or otherwise circulated in any form of binding or cover
other than that in which it is published and without a
similar condition including this condition being imposed
on the subsequent purchaser.

The right of Dick Kirby to be identified as the author
of this work has been asserted by him in accordance
with the Copyright, Designs and Patents Act, 1988

A copy of the British Library Cataloguing in
Publication Data is available from the British Library

ISBN: 978-1-84529-569-1

1 3 5 7 9 10 8 6 4 2

To Ann
All the way to the moon and back

Contents

Contents

Introduction

Despite the title of this book, not all of the stories contained in it originate from villains. Of course, many of them do, but the sources of other stories, where the central characters are villains and villainesses, are former police officers and the ordinary people of London. Of the latter, those who were permitted to peek inside the door of criminality for once in their lives treasured the moment and passed their experiences on to me.

Where it has been possible for me to authenticate these stories I have done so but quite often this proved to be impossible; furthermore, my sources were sometimes unaware of the identities of some of the characters who formed part of these tales and therefore I have provided them with aliases.

The vast majority of the persons named in this book have had their names and descriptions changed. In addition, the dates and the locations – sometimes even the country – of these occurrences have also been altered. One reason for this is to save the characters (venal or not) concerned, and their families, embarrassment. Another is that if the correct names and locations had been used, the central villainous characters could, without too much bother at all, correctly identify the source of the story. And in many cases, the principal characters are implicated in crimes for which they were acquitted or never even charged and to disclose their real names might result in a legal mine-field. Some of the stories were told on the understanding that they were not to be retold until some of the central characters were dead and, as far as I am aware, this has been adhered to.

Neither the villains nor many of the police officers who had dealings with them emerge with much credit but there is good and bad in all of us and, sometimes, despite the wickedness of some of the most iniquitous criminals ever to grace the lists at the Old Bailey, a glimpse of selflessness shines through. A case in question is where Ronnie Kray displayed compassion to one less fortunate than himself. But Ronnie purists need not worry; he returns in a separate story at his demonic worst.

These tales are separated from each other by many years but there is one common factor: in those days people were more inclined to speak to each other, even police and criminals. Extraordinary exchanges took place, and some have found their way into this book.

In consequence, these pages are littered with accounts of contract hit-men, gunmen, murderers and strong-arm men. There are tales of lorry thefts and those who received their contents. Armed blaggers, screwsmen, fraudsmen and forgers mix easily with prostitutes, arsonists and car thieves. There are stories of the unscrupulous people who imported drugs and those who dealt them to the unfortunates who ingested and injected them. Those who were caught for their misdeeds and, deciding that prison life was not for them, went 'over the wall' have their stories told. You will be introduced to the art of the van dragger and the peterman, as well as those who were 'at the corner', 'at the Creep' or 'at the jump-up'. And snouts, who infiltrated the ranks of all of the foregoing and stuck them up for all differing reasons and rewards, feature everywhere.

Savour the moment; such social intercourse between detectives and villains does not happen now, nor do I believe it will ever happen again.

Dick Kirby

Wheeling and Dealing

Almeria is situated more or less on the most south eastern tip of Spain. Up the coast to the north-east is Barcelona and the coast road in the opposite direction leads into Malaga. Around the town of Almeria are dotted small villages and a good many farms. One such farm is off the beaten track. Once it was smart and quite prosperous, with a healthy olive crop, but now the farm is deserted. It has a look of general decay about it, the paint is peeling and a shutter hangs on just one hinge; it is only a matter of time before a strong gust of wind sweeps in from the Golfo de Almeria and blows it right off. The olive trees are no longer regularly pruned or tended and the whole farm is overgrown with weeds and has a flyblown look about it. One day, a property developer will apply to build on the site and, given the cavalier approach that the Spanish have regarding an outsider's property, I should think it will take all of five minutes before an agreement is reached and the bull-dozers commence levelling the site.

It will make little difference; the owner is never coming back.

This story begins over twenty years ago, although it was ten years before that that Jimmy Munson had acquired the farm. During those ten years, Munson had carefully tended the olive groves. He had hired local help to gather in the crop and later the European Union paid out handsome subsidies to the owners of olive groves.

It gave Munson a general air of respectability. He was in his late fifties, a short, slim, dapper man with a ready smile which some people thought was genuine but others found less convincing. He had been born in Kentish Town, and during his youth he had collected a few minor convictions for general dishonesty, although none was serious enough to merit imprisonment. He had acquired a good, working knowledge of the Spanish language and when he walked into the local village, to take a drink at one of the bars or to dine in the restaurant, the locals would smile and nod at him and some would call out, *'¡Hola, Señor Jim!'*

But despite this façade of respectability, Munson acquired his money by fraud, thievery and trickery. He could quite easily turn his hand to any dishonest enterprise. His knowledge of the British criminals who had fled to the warmer climes of the Costa del Sol – they were referred to as 'the chaps on holiday' – was extensive and he was well acquainted with the more 'white collar' English criminals. These were the long firm fraudsters, the tax and VAT evaders, the distinctly dodgy timeshare merchants who tended to live in the more respectable area of Calpe, just north-east of Alicante.

The former robbers who lived on the Costa del Sol had a great deal of money from their criminal enterprises. When this was laundered they needed advice on how to invest it. Munson brokered introductions to the residents of Calpe to do just that, for which he was paid a decent commission. Over the years, he had built up credibility with the ex-pat criminal fraternity as a wheeler and a dealer. If something needed to be sorted out back in the old country, where it would have been distinctly inadvisable for many of his Costa del Sol clientele to venture, Munson would carry out the task, quickly and efficiently. In addition, errands needed to be carried out in Europe and more distant parts of the world and this too Munson willingly agreed to do. So Munson made a good living from the criminal fraternity and often he would invest his own money in one of their enterprises when he felt it would provide a good return. He was seldom let down. With his ready smile, his steady stream of patter, Munson was well-liked. It was therefore just as well that none of his clientele were aware of a couple of his less desirable traits, one of which was that he was a grass – a high-ranking one, too.

It was Munson's first action, upon disembarking from his flight at Heathrow to telephone his handler, Detective Inspector George Chilton of No. 9 Regional Crime Squad to arrange an urgent meeting. Chilton had handled Munson since he was a detective sergeant and had received some top quality information from him. The successes which arose from the information were in no small measure responsible for his promotion. Now, Chilton had his sights fixed on the rank of detective chief inspector and promotion boards for this rank were only a couple of months away. Therefore, another outstanding success, just before he appeared at the board, would almost certainly prove a clincher to his advancement. Greed, for money, social standing and crumpet, can make many men, including police officers, blind to many aspects of a delicate situation, when they should be alert to the slightest hint of duplicity.

Munson was his normal, effusive self as he and Chilton shook hands in the bar on the twenty-eighth floor of the Park Lane Hilton and, after pleasantries were exchanged, he got straight down to business. 'Interested in an importation of about three tons of cannabis, George?' he asked, casually, noticing the gleam in Chilton's eyes.

The information that Munson had on offer was that Dave

Baxter, a businessman who had owned a small chain of hotels in England and had sold up, at a vast profit, and gone to live in Spain in the 1970s, was financing a massive importation of cannabis resin into the United Kingdom. It was Baxter's intention to fly to England with his wife, hire a car and to visit addresses all over the London area to finalize the deal and also – and this was most important – to go to Brentford Car Auctions to purchase a large, four-wheel drive vehicle which would figure prominently in the importation. The purchase would be made in cash, so that ownership would not be attributed to him, and the vehicle would be driven across Europe back home to Spain.

The following day, Chilton checked Dave Baxter's details on the C11 computer; it revealed that he was 'flagged' to Her Majesty's Customs and Excise. Since HMC&E had declared an interest in Baxter, Chilton arranged a meeting with them, when it was discovered that they, too, had received almost identical information from one of their informants.

This confirmation was sufficient to form a joint operation between the Regional Crime Squad and Customs and two days later, when Baxter and his wife flew into Gatwick (just when Munson said they would), the RCS surveillance team was in place to follow them all over London for the next four days. All of the addresses that they visited were logged and, on the fourth day, Mr and Mrs Baxter were followed to Brentford Car Auctions where a large and impressive four-wheel drive was purchased by Baxter, in cash. Mrs Baxter, who was a pneumatically-built, bleached blond Yugoslavian named Luba, was especially delighted with the purchase. She clapped her hands, bounced up and down and enthusiastically kissed her husband, who was several years her senior, on the cheek. All of this was noted and photographed and most of the surveillance team came to the conclusion that not only was Mrs

Baxter deeply involved in the whole importation business, she was probably the brains behind it.

The Baxters drove off, her in the four-wheel drive, him in the hire car, back to the local office for the hire car to be handed back and then to Dover, where the four-wheel drive was loaded on to the ferry. As the ferry sailed on the evening tide for warmer climes and the surveillance team made its way back to London, Chilton decided that things were looking definitely up.

The following day, Munson had another meeting with his handler. 'How'd everything go, George?' he asked.

'Right as ninepence,' grinned Chilton. 'All we need to know is when matters are going to get underway in Spain.'

Munson flashed his reassuring smile. 'Leave that to me, George. However, I've laid out quite a lot of my own dough on this job and I really would appreciate a few readies.' Chilton frowned. It was highly unusual for an informant to be paid prior to arrests being made. Munson noted the hesitation. 'That is, if you want me to follow it through.'

Chilton nodded. Everything was falling into place, Munson had been an impressive enough snout in the past and there was that forthcoming DCI's board to consider. This job *must* be followed through to its conclusion. Actually, there was a precedent for informants to be given an ex-gratia payment in circumstances such as this, due to a report which had been submitted to the commissioner of the Metropolitan Police forty years previously.

At the end of World War Two, England was in a shocking state. It had been bombed out (in London alone, 116,000 houses had been destroyed, with well over twice that number needing major repairs), and almost 30,000 Londoners had perished in the air-raids. The Black Market was booming, since just about every saleable commodity required coupons in order to obtain their purchase and the country was practically bankrupt. Recruiting for the Metropolitan Police recommenced in January 1946 but the force was still 4,000 men under strength. Indictable offences rocketed to an all-time high of 128,954 and it was clear that something pretty dramatic would have to be done in order to combat the spiralling crimes of coupon counterfeiting, warehousebreakings and lorry hijackings. Something was.

Percy Worth MBE, the Chief Constable of the CID had come up with the revolutionary idea of striking off four officers from their routine duties to get them to infiltrate the underworld with their informants. It was phenomenally successful. In the three years and nine months of its existence, the Ghost Squad, as it was known, was responsible for 789 arrests, the solving of 1,506 cases and the recovery of goods, totalling £253,896.

In his initial report to the commissioner, Worth wrote: 'We should encourage the securing of reliable information and be prepared to pay – win or lose. This of course has its dangers and is not one to be encouraged generally. Each case must be judged on its merits, but the one I have in mind is where the informant is reliable, his information valuable, and his circumstances are such as to merit financial support.'

Well, it appeared that Chilton felt that Munson was well qualified on all counts. In order to facilitate his travelling to and from Spain and to provide a reasonable standard of living whilst he was temporarily in the United Kingdom, when it was deemed necessary, Munson suddenly discovered that he was richer by several thousand pounds.

However, if the thought of a Scotland Yard nark running around with a couple of grand in his pocket causes you as much disquiet as it does me, Chilton decided to use a safeguard and this, too, stemmed from the Ghost Squad. The divisional detective inspector in charge of the Ghost Squad was one John

Richard Capstick and his nickname, with some justification, was 'Charley Artful'. Instead of infiltrating a gang with one informant, Capstick used two. He believed that each would encourage the other to bring about satisfactory results and when the gang was eventually arrested (and the two informants would naturally escape) Capstick would dissolve the partnership and introduce the two men to other partners, to infiltrate gangs in other parts of London.

So now, Chilton introduced Munson to Vince Young; the reason, he told Munson, was that he (Munson) was such a valuable commodity that he wanted nothing to happen to him. Of course, in addition Chilton wanted Young to report back to him about any other irons which Munson might have in any number of other fires. Munson objected but Chilton insisted; it was either that or he didn't get the money so, with bad grace, Munson accepted Young as his minder.

Initially, he did think that Chilton had planted him with an undercover detective but, at five foot six, Young would never have met the five foot eight minimum height requirement, demanded then by the Metropolitan Police. And apart from that, on their first night out, Munson asked Young if he'd care to snort a line of coke. 'Sure, why not?' replied Young and did just that, thereby establishing his bona fides. After that, Munson and his diminutive, broad-shouldered colleague (who did have a fair amount of form) got on well. Young drove him all over London in a hired, top of the range Jaguar and Munson kept meets with some exceptionally serious villains in pubs, clubs, motorway cafes, plush hotel suites and, on one occasion (at the other party's insistence), in a church. Initially, there might be some suspicion upon meeting but Munson's breezy charm, together with knowledgeable references to 'Ronnie', 'Cliff' and 'Fred', accompanied with personal stories concerning those characters, plus their wives and girlfriends quickly ensured acceptance for both Munson and Young. Deals were done, messages were passed on and accepted for onward transmission.

Two weeks went by, with Munson contacting Chilton at agreed, regular intervals. 'Had a bit of info, George,' said Munson. 'There's a yacht named *Baby Blue Eyes III* that I think has been nicked. Can you check it out for me? Because if that's the case, I know where it is.'

Chilton did, and discovered that such a yacht, worth £100,000, had been purchased by means of obtaining a marine mortgage from someone who had tendered some very dodgy particulars. The owner had sailed it to Spain where it had been re-registered and where it was now quite happily bobbing up and down in the Marbella harbour of Puerto Banús. Munson had obtained the information after overhearing a very pissy conversation between two south London villains in a pub off the Walworth Road.

Munson demanded a meeting with the mortgage company and since such a meet between informant and an interested third party is strictly forbidden by police regulations, this caused Chilton some misgivings. But there was a lot riding on this drugs job, so Chilton put his reservations to one side and the meeting went ahead. Although Chilton was present, Munson made it clear that the negotiations were between him and the insurance company. The meeting took just one hour; at the end of that time, it was agreed that Munson would fly back to Spain at the earliest opportunity, naturally at the mortgage company's expense, to meet with the Spanish representative of the company. Two days later, Munson brought the hire car to a halt on the Avenida Duque de Ahumada and looked down into the sparkling blue waters of the Mediterranean. 'There it is,' he said, handing the binoculars to the company representative. 'Fifth one in.' And that was that. *Baby Blue Eyes III* was correctly identified, the company ensured that an arrest warrant was nailed to the mast and Munson was £5,000 richer.

Back in the United Kingdom, Munson was looking for a long-term place to stay. He had been sleeping in the spare bedroom of Gerry Beaumont's flat in Bow, and Beaumont, a former armed blagger, still possessed serious criminal connections at home and abroad. He had been travelling constantly between England and Spain but of late he had decided to spend more time at home. Therefore, it would be inevitable that Beaumont would want his guest to vacate the spare bedroom and this was definitely not to Munson's liking.

'I've got a bit of business in Wickham Market,' said Beaumont, one morning. 'Shouldn't take too long – be back tonight or tomorrow, at the latest.'

Munson nodded. 'Take care, Gerry. Catch you later.' A quarter of an hour later, he waved goodbye as Beaumont drove off in his silver Mercedes 280, of which Munson had carefully noted the registration number. He watched the car until it disappeared in the general direction of the Bow flyover, before he strolled back to the flat and picked up the telephone.

'George? Listen. Gerry Beaumont's on his way up to Suffolk – a place called Wickham Market. Don't know where he's going exactly but it's to do some business. Underneath his driving seat he's got a pack of what I'm told is 96 per cent pure cocaine, plus a loaded shooter. He's got the right arse about something – don't know what – but he was heard to say that he'd fix that bastard for good.' Munson then provided the description of the car, plus the registration number.

After that, things happened very quickly, indeed. With Beaumont in possession of drugs and a loaded firearm, possibly en route to assassinate some unknown person at an unknown location, he had to be arrested, fast. The Metropolitan Police helicopter, India nine-nine, was scrambled and, working on the assumption that Beaumont would be taking the most direct route to Suffolk, the crew focused their attention on the A12 trunk road. Within a very short space of time, they identified the Mercedes as it approached Marks Tey and both the control rooms for Essex and Suffolk constabularies were alerted. Armed response units from both constabularies got on the move but Essex were too far away. Suffolk, emerging from Ipswich, was not and a rolling road block, just after one of the roundabouts at Martlesham Heath, resulted in the arrest at gunpoint and the seizure of drugs and a loaded firearm of one very surprised former armed robber.

Munson had been seeing Peter Hemmings whilst he had been 'doing the rounds' and Hemmings, who had recently been released after serving just over half of a five year sentence for receiving, had been making some attractive noises with regard to the sale of funny money. Munson had contributed to the conversation with a series of nods, grunts and shrugs as though he was fairly uninterested and was merely showing signs of politeness, whereas, of course, the opposite was true. Finally at one of their meets, Hemmings produced a forged £50 note. 'What'd yer think of that, then?'

'Looks pretty good to me,' acknowledged Munson and, to his reasonably expert eye, it looked very good indeed.

'I'm knocking these out for a tenner apiece,' casually commented Hemmings.

'That sounds a bit pricey to me,' replied Munson, 'but I dunno.'

This was the truth and a lie. It *was* pricey and Munson *did* know. He knew the going rate for snide £50 notes was six quid, although some buyers could knock the price down to four and, on impressively funded deals, it had been known to go down to two quid.

'I'll tell you what, Peter,' said Munson. 'I've told you, I'm really not interested in buying a load of snide fifties but I do know someone who wants to make a shrewd investment like this. I can put him into you if you like, for a drink.'

Hemmings nodded.

'Can I take the sample with me? He'll want to make sure about the quality before he meets you and if he likes what he sees, there's no reason he couldn't make a deal with you for – what? What've you got on offer?'

'If he made the right sort of offer, I could unload a hundred grands' worth of snide fifties on him,' replied Hemmings, decisively.

Munson whistled. 'A hundred grand! Bloody hell, Peter, I could be looking at a right nice drink out of that! I'll be in touch.'

The following day, Munson met Chilton, having come from the Bank of England. 'Looks like you've hit the jackpot, Jim. That sample note is one of a big series going the rounds. If it's at all possible, we'd like to get our hands on the printing press. Well, let's get things rolling. Tell Hemmings that your man is interested and make a meet so that you can introduce the buyer to him. After that, you can fade out of the picture.'

Munson nodded. That suited him just fine. If the funny-money job came off, the reward from that, plus the reward for sticking up Gerry Beaumont, should keep him ticking over nicely for a bit. Which reminded him . . . 'By the way, George, what happened about Beaumont?'

'Beaumont?' replied Chilton, casually, but nevertheless watching Munson's face for any sign of duplicity. 'Oh, he was nicked and charged. Screamed the place down, when he got a lay-down, apparently. Reckoned he'd been fitted. Know of anyone who'd got the hump with him?'

Munson shook his head. 'Can't say I do.' As he walked

away, Munson was smiling. Everything had worked out just right – and now for some fun.

On the morning of the meet with Peter Hemmings, it had been decided that Munson and Vince Young would turn up at the service station on the M1 in the hired Jaguar and 'Sean', one of the Yard's top undercover men, would arrive in his Rolls Royce. Munson failed to arrive in the Jaguar at their agreed meeting place at Mile End Underground station and, after waiting nearly twenty minutes for him, Young went to a public call box and telephoned Chilton.

'The job's off,' replied Chilton shakily. 'Jimmy's been nicked. Call me later.'

For thirty years, Police Constable 811H Morrie Crane had patrolled the streets of Bow. He had joined the Metropolitan Police straight from his National Service in the Army and his entire service had been spent at Bow police station. He had never sought advancement through the ranks nor had he wished to expand his talents through any of the specialist departments. He was quite happy to serve the community by walking the beat and he was regarded by his superiors and the public as being a fair man, who was also a hard, conscientious worker. And now, the evening before the meeting of the two snouts, the funny-money provider and the police undercover officer, PC Crane was not only coming to the end of his career with the police, he was also coming to the end of his shift. It was half-past nine when he turned on his heel to commence the walk back to the nick, where he would arrive at a couple of minutes before ten, just in time to book off duty, providing of course that nothing happened. Something did.

'All units Hotel Whisky, Hotel Whisky five and Hotel one-one,' was the transmission on the personal radio from Bow Police Station. 'Male IC1 seen pulling a young girl from a car into a block of flats.' As the controller gave the address, PC Crane suddenly realized that he was almost outside the block of flats. '811 on scene and dealing,' he acknowledged and broke into a run. As he entered the flats, he looked wildly round – there was no one, of course, to tell him which flat. And then, providentially, he heard a scream – the scream of a terrified young child. 'No!' screamed the voice. 'I don't like it!' The child's voice had come from behind a closed door, just along the hallway. PC Crane did not theorize, temporize, agonize, call for armed back-up or ask his sergeant what to do – he acted precisely in the way he had been taught and introduced his size twelve boot to the front door of the flat which smashed it right off its hinges. Running instinctively into the nearest bedroom, the sight that greeted his eyes was that of a naked girl, aged about ten, tied wrist and ankle to a bed and, advancing towards her, similarly naked in an obvious state of excitement and arousal, was Jimmy Munson, holding a piece of cloth in both hands for the purpose of gagging the child.

PC Crane's colleagues were later mightily surprised when they learnt that the former army PTI's only comment as he bent to untie the sobbing girl, was to say quietly to Munson, 'Get in the corner where I can see you, and get dressed.'

It could well be that Munson thought that the rest of his time, whilst he was in police custody, he would be treated in the same courteous manner. If so, he was in for a rude awakening.

When the Police and Criminal Evidence Act was introduced it meant that when a criminal was arrested, it was rather as though he had just entered a fairly up-market hotel where his every demand was not only expeditiously dealt with but also often anticipated. This was to ensure that the whining type of allegations of ill-treatment by prisoners might be eradicated and also so that solicitors and social workers could line up to fuss over them.

Unfortunately for Munson, at the time of his arrest the act was a year away and, consequently, things were about to go dramatically wrong. First, although Munson had, for many years, had dealings with the police, it had been on a fairly even footing. In fact, his requests to them had, of late, more or less turned into demands. And second, the times when Munson had been brought into a police station under arrest were so long ago that they were no more than a dim, distant memory.

So as Munson walked into the charge room at Bow police station, and everyone in the nick was aware of what had happened, it was the height of recklessness for Munson to say to the station sergeant, 'I demand that you telephone Detective Inspector Chilton of No. 9 Regional Crime Squad, immediately. Then I shall want my doctor advised of my detention.'

The station sergeant who was of the same school as PC Crane simply looked at Munson, before strolling round the charge room desk, casually picking up his thick, ebony ruler and cracking him right across the shins with it. Munson screamed and crashed to the floor. 'Get him up, Morrie,' said the sergeant as he resumed his position behind the desk. To the white-faced Munson, he said, 'Perverts don't make demands in my police station, mister,' adding, 'although I think you're right about calling a doctor. Reckon you're going to need one. Name?'

Half an hour later and Munson, none of his requests complied with, was in the CID office, sitting at the desk of the detective sergeant. Also present was an aid and a detective constable. 'OK, pal, this is the way it is,' said the very hard-faced detective sergeant. 'You, you dirty fucker are going to tell me chapter and verse, about everything that happened tonight between you and the kid. Got it?' He paused and slid open his desk drawer. From it, he took a dining table candle, about nine inches in length, ominously spotted with red at the tip. Holding this out towards Munson, he added softly, 'Three guesses as to where I'm going to shove this, and two more like it, if you don't!' Munson stared, mesmerized, at the candle before he swallowed. In almost a whisper, he started to reply, 'I demand to speak to detective inspector—'

'That's it!' snapped the sergeant. Rising to his feet, he pulled off his jacket. 'You!' This, to the aid. 'Get over to the door and mind it – make sure nobody comes in!' As the aid headed towards the door, the sergeant rolled his sleeves up, went to the desk next to his and with one brawny arm, swept the 'in' and 'out' baskets, together with the correspondence contained in them, flying across the floor, together with the blotter and the telephone, which was smashed to pieces. Turning to the detective constable, the sergeant said, 'Right, you. Bend him over that desk. Get his strides down, then hang on to his wrists!'

Munson screamed, then, two seconds later, he started talking. He was permitted to sit down. He told them all about the abduction of the little girl. He then told the sergeant about two other little girls, one from Hammersmith and one from Bromley who had been nowhere as near fortunate as their Bow counterpart. The sergeant picked up the red-spotted candle and looked at it reflectively. 'What else?' It was all the impetus that Munson needed. There had been another girl, in France in Aix-en-Provence, two more in Holland, one in Utrecht and one in Haarlem. Then there was one in Hamburg. All of the others had consented. Especially when he went to Vietnam. Those three in the bar in Ho Chi Minh City had *definitely* consented. Well, probably.

The detective sergeant who was Munson's interrogator possessed a fine flair for the theatrical. Although he used the candle threat on many occasions throughout his career, never once did he need to follow through. The glistening red marks at the business end of the candle were supplied, by the CID typist's lipstick. The other members of the office thought he was a great copper.

This view was not shared by G9 (Accident Claims) Branch at the Yard, due to the number of reports which the sergeant submitted to them, requesting replacement of broken telephones. 'Look at this!' snapped an exasperated higher executive officer from G9 Branch to a colleague. 'This is the eleventh request he's submitted this year! He must be the clumsiest officer in the Met!'

When no one turned up at the meeting, Peter Hemmings immediately suspected a ready-eye and made himself scarce. Although all of Munson's work was shelved as soon as the sickening details emerged regarding the offences for which he was charged, surveillance was carried out on Hemmings and his telephone calls were intercepted, both without success. If he did have access to a considerable amount of forged currency, it was not found in his possession and the plates were never discovered.

Dave Baxter, who really kicked off this story, was not a drugs dealer. The Customs and Excise informant's name was Ian Gibson. He had given this story to them, in conjunction with Jimmy Munson as back-up, because he wanted Baxter out of the way since he, Gibson, was completely and utterly besotted with Baxter's wife, Luba. Gibson knew that the Baxters would be going to England to visit various people and for the purchase of the four-wheel drive, because Luba had told him they were going. After they returned, Gibson intended to invent an excuse for Baxter to return once again to England. He would inform Customs of the date when Baxter would arrive and Munson would do the same with the police. If Baxter did travel in the four-wheel drive, all well and good; he would ensure that the door panels would be packed with drugs. If not, then Munson would plant a gun and drugs in the hire car which he would acquire once he had arrived – Gibson had already supplied both to Munson to cover that eventuality – and Baxter would be nicked and out of the way.

What Gibson did not know was the main reason why Baxter was travelling to the old country. Yes, it was to acquire the four-wheel drive but that was because Luba coveted one; and whatever Luba wanted, Luba got. In any case, it was far cheaper to purchase one in England and have it shipped over, than to purchase one in Spain. But the other reason was because Baxter was dying. He had an incurable heart disease and he was simply saying goodbye to relatives and old friends.

Within months of returning home to Spain, Baxter died. An overjoyed Gibson immediately moved in with Luba but unfortunately the relationship festered. Luba became disenchanted with Gibson and took up with an impoverished scuba diving instructor named Jean-Pierre, who was handsome, muscular and fifteen years her junior. Gibson was later found dead with a bullet in his head. The reason for his demise was never satisfactorily resolved.

Vince Young faithfully corroborated much of the information supplied by Munson and contributed some of his own which, for one reason or another, Munson had neglected to pass on. It was disseminated to various departments at New Scotland Yard and some constabularies and Young is still regarded as one of the Yard's top informants.

George Chilton did attend the board for detective chief inspector but, although the only CID officer who sat on that board tried to make a case for Chilton's advancement, he was passed over. Oh yes, commented the very senior officer who was the board's chairman, Chilton was a good thief-taker all right and, it was true, he did have an impressive number of commendations but his handling of informants was just a little . . . well, shall we say – reckless? No, perhaps reckless was too strong a term but perhaps . . . imprudent. However, the other contender was a much sounder prospect. True, he had spent his entire career in uniform and he did have just the one commendation and that was for his input into the structuring of a suite for rape victims but he did have a first in PPE at Cambridge and that was the clincher. He was the sort of chap who was wanted for the rank of detective chief inspector. He was altogether more . . . sound. His lack of expertize regarding detective work could easily be rectified. All he needed was a good tutor and he could, well . . . you know . . . pick it up as he went along. There was a vacancy coming up for a DCI at Bow. In fact, there was a pretty reliable detective sergeant there already, who could certainly take him under his wing.

During the many years in prison which inevitably followed, Munson was never offered parole, neither did he seek it. Always in the back of his mind was the thought that if he were to be released, Vietnam would seek his extradition where, for the type of offences for which he would undoubtedly be convicted, the punishment was death. Anyway, he was reasonably happy where he was. The other paedophiles were such great company; they could swap stories all day long. But at times, he longed for the farm at Almeria, the smell of the olives, the warmth of the sun and this, and despite his solicitor's assurances that he would not be extradited, caused him to become profoundly depressed. Before he toppled over the brink into insanity, God offered him the best deal of his life and Munson gratefully accepted a fatal heart attack. It was a happy release which the majority of people with whom he had had dealings considered he really did not deserve.

Not a Shred of Evidence

Nicky Baldwin came from what is colloquially known as 'a right family'. His father, George, had taken a spirited part in the short-lived riot at Dartmoor Prison in January 1932 where he had been serving a four year sentence for robbery with violence; an offence for which the punishment had also included 'a bashing' – or flogging. George was correctly identified as one of the ringleaders of the riot and was one of several cons convicted of riotous assembly in Princetown, three months later . He had another four years added to his sentence. Nicky Baldwin's conception was neatly slotted in between his father's release for that offence and his incarceration for the next, which was George's last sentence; he expired in the punishment block at Parkhurst after belting one screw too many.

Nicky grew up in north London where his mother's brothers took an avuncular interest in his well-being. A large, naturally aggressive boy, his belligerence was channelled into the world of boxing and, although his cold-blooded ferocity was often curtailed under the stringent rules of amateur boxing, several observant managers detected the strong whiff of 'a great white hope' in Baldwin.

But before he could turn professional, he was called up for National Service and, as a result of a number of serious clashes with authority, he spent a considerable time inside a military prison. When he emerged into civvie street, the latter part of his military service had made him more brutal, more vicious than ever before and, given his record, a career as a professional boxer was out of the question.

He had already dabbled on the fringes of criminality; now he went in for it full time. He was not over-intelligent but he was extremely cunning and, given his height of six feet one, his enormous strength and pugilistic ability, and with his battered face exuding menace, he was the perfect instrument for the gangs who were seeking prominence in the early 1970s, following the fall of the brothers Kray.

Nicky Baldwin was an 'enforcer'. When weekly payments to his masters were not forthcoming from those who paid them a 'pension' in return for providing protection for their premises, Baldwin would be sent to collect the outstanding sum. In accordance with the shop or club owner's track record regarding payments, the collection might or might not be accompanied with a 'slap' to encourage a more rapid disbursement in future. It was far different when a rival gang actually demanded protection from premises which were already being 'looked after' by Baldwin's employers. Then, there was no question as to whether or not violence should be applied; the level of impertinence would be punished with a severe beating, a slashing or, often, a shooting.

But the police had been keeping an eye on Baldwin and his employers and had steadily been gathering evidence and when, early one June morning, the police bashed in the door of Baldwin's tenement flat, it was sheer bad luck that underneath the floorboards of his bedroom was found a fully loaded Mauser automatic pistol. Worse still, a ballistic test revealed that a bullet retrieved from the leg of one of Baldwin's victims had been fired from that same gun. Victims were starting to talk and, although it was often difficult to differentiate between the morality of victim and perpetrator, Baldwin and a number of his associates were charged. The following May, after a long and bitterly contested trial at the Old Bailey, Baldwin was one of those found guilty and he was sentenced to twelve years' imprisonment. A number of members of society – mainly police officers and owners of premises, both licensed and unlicensed – gave a collective sigh of relief. One singularly dangerous bastard was out of the way.

At the beginning of the 1980s, Baldwin was released; it would have been sooner, except that some unacceptable behaviour had landed him in the Special Segregation Unit at HM Prison Albany and this had extended his stay. He was welcomed back to north London by his peers and then matters went rather quiet. He must have come into some money because he was able to purchase a smallholding on the Essex/Hertfordshire borders. The property had the benefit of having no close neighbours and, with the bungalow elevated slightly from the surrounding estate, it commanded a 360 degree view of the countryside which included the ability to spot anybody approaching the premises. For an honest man who valued his privacy, this would have been a bonus. For someone of Nicky Baldwin's talents, it was essential.

Criminal Intelligence at Scotland Yard – C11 Department – wished to update their file on Baldwin, but no information was coming in from their informants nor was his name mentioned on any of their current telephone intercepts. With this type of inaction, there was absolutely no justification for applying to have Baldwin's telephone calls intercepted. Long-range cameras photographed vehicles on the driveway outside the bungalow but registration checks revealed that the vehicles either belonged to Baldwin or to local tradesmen. When a reconnaissance aeroplane was sent up from Southend Airport on a completely disassociated matter, the C11 photographer suddenly remembered

Baldwin's smallholding and got the pilot to circle over the property and took several shots of the premises and the surrounding area. The film was developed and the prints were placed in Baldwin's folder. And that was that.

Baldwin had acquired a following in north and east London and, like many other prominent villains, his bad points were minimized and his virtues (such as they were) paraded triumphantly. One story which gained prominence at that time was that Baldwin had saved a young child from drowning in the River Thames. According to East End folklore, Baldwin had been walking across Tower Bridge when he saw the child in the water in obvious distress and, without a second thought, he had dived off the bascule bridge and, following a nifty bit of lifesaving, had restored the soaking child to the bosom of her family.

The story was bollocks. The depth from bridge to water is twenty-nine feet. Would you dive, headfirst into the evil-smelling Thames, to land on top of the flotsam and jetsam that floats on top of, and sometimes underneath, the river? No, and neither would I. And neither did Nicky Baldwin. And before outraged readers (many of whom assert that they were actually present at the investiture when a medal was pinned on Baldwin's manly bosom) retort, ''E fucking did!' it would be as well to point out that Baldwin was unable to swim. So there you are; no death-defying dive, no sodden child rescued and no gong. But that's not to say that Baldwin did not possess a compassionate side; that will be referred to much later in this tale. Baldwin was noted for his bad deeds far more than his benign ones and the tale which follows illustrates his demonic personality.

The Flying Squad switchboard used to be manned twenty-four hours a day. At about three o'clock one morning, when the switchboard operators were dozing, the telephone rang. The caller sounded as though he had been drinking heavily (as indeed he had) and what he said was this: 'Ronnie Castle's dead. That Nicky Baldwin done it. I saw it. He fed 'im, feet first into a shredder. It was 'orrible; Ronnie didn't deserve to go like that – 'e was screaming. Blood everywhere. Hope you nick the bastard.' He then burst into tears and rang off.

The switchboard operator stared. Then he checked the Yard switchboard. Had the caller dialled the famous 1212 number and asked to be transferred to the Flying Squad? No. The Squad number had been dialled direct. Therefore, the caller must have had some connection with the Squad in the past; a snout, perhaps. The operator then wrote down what had been said, word for word. Then he dialled the number of the Duty Officer of C1 Reserve, to whom all allegations of serious crime are referred and repeated what he had heard. The Duty Officer was just as sleepy as his Squad counterpart but questioned him carefully. With the limited information at his disposal, he telephoned Criminal Records Office and searched on the two names and obtained their files. These he left on the desk of the detective chief superintendent with the details of the message.

Later that morning, the detective chief superintendent raised a sceptical eyebrow at the content of the message and then checked the files. Ronnie Castle was a thief and a con-man with a string of convictions for petty and minor offences. On his CRO 100A (or antecedent) form, one officer had noted that he was 'an indiscriminate womanizer'. Then he checked Baldwin's file. No obvious connection between the two. Was Castle alive or not? That was the first thing to find out. He decided this was one for division and he reached out for the telephone to speak to his opposite number at H Division.

The detective constable who politely enquired of Mrs Castle

as to the whereabouts of her husband received a volley of abuse. This was the third fucking time this year he'd fucked off with some little tart and she was fed up with it. No, she didn't know who she was, no, she didn't know where he'd gone and no, she couldn't fucking care less if she never saw the no-good fucker ever again. And he (the detective constable) could tell him that. Did she wish to report him as a missing person? No, she didn't. Now, fuck off!

The enquiry now shifted to Baldwin's address. Did he know Ronnie Castle – and if so, had he seen him lately – and if so, in what circumstances? To each question came the reply, 'Speak to my solicitor.' Asked if Baldwin minded if the police had a look around his property, both inside and out, they were told that he did. 'Got a brief – no? Right – fuck off.' And because all this happened in the days before the Police & Criminal Evidence Act when it was not possible to obtain a warrant to search for evidence, the police did just that, and fucked off.

The detective chief superintendent of H Division pondered the matter briefly; there was no evidence of any crime having been committed and certainly not on his division. He wrote out a crime book entry alleging murder, classified it as 'No Crime' and then sent a short report to the commander of C1 Department, via the commander of C11 who noted the report and checked his own indices; Ronnie Castle was not in the system although Baldwin, of course, was. He checked his file and saw the aerial photograph which had been taken some time previously. Just to be on the safe side, he had a C11 photographer fly over Baldwin's smallholding and take fresh pictures. The newly developed prints were meticulously compared with the previous print. If something, or someone had been buried there, it would have showed up. When it was revealed that there had been no soil displacement whatsoever, there the matter ended, as far as the police were concerned. There was not even a 'Missing Person' report on a small-time crook who nobody cared about.

The truth was that Ronnie Castle (that indiscriminate woman-izer) had taken a fancy to a young woman named Sheila, and she to him. This might have blossomed into a torrid affair which could have lasted a few weeks before one tired of the other and Ronnie would then have wandered home to his wife and implored forgiveness, and he might or might not have been accepted back into the family fold. But not this time. Sheila was the daughter, and the apple of the eye, of a gang-land boss who most definitely did not want his daughter involved with a married man, particularly one as charmless as Castle. Without the knowledge of his daughter, he took Castle to one side and told him to make himself scarce. Castle was reckless enough to ignore him and when he disregarded a second warning, the gangland boss decided that sterner meas-ures would have to be taken. He instructed an associate to contact Castle on the pretext of shifting some stolen property, to which Castle agreed. The boss then contacted Baldwin, explained the problem and asked him 'to take care of it'. Perhaps he should have been a little more explicit in his instruc-tions but given the deserted place which had been nominated and the lateness of the hour, 'taking care' of someone in those circumstances meant only one thing to Baldwin.

The unfortunate Ronnie Castle realized that the industrial-sized shredder at the car breaker's yard was not the dodgy gear which he had been commissioned to move as soon as Nicky Baldwin started it, then grabbed hold of him in a vice-like grip and began to feed him, feet-first into it. It took quite a long time to completely dispose of him but his agonized screams had abated long before he finally disappeared. The horrified go-between who had witnessed the whole thing stayed long enough to see the dreadful look of satisfaction on Baldwin's face before shuffling away (a) to be mutinously sick and (b) to get staggeringly drunk. He was certainly staggering when he made the telephone call to the Flying Squad office. He had been a Squad grass before but this would be the limit of his involvement.

When Ronnie Castle suddenly disappeared without a word, Sheila was inconsolable for all of three or four minutes.

So the mincing of Ronnie Castle passed into Nicky Baldwin folklore and it was accepted just as readily as the fallacious story regarding the rescue of the little girl from Old Father Thames.

Vilamoura was one of the first holiday resorts to be built in the Algarve region of southern Portugal. It is just half an hour from Faro Airport and, with the marina complex capable of providing one thousand berths, it is very attractive to holiday-makers. There are many properties in the area, including a number of purpose built flats, with communal swimming pools for the residents.

One such flat had been sub-let to a verminous bunch of yobs from Canning Town. Their names were Trevor, Alan and Jimbo. During the two weeks of their stay, they had met up with a group of sluts whose identities are unimportant to this story. Between the six of them, they made the other residents' lives a misery. The hi-fi blasted out all night long; it was not turned off because the occupants inevitably succumbed to an excess of alcohol. Their language was a disgrace and the other residents were swiftly discouraged from using the communal swimming pool whilst Trevor & Co. were in the vicinity. Their main delight was to leap into the pool and 'bomb' whoever might be in or around that area; on one auspicious occasion, this was achieved from the height of their first-floor balcony. The 'bombings' were interspersed with the six of them 'streaking' around the pool, shrieking with laughter at their antics and throwing each other into the water, irrespective of who might be present. On two occasions, sexual acts were performed by the pool in broad daylight. Three families left in the first week.

Ted Davies had been quite a hard man in his heyday, having been a member of Jack Spot's mob. But those days had long gone and now, at seventy-two years of age, he was mildly diabetic and had suffered two heart attacks. He and his wife had taken their grandchildren on holiday with them and Ted had very quickly become extremely vexed at the group's behaviour. He remonstrated with Trevor at the poolside, believing that the menace he had exuded all those years before still held good. Sadly, it did not. Alone, it might have done, but of course Trevor had Alan and Jimbo to back him up and after some pushing, shoving and extremely abusive language, Trevor, pulled open the front of Ted's swimming trunks and Alan poured a can of lager into them. 'Look, 'e's pissed hisself!' shouted Jimbo and the sluttish trio sobbed with uncontrollable laughter. This was almost the end of the line for Ted but there was worse to come. He had retired to the flat – the music from upstairs had just started up again, full blast – when his five year old granddaughter tugged at his arm. Ted looked up. 'What is it, dear?'

'Granddad, what's a wanker?' she asked.

'What!' gasped Ted.

'That boy – the fat one,' (she was referring to Tevor) 'he said, "go and tell your granddad he's a wanker".'

For Ted, this was the last straw. Tears pricked his eyes at his mortification and he was about to pack their suitcases and go home when there was a knock on the door of the apartment.

Cautiously, he opened it, expecting some fresh humiliation. 'Ted, who is it?' anxiously called his wife from the kitchen. In the hallway, Ted stepped back from the door as he saw who the visitor was. 'It's all right,' he called back. 'It's an old friend.'

In the kitchen, over tea, the whole sorry story came out. The owner of the block of flats listened carefully, saying little, nodding often. 'To be quite frank with you, when you knocked on the door, I was all set to pack up and go home,' admitted Ted. The apartment's owner smiled and patted the old man's arm. 'No,' he replied. 'There's no need for that. Stay here.' And with that, Nicky Baldwin rose and walked up the flight of stairs towards the very noisy flat on the first floor and knocked very loudly on the door.

It was Trevor who opened the door. 'Yiss?' he enquired, aggressively. It sounded like steam escaping from a boiler. Baldwin's right hand shot out and grabbed him by the throat and with consummate ease pushed him back into the room. Alan emerged from a bedroom and belligerently asked, 'Problem?' Baldwin responded by smashing the back of Trevor's head into the bridge of Alan's nose. Alan crashed to the floor, blood fountaining from his face and, at the same moment, Baldwin released his grip on Trevor's throat; he too, sank to the floor, gasping for breath. At that moment, Jimbo entered the room. Baldwin glared at him. 'Turn that shit off!' he growled, indicating the hi-fi. Jimbo merely goggled at him and his reluctance was rewarded with a heavy punch in the solar plexus; the noise problem was cured by Baldwin stamping on the hi-fi. The first of the three girls, all of whom were stark naked, was attracted by the sound of violence and she erupted from the bedroom. She looked aghast at the three slumped bodies who were displaying various signs of distress. ''Ere, woss fuckin' goin' on?' she screeched and that was as far as she got before

31

Baldwin grasped her by the nape of her neck and swiftly propelled her, shrieking towards the front door. She was unable to properly keep up with him and gave a fairly convincing impersonation of a wounded antelope in mid-gallop, before they reached the doorway and Baldwin planted an enormous kick on her buttocks. The kick propelled her, screaming, right over the banisters. Her body described a complete parabola and she landed, flat on her back, just outside Ted's door, one floor below. It was amazing that no bones were broken and she only suffered mild concussion and extensive bruising.

Back in the apartment, the terrified faces of the two remaining girls peered fearfully around the bedroom door, until Baldwin growled, 'Get back in there, you slags!' and they did.

And now he turned to the three terrified youths, athletes, imbibers and Lotharios no longer, who were still on the floor, having managed to prop themselves up by the wall. Baldwin leant towards them and they collectively flinched. 'Know who I am?' he enquired, softly. 'Nah,' fearfully wheezed Jimbo. Trevor, with his injured throat was still having trouble speaking and Alan was attempting to staunch the flow of blood from his nose so they simply shook their heads. So Balwin told them. Their eyes bulged at the very mention of his name; they, like all of Canning Town's low-life, had heard the tale of the shredder.

'And now, you listen to me,' continued Baldwin, still speaking quietly. 'You cunts have been taking the piss, big-time. I want you all out of here – you and those slags – by tomorrow morning. And now I'm going to tell you what's going to happen if you don't.'

And Baldwin told them; in graphic detail. At the end of his brief discourse, Jimbo had lost control of his bladder, Alan was displaying all the symptoms of combat fatigue and Trevor burst into tears. Baldwin stood up to go and then, given the misery they had caused to the other residents of the flats, realized he had let them all off far too lightly. First, he unzipped his fly, and urinated over the three of them. Not one word in protest was uttered. Next, he dropped his trousers and defecated on the floor. As the three low-lifes stared at the smoking faeces, so Baldwin pulled up his trousers and headed for the kitchen. He returned seconds later and threw down three forks and a bottle of HP sauce. 'Eat it up,' he growled. There was just a moment's hesitation before the three cowering youths liberally doused the excrement in sauce and tucked-in. Baldwin stood there to ensure that every scrap was consumed.

'Right,' he said, approvingly. 'I can see you've learnt your lesson. Time for you to be rewarded. Who's got some Vaseline?'

Three horrified pairs of eyes stared at him as they realized the implication of Baldwin's last statement.

'No?' queried Baldwin. 'Never mind. I know where I can get some. Be back in five minutes.'

Within minutes of Baldwin leaving the flat, Trevor & Co. had gone. Rushing to the airport, the six discovered that there were no more flights that evening; it made no difference. They slept in the airport lounge at Faro and then, fearfully looking over their shoulders to ensure that they were not being followed, they boarded the first outgoing flight. Providentially, it was heading for England but they would not have cared if its destination had been Nairobi.

One day, the owner of a certain scrap metal yard will die and this will come as no surprise to those who know him, because he drinks like a fish. Because he has no kith and kin, his estate, including his yard, will revert to the Government. Perhaps the local council will accede to the protests of the local residents who for years have campaigned to have the site removed, because they consider it to be a blot on the landscape. And if this is the case, when the neat rectangles of squashed-up cars are removed, buried underneath they will discover a very old industrial-sized shredder. It will appear to be covered in rust but a forensic examination will disprove that notion. If anyone with knowledge of this type of machinery examines the apparatus, they will discover that the screen has unusually been removed. It is against the screen that the 'flails' which shred the material is normally hammered, to force the residue through. Before a further examination of the discharge elevator is made, the smell alone will suggest that it encloses a ghastly secret.

But that day has yet to arrive. Nicky Baldwin's culpability has yet to be challenged by the judicial process of law. So until that fateful day dawns, there's not a shred of evidence against him.

The Ruling Class

Can Toffs become villains? Well, why not? Being born in Cheltenham or Aldgate Pump is just an accident of birth; after that, it's all in the genes. Toffs can certainly fall foul of the law. The Marquess of Blandford has fought a battle against drug addiction over a period of years and has been sentenced to periods of imprisonment on four occasions. The trustees of the family estate at Blenheim have ensured that he will not inherit control of the estate but he will inherit the Dukedom. Lord Brockett copped five years for an insurance fraud in the 1990s but could he or Jamie Blandford be truly termed villains?

One toff who was, without doubt, a villain in every sense of the word, was Peter Martin Jenkins. Precisely what prompted Jenkins to go off the rails is unclear. He had all the advantages of good looks, a suave personality and a stable background and he lived in an opulent flat in Mayfair's Half Moon Street, but off the rails he certainly went and with considerable style, too.

The case, which became known as 'The Mayfair Playboys', commenced in December 1937 when one of Jenkins' four-man gang booked a suite at the prestigious Hyde Park Hotel. Next, and just five days before Christmas, a leading Bond Street jeweller's received a telephone call from the suite's occupier, requesting to see a collection of jewellery. The director of the company duly arrived at the hotel, carrying an attaché case containing rings valued at £16,000 and he was shown into the suite. There, he was savagely attacked by Jenkins, wielding a life preserver (a curiously named short stick with a heavily loaded end – in other words, a cosh) and when, later that afternoon, the jeweller was found by the hotel staff, lying in a pool of blood, both the attaché case, and Jenkins and his associates had vanished.

Jenkins was identified from his photograph, taken in a night club and published in *The Tatler*, by a snout who had seen Jenkins in possession of the rings and this put Detective Inspector Bob Fabian ('of the Yard') on his trail. A visit was made to Jenkins' sumptuous flat. This revealed packets of cigarettes, seldom seen in England at that time, which corresponded with cigarette ends found in the suite at the Hyde Park Hotel. Even more interesting was a receipt, acknowledging the sale of three life preservers. When Jenkins returned to his flat he made the most terrific fuss, threatening the detectives with legal action but it did him little good. Two more of the gang were arrested in Oxford and, when the third was also brought in, Jenkins, who had probably discovered the folly of screaming threats at a very tough detective like Fabian, helpfully showed him where the rings were hidden.

The public gallery at No. 1 Court at the Old Bailey is not particularly large and it seemed that all of the *glitterati* of Mayfair wanted to see the four toffs get their come-uppance so admission to the gallery was by ticket only.

Before passing sentence, Lord Hewart, the Lord Chief Justice had this to say: 'The word education has been used about each of you. If I believed that you really were educated men it would be necessary for me, on that account, to be more severe. Probably, all that is meant is that somebody has spent money in providing you with certain conventional opportunities of education. The results are not impressive.'

Jenkins' three associates were then respectively sentenced to five years' penal servitude and fifteen strokes with the cat o' nine tails, three years' penal servitude and eighteen months' hard labour. As the leader of the gang, Jenkins received the toughest sentence: seven years' penal servitude and twenty strokes of the cat o' nine tails.

Jenkins did not cope well with prison; not even his schooling at Winchester had prepared him for anything like this. But his time spent behind bars did not prove to be the reformative exercise that Lord Hewart might have hoped for.

In 1945, following his release, Jenkins was stopped in the street by Detective Inspector Bob Higgins who wished to know the content of a parcel which Jenkins was carrying. When it transpired that it was a fur coat – a stolen one – and Higgins demanded to know its provenance, it seemed the height of recklessness for Jenkins to reply that he had 'found it hanging from a tree in Hyde Park.' It earned him another three years' penal servitude. Higgins' actions were recognized by a death threat from Jenkins and a commendation from the commissioner.

Still Jenkins failed to learn his lesson. When Gainsborough's portrait of Lady Georgiana Spencer, Duchess of Devonshire was cut from its frame at the Chelsea home of the Earl of Carlisle in 1948, it wasn't too long before a Ghost Squad snout fingered Jenkins and his associate, Harry Mann, for the housebreaking. They were caught red-handed, trying to sell the painting to a 'buyer' and both went away for four years' penal servitude.

Dartmoor finally broke Jenkins' spirit. He died in a lodging house, penniless, from alcohol abuse.

You'd think that the downfall of Peter Martin Jenkins would be included in the curriculum of every public school as a cautionary tale, wouldn't you? 'Don't go down that road, m'lads or that's what'll jolly well happen to you!' A bit like the sport's master pointing out the perils of masturbation.

A pity really that the Honourable Giles St John Armsby-Croake, youngest son of the Right Honourable, the Viscount Henry Armsby-Croake didn't hear of the sad plight of Peter Martin Jenkins or if he did, failed to heed it.

Giles Armsby-Croake was sent down from university for embezzling money. He really didn't need to rook his fellow students for their hard-earned cash; he knew there was a never-ending supply of funds from his parents. Oh, they might be grudgingly given, but there was never any danger of him becoming destitute. No, the reason he did it was not just because he was a self-opinionated little snob. It was because he utterly despised just about everything and everybody. Certainly, he despised his parents but he hated the dean, for being a fucking grass. He hated the police too, with their supercilious ways when they pulled him up in his MG. So that evening, at Annabel's night club, when he met up with Billy Farquarson, whom he had known at Eton, Giles was presented with a ready-made solution to display his contempt for Farquarson plus his hatred of police in one easy lesson.

'Giles, I'm in such a bloody mess!' wailed Farquarson. 'I was caught dealing some coke to a couple of chums; then the fuzz found some more round my flat – oh, Christ! I managed to get bail but my solicitor says that I could be looking at four years!'

Giles attempted to keep the look of contempt off his face, but didn't try very hard. 'I think I may be able to help you, Billy,' he said, slowly as the idea formed and expanded in his mind. 'Of course, it'll cost you,' he added.

'Anything, Giles, anything!' gasped Farquarson.

'Right, what's the name of the officer in charge of your case?' asked Giles and Farquarson told him.

The following day, Giles made a phone call from a public telephone box to Chelsea police station and was connected to Detective Constable Ford, who was in charge of Farquarson's case. Telling him that he had some up-to-the-minute information regarding the West End drugs scene, he arranged a meeting with the officer at a nearby public house.

During the meeting, Giles came straight to the point and told the officer that there was five hundred pounds on offer for the evidence against Farquarson to be impressively watered-down. The detective evinced interest and a further meeting was made for two days' time at The World's End pub.

The young officer returned to Chelsea police station and immediately informed his senior officer of what had occurred. Detective Chief Inspector Tony Fenner was a very good policeman indeed, and one who had a hatred of corruption. 'Right, son,' was his response. 'Write down a statement of everything that happened between you and this little bastard, straight away.' The officer did so and DCI Fenner witnessed, timed and dated it, before locking the statement in his safe.

As soon as he left the meeting with the detective, Giles made his way to Scotland Yard. It was at this time that Robert Mark had been appointed deputy commissioner and he was determined to break the power of the CID, the vast majority of whom he considered to be bent. He had formed an anti-corruption department which was known as A10 and he staffed it with a mixture of uniform officers (who hadn't a clue about investigation) and CID officers who had. Some of these officers were unwilling to perform this type of duty and were simply told to get on with it; others jumped at the chance. One of the latter officers was Detective Chief Inspector James Wade. He had never been regarded as a thief taker and had previously immersed himself in long, boring investigations, usually involving long columns of disputed figures. He was malevolent and vindictive and, being no leader of men by any stretch of the imagination, he was thoroughly disliked by the rank and file. Now, Wade was in his element. He could exercise real authority over detectives and watch them squirm. It was little wonder that one junior officer referred to him as 'that despotic fuck-pig.'

So Giles, who was fully aware of the existence of A10, thanks to the publicity which had been generated as a result of its commencement, found himself ushered into the office of DCI Wade at the Yard.

'Honestly, Chief Inspector, I was shocked,' Giles earnestly told Wade. 'I know that Billy Farquarson's a chum of mine – after all, we were at school, you know – but to get a phone call right out of the blue, like that from DC Ford and then, when I met him, telling me he wanted five hundred pounds to go easy on poor Billy. Well, I suppose Billy had told him that my people are quite well off. You do know that my father's Viscount Armsby-Croake, don't you?'

Wade didn't but he all but rubbed his hands together with glee. Sorting out this bent little bastard of a DC would do him no end of good.

On the morning of the meeting, DCI Fenner took DC Ford to a certain department at the Yard, where he requested a Nagra or concealed tape recorder. The detective sergeant at the desk handed it over. 'Here you are, Guv. Sign here, please. Hope we don't run out; this is the second one I've issued today.'

Both Giles and DC Ford had been issued directions on how to react when the five hundred pounds, in marked notes was handed over, by their respective detective chief inspectors. As they sat at a table in the bar of The World's End, sipping their drinks, their respective tape recorders whirring away, Giles felt a sense of triumph as he slid the envelope containing the money across to DC Ford. 'This is what you want, I think,' said Giles with a smirk and at the same time, slid his finger inside his collar, which was his pre-arranged signal to the A10 personnel.

'Thank you,' courteously replied DC Ford, gathering up the envelope in one hand and pinching his nose with the other, which was his signal to DCI Fenner and *his* personnel.

The next moment, pandemonium broke loose in the bar. DC Ford was seized in a bear-hug by a police sergeant from A10 who was still giddy with excitement at being allowed to put 'detective' in front of his rank and also because this was the first arrest he had made since he'd nicked drunks as a constable. DCI Wade snatched the envelope from DC Ford's hand, opened it to reveal the money and said, 'Right, I'm Detective Chief Inspector Wade from A10 Department and I'm arresting you—' and that was as far as he got, before the money was snatched from *his* hand.

'No you're not, pal,' said DCI Fenner, 'because this little bastard,' and here, he indicated Giles who was struggling in the grip of two of DC Ford's colleagues, 'is under arrest for attempted bribery and this,' and he waved the envelope stuffed with money under Wade's nose, 'is what's known as evidence and I'm hanging on to it.'

'That's our money!' howled Wade. 'Give it back!'

'Bollocks,' replied Fenner, 'and tell that prick to let go of my officer or he'll get a dig in the face.'

Matters by now had become a little fractious and the management of the pub were relieved to see the uniform turn up, which was fortuitous as far as the licensee was concerned but which turned into a rather embarrassing three-ring circus as far as the police officers were concerned.

Giles was taken into Chelsea police station where he and DC Ford surrendered their Nagras but where only Giles was chucked into the cells. A10 took their demand for the return of their money up to deputy assistant commissioner level but in those days the DAC was former SAS man and committed detective Ernie Bond, who privately thought the whole concept of A10 was distasteful and openly thought that this particular case was hilarious and told A10 to get stuffed.

However, A10 did get their money back. Fenner submitted a report to the Director of Public Prosecutions who declined – and the reasoning for the refusal was unclear – to prosecute Giles. Instead of expelling a sigh of gratitude at being left off the hook, Giles simmered with rage at Fenner's treatment of him. His details were entered into the now-defunct 'ACC's Consolidated Instructions', the maroon book issued to every CID office which included details of dangerous informants of which Giles was rightly considered to be one. Billy Farquarson's worst fears were realized when he did indeed cop four years for his dealings in prohibited substances.

Giles' next undertaking was quite breathtaking in its stupidity and the reasoning behind it has never quite been understood by anybody who knew him. He decided to become a licensed taxi driver.

In case the contents of my last paragraph should be misconstrued, I should make it quite clear that I am not suggesting that anybody who wishes to become a black taxi driver is stupid, or that it is a stupid profession; it is not. Fledgling cabbies have to spend several years doing The Knowledge which necessitates knowing every street in the Greater London Area and, what is more, the most direct way to get there, through a mass of streets which are often one-way, before passing a very stiff test indeed. But Giles did not wish to spend years travelling around London on a moped before being rigorously tested on The Knowledge and his good character (both of which would have presented certain difficulties) at the Public Carriage Office (PCO) in Penton Street, Islington.

Instead, he started hanging around cab shelters, those green huts which serve meals and hot drinks to London cabbies and picked up a sizeable amount of the cab drivers' jargon. When he felt that he had accumulated sufficient cabbie *patois*, Giles next broke into a parked-up cab and stole the driver's badge and his licensed bill and, armed with these items, he made his way to a licensed proprietor.

A licensed bill is issued by the PCO and it proves that the cab driver referred to has passed the test. A licensed proprietor is licensed by the PCO to supply cab drivers with a cab. Giles, with his cabbies' jargon and confident manner, plus of course the badge and licensed bill, easily persuaded the proprietor to part with a cab, which he hired on 'full flat' which meant that he could use the cab twenty-four hours per day, as opposed to 'half flat' which meant he would have shared the cab with another driver.

Off went Giles in the cab and instead of paying rental to the proprietor each week, kept the lot for himself. The licensed proprietor reported the matter to the police, who quickly discovering that the badge and licensed bill were stolen, circulated the cab's details on the newly introduced Police National Computer. Six weeks later, Giles was nicked in the cab and was brought to the police station. He was chucked into a cell and detained overnight, to await the arrival of the investigating officer, Detective Constable Bill Laine. So Giles sat and fretted in his cell all night, cursing an unkind cut of fate which had brought him into this predicament. He was more unfortunate than he knew. A new detective chief inspector had just been posted to that station and his name was Tony Fenner.

As soon as DCI Fenner discovered that Giles Armsby-Croake was in the cells, he informed a very surprised DC Laine that he would be conducting the interview with him. As Laine led Giles into the CID office for interview, he took one look at DCI Fenner before he screamed for a solicitor to be present and not just any old brief, either; he demanded that the acerbic barrister, George Carman be summoned. DCI Fenner shrugged his shoulders. 'Fine,' he said. 'Call him.'

Giles bellowed with indignation down the telephone at the clerk in Carman's office who told him that Mr Carman did not deal with legal aid work and the mention of the prestigious Armsby-Croake name did not alter things by one jot. She suggested he try the Yellow Pages – under S for solicitor, she added, sweetly.

Giles was charged with a number of offences and DCI Fenner took a heaven-sent opportunity to telephone his opposite number, DCI Wade at A10 to tell him of the arrest, that Giles would undoubtedly be on the phone to him alleging that he and DC Laine had tried to get a few bob out of him, in return for bail so if he wished, he, Wade, could turn up at court the following day and witness a real detective getting a slimy little shit remanded in custody.

Wade did not make an appearance at the local Magistrates' Court the next day but Giles was given a lay-down for a week and decided that HM Prison Brixton was a beastly place. His family eventually got the matter in front of a judge in chambers and bail, with some stringent conditions, was allowed.

Giles could have contested the matter at the Magistrates' Court but elected trial by jury at the Crown Court. The chance to belittle the police in front of a jury of his peers – well, not his peers, of course, more a bunch of council estate oiks, but they would suffice – was too mouth-watering to pass by. It mattered little to him that the evidence for the prosecution was very strong. He had been arrested whilst driving the cab. He was wearing the stolen badge at the time of his arrest and the stolen licensed bill was in his pocket. The licensed proprietor had positively identified him at an identification parade and Giles' fingerprints were on the written hire agreement.

Giles' defence barrister strongly suggested that he should plead guilty to everything, throw himself on the mercy of the court and let him, the barrister, do the best he could. Giles, quite predictably, would have none of it and, in ringing tones, declared to the court that he was 'not guilty'.

No real defence was put up against the charges. Giles stated that he had for some time been a crusader against corruption in the Metropolitan Police which, he averred, was 'rotten to the core'. He referred to the case in Chelsea and stated that this whole present case was one gigantic frame-up, orchestrated by the Metropolitan Police in general and DCI Fenner in particular.

But in the end, it was a minor point, a bit of silly boastfulness that was to cause Giles' downfall.

He was being cross-examined by his barrister on his antecedents and Giles carelessly stated that he was the recipient of a Bachelor of Law degree and the trial judge suddenly stopped the proceedings and sent the jury out.

'Tell me, Mr Armsby-Croake,' politely enquired the Judge, 'at which university did you read law?'

'It was Trinity College, Cambridge, in 1972,' replied Giles, smoothly.

The judge raised his eyebrows. 'Really? How interesting. Would you leave the witness box and return to the dock, please?' And then he turned in his seat, to face DC Laine who was observing the proceedings and asked him to enter the witness box.

'Mr Laine, I should like you to telephone Trinity College, Cambridge and speak to the dean. Pray give him my compliments and ask him to check the records for 1972 to establish whether or not the Right Honourable Giles Armsby-Croake did in fact receive an LLB in 1972. Oh, and Mr Laine, should you have any difficulty obtaining that information, would you remind the dean that it was at Trinity where I received my degree, albeit somewhat earlier,' he added with a thin smile, 'than the defendant, of course.'

Just as DC Laine was about to leave the court, he saw Giles' defence barrister rise to his feet and address the judge in a somewhat agitated manner. It appeared that he had just received fresh instructions which were both 'sudden and urgent' from his client, who now wished the charges to be put to him again. They were, and Giles pleaded guilty to everything.

What a pity, sighed the judge that the Honourable Giles St John Armsby-Croake had not established a little credit by pleading guilty at the earliest opportunity, instead of turning the courtroom into a stage for a two week vituperative (and totally unjustified) attack on the police. The very least sentence that he felt that he could impose, given all of the circumstances, was one of fifteen months' imprisonment.

As the train roared through the night towards Bath, and home, the judge who had just finished a quite passable dinner and was now sipping a large brandy, smiled at his reflection in the dining-car window. Three matters were in the forefront of his mind. The first was that he had obtained his degree at The Queen's College, Oxford, not Trinity College, Cambridge. The second was that a proper sentence for that type of offence was one of six months' imprisonment and that's what that young man would have received had he not have been such an obnoxious little shit. And the third matter was that when he, the judge, had been a small boy at Harrow public school, long before the war, it had been his misfortune to be a fag to a disgusting, perverted sixth-form bully. The Honourable Henry Armsby-Croake, later to achieve the peerage, was the bully's name.

Messing about on the River

The River Crouch in Essex has, for centuries, been the haunt of smugglers. The river rises at Noak Bridge, near Basildon, and between there and Battlesbridge the river is little more than a stream. From the lock gates at Battlesbridge to where the river empties into the North Sea, between Holliwell Point on the north bank and Foulness Point on the south, the river is tidal and the upper reaches dry to mud on the ebbing tides. Also on the south side, the river is fed by the River Roach.

En route to the North Sea, is the town of Burnham-on-Crouch which is situated on the north side of the river. A former Roman fishing port, it is a town steeped in sailing history; it hosts a regatta, dating back to the early nineteenth century and, at one time, boasted a sailing club as well as three yacht clubs of which one, the Royal Corinthian, boasted no less a revered personage than the Right Honourable Sir Edward Heath MP as a member.

To the south of the river is the area known as Wallasea Island, which is separated from the mainland by a creek, no more than ten feet wide. A pub, named the Creeksea Ferry Inn is situated close to the river's edge. Now ultra respectable, it is understood to have had a troubled past. Over forty years ago, the brothers Kray were said to have had an interest in the premises. Alongside the pub is a slipway into the Crouch, used from time to time to launch small boats into the river and also, it is rumoured, once used to convey the corpse of someone whom the Twins found to be tiresome, into mid-channel. But perhaps this is a bit unfair. The Twins seem to get the blame for everything.

To the east of the pub is the Essex Marina: It's not quite as grandiose as its north shore counterparts – it can boast neither the former prime minister nor the bandleader of the same name amongst its members – but it is very popular with many decent sailing enthusiasts from all walks of life. The centre-piece of the marina is a large building housing the Wardroom Restaurant and a bar on the upper floor. Unfortunately, during the 1970s, some of the less desirable sailors and yachtsmen from Essex and east London – thieves and layabouts – were also regular frequenters; one tender tied to a pontoon was named *Dun Robin*.

Between the Marina and the pub were a timber yard and a quayside known as Baltic Wharf. There, freighters from Russia would dock and unload their cargo of timber before being loaded with grain for the return journey. The Russian sailors were often seen in the pubs in the nearby village of Canewdon.

Since the area was notorious for its smuggling activities, during the eighteenth century two vessels were used by the authorities on the River Crouch. The *Kangaroo* was moored by the north bank, the *Beagle* by the south and they were manned by the coastguards and customs officers to police the smugglers.

But during the 1970s, the whole area of Wallasea Island was covered by just one police officer whose enormous beat included the outlying villages of Paglesham, Eastend, Churchend, Stambridge and Canewdon. At Southend airport, seven or eight miles away to the south-west, four Special Branch and two Customs officers were stationed; and a representation would appear only as and when a Russian ship was due to dock.

*   *   *

Terry Connelly was a second-hand car dealer from Victoria Dock Road in Canning Town. The clapped-out, oil-guzzling dilapidated old bangers and the highly dangerous 'cut 'n'shuts' which Connelly sold to an unsuspecting public probably represented the height of his openness and candour. Apart from that, Connelly was crooked through and through. In and out of prison for fairly moderate sentences as the result of all types of crooked deals, his latest enterprise was to be the importation of large amounts of cannabis.

After a series of introductions, Connelly met two men in Amsterdam who were willing to supply him with this commodity.

'We can supply you with resin, no problem, Terry,' said Dik, the larger of the two. 'For one hundred kilos, it will cost – excuse me—' Here, he produced a pocket calculator and punched the buttons. 'Yes, £1,300 per kilo.'

'That is a good deal,' added Paul, who was shorter, with dark, curly hair. 'Good health!' he toasted their visitor, raising his glass of *jonge jenever*.

Connelly nodded. 'Cheers,' he replied, sipping his beer and looking out along the bustling Weesper Straat. He appeared to be giving the matter deep consideration but he knew Paul was right; it was a good deal. He was fully aware that, at that time, good quality resin in the United Kingdom was trading at between £1,800–£2,300 per kilo. For a capital outlay of £130,000, he was looking at a profit of between £50,000–£100,000. Of course, Connelly's problem, like all smugglers, was how to import it safely into the United Kingdom.

Dik appeared to be reading his mind. 'We can guarantee you a delivery service, Terry. Of course, because the risks are all ours, this naturally comes at a price. We charge £150 per kilo.'

Connelly nodded, again and thought, 'You didn't need your

calculator that time, did you, pal?' And Connelly didn't need a calculator to reveal that if he accepted the offer, his profit margin would be reduced by £15,000. That was not a huge consideration; but what Connelly knew was that there was no guarantee of delivery. He could hand his one hundred and thirty grand over in an Amsterdam 'brown cafe' – a coffee house, so-called because of the tobacco staining on the ceiling – and never see his consignment arrive.

'Of course,' said Paul, smoothly. 'That is only something that we mention, purely for your convenience. Doubtless you have your own arrangements.'

Connelly smiled thinly, stood up and shook hands with both men. 'I'll be in touch.' As he strolled off towards the junction with the Maurits Kade, he was thinking furiously as to how he could overcome the problem with the importation. By the time he had boarded his KLM flight at Schiphol airport, he thought he had the makings of an idea.

Trevor Merchant was the skipper of *Attaboy IV*, a sleek, twenty-seven-foot motor yacht. He held a master's ticket, so he was certainly a competent sailor and he had taken a deep-water mooring at Essex Marina, where he was a frequent visitor most weekends. Merchant had no previous convictions but he had mentioned once or twice that he would be prepared to dip his toe in a criminal enterprise if the price was right. Of course, as we all know, once one's toe is dipped in, it has to go in all the way. He was about to be guided along the whole route, since he was also the brother-in-law of Terry Connelly.

'Are you serious?' That was Trevor Merchant's initial reaction upon being asked to smuggle one hundred kilos of cannabis resin on board his yacht. 'Fuck off!' was the second.

The discussion took place in Connelly's living room, late at night; after his wife had gone up to bed. With the prospect of a profit of up to one hundred grand in the offing, Terry Connelly could be very persuasive. He did not think it necessary or desirable to actually mention his profit margin to his brother-in-law, so when Trevor Merchant asked, 'What's in it for me?' all Connelly said was, 'Ten grand's a nice little earner for a night's work.'

Put that way, to someone who had no concept of the whole-sale and retail prices of cannabis resin, it was.

The trip across the Channel would present no problems to Merchant, since he had made crossings to France and Belgium on a number of occasions. However, now that he had entered into a criminal enterprise, he started to try thinking like a criminal.

'Terry, I don't like the idea of a crossing from Holland to the UK; to me, that's asking for trouble,' he said.

'You've got a point, there,' admitted Connelly. He thought for a moment. 'How about sailing from a Belgian marina – say Blankenberg? That'd be better, wouldn't it?'

'Yachtsmen are supposed to give twenty-four hours' notice of arriving from outside territorial waters to the Harbourmaster at Burnham,' replied Merchant, doubtfully.

'Why – so's he can inform Customs and Excise, just in case they want to turn you over? I'll tell you what,' winked Connelly and ruffled his brother-in-law's hair, 'let's not fucking tell him, then!'

And on that optimistic note, the meeting broke up.

Over the next couple of days, Merchant and Connelly cobbled together a plan.

'Terry, the best time for me to return to the mooring is on a Sunday afternoon,' said Merchant, on that April evening at Connelly's Forest Gate home. 'That's the first thing. The second is that it must be done between May and October. The North

Sea can get right fucking choppy and I want the best sailing conditions possible. And when I get back, I want loads of people about; late spring, early summer, on a Sunday, will be the best bet for that.'

Connelly nodded. 'I can't see anything wrong with that. Now, I'll tell you what I've got in mind. First of all we're going to need a bit of help, both in Amsterdam and Blankenberg, as well as back here. A mate of mine, Ronnie James'll do it; he's good as gold. This is the way I see it. Early on a Friday morning, you set sail for Blankenberg. That'll take you – what? How long?'

'It's about a hundred nautical miles to Blankenberg,' mused Merchant. 'Depending on the sea conditions – maybe ten hours, fifteen max.'

'Right, so while you're doing the crossing, Ronnie and me'll meet the Dutchmen and collect the gear. We'll meet up on the Saturday morning and load the puff into your yacht.'

Merchant nodded. 'All right so far.'

'Then Ronnie and me go down the coast and, on the Saturday evening, we'll catch the ferry from Calais to Dover. Now, early on the Sunday morning, you slip your berth at Blankenberg and make the return crossing. You'll be aiming to reach the mouth of the Crouch in the afternoon, say between two and four.'

Merchant nodded again. 'Go on.'

'On the Sunday morning, I'll hitch up my speedboat to the Range Rover and me and Ronnie'll drive to Wallasea Island and launch the boat into the river, round about one. Then we drive the speedboat through the moorings and when we get to the Roach, we hold it there, call you up on your mobile and as you come alongside, you chuck the parcels over.'

'How long'll the exchange take, d'you reckon?' asked Merchant.

'A minute, maximum,' replied Connelly. 'They're going to be in four holdalls, it'll take no time at all. Then me and Ronnie shoot off back to the slipway, winch the boat back up, hide the gear under the seat and back to London, you return to your mooring, same as usual and nobody's any the wiser.'

Merchant beamed. 'Great!'

Then it was a matter of checking the tide tables and, eventually, they came to the conclusion that, providing the weather conditions were favourable, the ideal time for Merchant to make the crossing to Belgium would be on the morning of 18 May.

Connelly made several telephone calls to Dik and Paul as well as two more trips to Amsterdam to confirm that the deal was still on and also to arrange for the exchange of money and drugs at a motorway service station, just north of Breda in southern Holland – just twenty miles from the Belgian border. He also checked the marina at Blankenberg. He found a little cafe down at the beachfront – close enough and yet sufficiently far from the marina – for the three men to meet. A last minute check of the weather on 16 May revealed that the conditions promised to be fine for a crossing on the Friday and that the outlook for the whole weekend was good. So it proved to be; Merchant experienced no problems whatsoever during the crossing.

Meanwhile, Terry Connelly and Ronnie James met their contacts, Dik and Paul at the service station near Breda. They had a driver with them who handed Connelly one of the 'soaps' of resin – so-called because when the resin has been pressed from the cannabis plant it goes into a mould to be set and the half-kilo mould resembles a large bar of soap – and he laughed and said, 'Good stuff, yes?' Connelly looked; there on the resin was an embossed mark. Many dealers had their own stamps made up; they were pressed into the resin at the point of sale, normally Morocco, and compared when they reached Amsterdam, to ensure that they hadn't been ripped-off.

Connelly smiled and nodded. 'Yeah, good stuff, mate.'

The payment and the exchange went off without incident and Connelly and James drove off in their hire truck, south towards the Belgian border – all customs posts between Holland and Belgium had been abolished years previously – and on to Blankenberg. In fact, everything had gone so smoothly, they found that they were actually ahead of schedule. The three men met up in the cafe late on the Friday evening.

'How'd it go, Terry?' asked Merchant, breathlessly.

Connelly grinned and winked. 'Sweet as a nut, mate. Tell you what. Why wait till morning? It's late enough and dark enough. Let's get the gear on board, now.'

They finished their coffee and went outside to the hire truck. Merchant and James took a holdall each. Connelly took the other two. Fifty kilos took a deal of carrying but Connelly did not want to risk making two trips to the yacht and, in any event, with his adrenalin flowing, he managed the journey easily. In the cabin, the men had a drink and chatted about the purchase and what each of them intended to do with their share from the sale of the cannabis. That night they slept on the yacht and the following morning, after a late breakfast, Connelly and James drove off towards Calais and England.

Merchant spent a stress-filled day on the yacht, not daring to leave it and tried to get as much rest as he could. He knew he would get little enough sleep that night. At four o'clock the following morning, his heart thumping, Merchant cast off from the pontoon and sailed out into the North Sea. The tide was running at about one knot in his favour, so with the fine weather conditions, he estimated that he would make the crossing in approximately nine hours.

Later the same morning, in Forest Gate, Connelly and James

were busy hitching up Connelly's speedboat, *Wicked Willy* to the Range Rover. The vehicle was not, of course, registered in Connelly's name; he had picked it up a few weeks previously at a car auction. With both men on board, the Range Rover headed east, along the Romford Road towards Essex.

Just after eleven, the speedboat was backed down the slipway and into the River Crouch. After Connelly pulled the boat round to the Essex Marina and tied up to a pontoon, James had a look around the marina and the repair yards. Everything seemed fine. Just a usual Sunday, with quite a few people just wandering about, most of them families, coming and going to boats on the jetties. And there were others, working at boats on the hardstandings. Yes, just a normal Sunday.

At one o'clock, Connelly and James headed *Wicked Willy* out towards Foulness Island, which lay between the River Roach and the North Sea. Shortly after two o'clock, Connelly's mobile rang.

'Terry? It's me. Just passed the outer Crouch buoy,' said Merchant. His voice was strained with the tension. It had been a calm enough crossing, but he had nevertheless thrown up, twice. 'Should be with you in an hour.'

Connelly turned into the River Roach and kept the engine idling as he drifted on the tide. Three-quarters of an hour later, Merchant called again. 'Terry, I'll be level with the mouth of the Roach in about five minutes. I've had a look round and all the other craft movement is light. Approach me on your port side.'

Connelly throttled the speedboat's engine and headed out into the Crouch and as he turned to the east, he could see Merchant's yacht approaching him, two hundred yards away. James took up position on the speedboat's port side as the two vessels slowly came alongside each other and he grabbed the gunwales of the yacht.

The holdalls were 'coopered' across – an old smuggling expression going back to the days when barrels of brandy were passed between boats on similar missions – and Merchant rapidly passed the holdalls across to Connelly, who was quite right in his assumption that the exchange would take about one minute.

In fact, it took fifty-seven seconds for the last holdall to be 'coopered', according to the log of the senior swimmer-canoeist from the Special Boat Service's M Squadron, who boarded both crafts and seized them.

The Special Boat Squadron (SBS) – it became known as the Special Boat Service in 1987 – had been the seaborne section of the wartime Special Air Service and they had carried out daring raids against the Germans and Italians in the Aegean. In 1946, they became part of the Royal Marines and the operatives were trained in parachuting, demolitions, survival training, swimming and canoeing. In later years, one of their maritime duties has been the protection of oil rigs – that, and assisting Her Majesty's Customs and Excise. M Squadron was part of the Marine Counter Terrorism team, skilled in covert operations, both on water and on land.

On this particular occasion, they had used three RIBs (rigid inflatable boats), each powered by a large outboard motor, lying low in the water; one on the northern bank of the Crouch, the second on a saltmarsh between Hullbridge and Wallasea Island. As soon as the speedboat had left its mooring at the marina, so this second RIB moved off after it. The third, and closest, RIB had actually been in the River Roach. The entire operation had been controlled by SBS personnel, dug in along the banks of the river; in overall charge had been a senior investigator of HMC&E who had been on board a covert motor yacht, used by the SBS. Two SBS diving teams had been on standby, in case the merchandise had been thrown over the side.

But of course, it wasn't, because of the almost invisible approach of the RIBs and the shocked crews of *Attaboy IV* and *Wicked Willy* gave up immediately. Given the fearsome reputation of the SBS (motto: 'By Strength and Guile'), it was the most prudent course of action: so was Connelly's and James' plea of guilty to the importation charge, for which they were each sentenced to seven years' imprisonment.

Merchant decided to contest the case, claiming that it was his understanding that they were smuggling tobacco. His barrister was working on the assumption that with the two principals convicted, the Crown would not wish to expose the evidence which had been gathered by covert means. It was a serious mistake.

The two Dutchmen, Dik and Paul, had been targets of the Dutch State Police who had worked in conjunction with HMC&E to effect the arrests. The Dutch prosecutor was not interested in locking up Dik and Paul for possessing one hundred kilos of cannabis resin; he wanted them convicted of racketeering. To this end, evidence was gathered by means of telephone interception, which can be used in Holland as evidence, and also by means of covert surveillance. But that wasn't all. The Dutch police had infiltrated the gang behind it all – import from Morocco, export to the United Kingdom – with an undercover police officer. In fact, he had delivered the cannabis to Connelly and James at Breda and followed them to Blankenberg. Cooperation with the Belgian authorities had resulted in a probe being installed in *Attaboy IV*'s cabin. The conversation between the three men on the Friday evening had all been recorded, which revealed that Merchant had been fully aware that it had not been tobacco which he had been importing. Anyway, one hundred kilos of cannabis resin in a twenty-seven-foot yacht is more than sufficient to stink it out.

So it was a sad blow for Merchant to be sentenced to nine years' imprisonment. That, plus the sequestration of his beloved *Attaboy IV* by HMC&E was almost too much to bear. At a cost of £30,000, that represented three times the amount that his brother-in-law had promised him.

Give 'em Both a Big Hand!

Jimmy Busby was born in Bethnal Green and he spent much of his life there. He was not handsome, tall or particularly bright but he was cunning and thoroughly reliable and since Jimmy was a persistent thief, this counted for much amongst Bethnal Green's criminal fraternity.

His criminal career had been punctuated with periods of incarceration in a number of His and, later, Her Majesties' places of correction but it was Jimmy's proud boast that he had never carried out a day's honest toil. After a period of Borstal Training, much earlier in his criminal career, he had been told that his licence could be revoked if he could not show that he was gainfully employed thereafter and therefore whenever he was arrested he inevitably stated that he was a self-employed painter and decorator. Over a pint in the Rose and Crown, he did admit with a grin that whenever his premises were turned over, any copper who discovered a single paint brush or a solitary pot of paint could quite accurately be accused of planting them there. One arresting officer at Old Street Magistrates' Court stated, 'He appears to have been living on his wits, Your Worship,' which was a rather polite way of saying, 'He's a thieving little bastard.' The latter, unspoken statement was one which was absolutely accurate.

Jimmy's physique – or rather, the lack of it – imposed certain limitations on his criminal career. Blaggings were out; firstly, violence was not his game and secondly, no victim would have been brought to a petrified and submissive state by the appearance of Jimmy's pigeon chest. Pickpocketting or whizzing was a science, requiring a skilful apprenticeship of several years and this was an expertize with which nature had not thought fit to endow him. No, Jimmy was a thief, pure and simple, who would nick anything which was not actually red-hot or riveted to the ground.

In 1956, Jimmy was thirty-four years of age and he had just carried out a raid on a warehouse on an industrial estate in Ealing. The prize had been carpets, worth three grand – serious money. Jimmy had acquired the services of a receiver, who had seen a sample carpet, declared himself very interested and had agreed to meet Jimmy in a drinking club. There, over a light ale, they would finalize the deal, Jimmy would arrange for the delivery of the carpets to the receiver's lorry and, after paying off the rest of the team, he would be several hundred, not unimportant, pounds the richer. Jimmy's eyes gleamed at the thought and in agreeing to meet the receiver in the club which was situated just off Dunbridge Street, he completely forgot that the thoroughfare was adjacent to Vallance Road. There, at No. 178, was the family home of Reggie and Ronnie Kray.

At the time of Jimmy's proposed meet with the receiver, the Kray Twins' social standing amongst the East End fraternity was already high. Born in 1933, the Twins' name had soon become synonymous with trouble with a capital T. Encouraged by their maternal grandfather, Jimmy 'Cannonball' Lee, they trained conscientiously as boxers, firstly at the Mansford Club and later at the Repton Club. In and out of brushes with the law – they were placed on probation after both attacking the same police constable – they turned professional and Reggie, boxing as a lightweight, won all of his seven bouts, with Ronnie winning four of his contests and losing two. Called up for National Service in 1953, they attacked a non-commissioned officer and casually strolled off home. Arrested the following morning they were returned to the Army and promptly escaped – again and again. Eventually, a uniformed police officer spotted them in Hackney and was duly assaulted as he tried to detain them. When the Krays were arrested, they were sentenced to one month's imprisonment for the attack on the constable. Returned once more to the military authorities, they wound up serving nine months' detention in Shepton Mallet military prison and, at the end of their sentence, they were ignominiously discharged from the Army.

The Twins demanded protection money on the racetracks, from bar, shop, and later club owners. When they desired a billiard hall for their headquarters, they selected one in the Mile End Road and simply moved in. No one tried to stop them, any more than they did when the Twins took over the Green Dragon Club.

But for anybody who did try to thwart them, in any way whatsoever, the penalties were frightful. With considerable justification, the Twins' family home was known as 'Fort Vallance'. Underneath the floorboards of the Twins' shared bedroom was a veritable arsenal; guns, knives, bayonets. Victims were shot, stabbed and, on one occasion, left for dead in a gutter. The weapon which had been used, a bicycle chain, was lying next to the victim, thick with his blood. And the violence was getting worse . . .

Jimmy Busby had a slight acquaintance with the Twins and wished to keep it that way. But as he sipped his light ale and waited for the arrival of the receiver, he was rather perturbed. Whenever a decent job had gone off, the Twins seemed to know about it and they demanded a cut of the take; sometimes as much as 50 per cent. It was those horrible queer little bastards, thought Jimmy – 'Ronnie's Boys' as they were known – who would make themselves busy and pick up scraps of information which they would excitedly impart to Ronnie at his club. But on this occasion, what with that warehouse job being pulled well away from the manor, Jimmy fervently hoped that he was safe. Both of the brothers were forces to be reckoned with – Jimmy had seen their handiwork on several occasions – but Ronnie was the worst. Ronnie was a *monster*.

Jimmy nervously looked at his watch again. The receiver was not really late; in fact, Jimmy had arrived early, but he did wish the receiver would hurry up. He could hear raised voices. There were two swarthy-looking blokes at the bar and they seemed to be having some sort of ruck with Timmy, the owner. Christ, they were a noisy pair – what were they, Greek? With those thick accents, he could hardly make out a word they were saying. Why didn't Timmy shut them up; or, better still, chuck them out? Noisy buggers. Jimmy lit a cigarette and started to look through some runners and riders in the midday racing edition of the *Standard*.

It was just at that moment that the doors to the club opened with a crash. Jimmy turned and saw that three men had entered. Two of them, whom Jimmy had never seen before, looked like real hard bastards. They stood either side of the third man, who had his back to the clientele, because he was busy ramming home the bolts, top and bottom of the doors. His task completed, the man slowly turned to stare at the punters at the bar. With a muted gasp of horror, Jimmy realized that the man at the door was his nemesis, Ronnie Kray.

It was much, much later that Jimmy was able to cobble together the reason for Ronnie Kray's sudden appearance. It had nothing at all to do with Jimmy's warehouse escapade.

Kosta and Stelios were just two of a large number of Cypriots who had come over to England at that time and they had made their home in Tufnell Park, north London. Both were tough and no strangers to violent conflict; they had served in the ranks of the EOKA terror gangs. They had decided to capitalize on their toughness and a number of Cypriot cafe owners in the Holloway area were paying them a 'pension' to keep trouble away from their doors. And all might have been well, had they remained in that area of London and not strayed to the south east, into Kray territory. The two Greek Cypriots had made their first appearance at the drinker the previous week.

It had been a quiet lunchtime when they barged in; Timmy, the owner was behind the bar, polishing glasses. The men demanded Scotch and as Timmy pressed each glass in turn under the optic, he immediately realized that these two meant trouble, that they were not there purely to drink Scotch (for which they obviously had no intention of paying) and that the reason for their presence was almost certain to put the bite on him. But, as he passed the glasses to them, and Kosta snapped, 'Where's the guv'nor?' in his thickly accented English, Timmy gave a silent sigh of relief. It meant they had no idea that he was the owner and that in all probability, they had mistaken him for the barman – which they had.

'Sorry, gents,' he replied, giving every indication of regret. 'The guv'nor ain't here; he's away in Blackpool for the week. On 'is 'ols, like. Won't be back till – er – next Tuesday.'

Stelios slowly looked round the interior of the club. The very few patrons present prudently raised their newspapers in the way that commuters do when a fellow passenger is being mugged.

'Nice little place you got here,' he said slowly. 'Sort of place that don't want no trouble; know what I mean?'

Timmy nodded vigorously.

'Be a pity if it were to get smashed up, know what I mean?'

Timmy nodded again. It was not difficult to be intimidated by this pair.

Kosta nodded as well. 'We can make sure there's no trouble. It'll cost your boss twenty quids a week – every week. Got it?'

For the third time, Timmy nodded so hard, it seemed his head would fall off. Both Stelios and Kosta looked hard at him and felt quite certain their message had got through. They drained their glasses, Kosta leaned over the bar, banged the 'No Sale' key on the till, extracted a handful of pound notes from the drawer and said, 'Next Tuesday – make sure you tell the boss.' Stelios stuck the heel of his hand under Timmy's chin and shoved; Timmy staggered backwards, knocking over some bottles as he did so. And with that, the Cypriots had gone.

In the silence that followed, one of the customers made a hurried exit; another called out, 'You all right, Tim?' Timmy nodded absently as he dusted himself down. He thanked his lucky stars that he'd had the presence of mind not to admit to being the owner. As he picked up the fallen bottles, he decided that a call round to 178 Vallance Road would prove advantageous. What was the point of paying out to the Greeks to provide protection when he was paying exactly the same amount to Ronnie Kray for the same service?

And now, it was the following Tuesday. The Cypriots had stopped arguing with Timmy and all was silent in the bar. Ronnie Kray, who despite the agreeable weather was wearing a topcoat over his well-pressed suit, spoke. He had a soft, lisping voice which made him sound all the more terrifying. Addressing Timmy, he said simply, 'That them?' and Timmy displayed agreement by simply showing the whites of his eyes.

Kosta, the bulkier of the two men was about to learn the hard way that it is one thing to fearlessly snipe at members of the British Army from the safety of the Troodos Mountains but quite another to meet an adversary who had already been awarded a First-Class Honours Degree for bar-room fighting from the school of hard knocks. He was nearest to Ronnie Kray and he started to move aggressively towards him but Kosta was a million years too late. Although he did not appear to move very quickly, Kray was across the club's floor in a second and his heavy right-hand punch caught Kosta just below his left eye and sent him crashing to the floor. Ronnie Kray ignored him. To his henchmen, he indicated Stelios with a nod of his head and said, 'Bring 'im over 'ere.'

Jimmy Busby swallowed loudly. He knew Ronnie Kray's track record and he was as certain as he could be that he was going to witness a 'striping' – that Kray was going to produce an open razor and lay the Cypriot's cheeks open to the bone, as a mark of his displeasure. He was wrong. In the Kray psyche, razors were now last year's fashion for displaying irritation and, furthermore, Ronnie Kray had dismissed razors as being 'babyish', adding that 'you can't get no power behind a razor.'

He now revealed the reason for wearing his unseasonable topcoat. 'Put 'is 'and on the bar,' he said to his associates and, opening his overcoat, he withdrew a cutlass. With the club's lighting glinting on the long, razor sharp blade, there was a sickening 'thud!' and the unfortunate Stelios had his hand severed. As he screamed from the pain and then slumped to the floor, fainting from the shock, Ronnie Kray, indicating Kosta, said, 'Get 'im up' and he was hauled by his arms from the floor. As his arm was duly held down on the bar, he stared at Stelios' hand, which by now was just a white claw on the bar and he screamed with terror at what he knew was about to happen. He did not have long to wait. The blade came crashing down, a fountain of blood shot into the air, Kosta's bloodless hand rolled towards what had been the terminal part of Stelios' right arm and he slumped, moaning to the floor.

'Get 'em up,' growled Ronnie and, as a henchman each pulled the dazed racketeers to their feet, Kray addressed both of them. Whatever was said, was spoken forcefully but quietly and Jimmy Busby could not catch exactly what was said. But from the look of terror on their faces, it was clear that apart from seeking urgent medical treatment, the pair neither wished to visit Bethnal Green ever again, nor did they wish to bother any of the inhabitants of that area of London. 'Get 'em out of 'ere,' was Ronnie Kray's instruction to his associates and as the two Cypriots were dragged towards the door, Ronnie Kray said the words which would be imprinted on Jimmy's mind for ever. 'Keep yer 'ands out of other peoples tills in future,' he said and picking up the severed hands from the bar, he stuffed them into the Cypriots' jacket pockets, 'and take these with yer!'

The two men were thrown out into the street and they were followed by Ronnie Kray and his associates who all went their separate ways. Miraculously, the Cypriots survived. Shortly thereafter, they returned to their native Nicosia where they had decided that life would be considerably more peaceful. Later that same year, in November, Ronnie Kray, who had been found in possession of a loaded gun, was sentenced to three years' imprisonment for inflicting grievous bodily harm. The victim's name was Terry Martin; Ronnie was never prosecuted for the attack on Stelios or Kosta.

But back in the club, there was silence save for the sound of vomiting from a particularly queasy customer in the corner. Jimmy got busy with a mop and bucket, the bar area claiming his attention rather than the bile in the corner of the room, which could wait. Five long minutes went by. Jimmy's heart was pounding, his breath was rasping and, with an unsteady hand, he picked up his bottle of light ale and poured the remainder of it into his glass. As he slowly drank it down, the glass rattled against his teeth. Suddenly, a hand clapped on his shoulder and Jimmy all but jumped out of his skin. Ronnie Kray had obviously remembered some unfinished business.

'Wotcher, Jim,' grinned the receiver. 'Sorry I'm late. Anything happening?'

The Third Man

In the forty-five years since it occurred, there have been a number of misconceptions surrounding the attack which occurred during the unscheduled stop at Sears Crossing, Buckinghamshire, of the Glasgow to London Mail Train at three o'clock in the morning of 8 August 1963, which became known as the Great Train Robbery.

Firstly, there is the 'Robin Hood' legend which sprang up almost as soon as the job was pulled which portrayed the persons responsible as a bunch of loveable rascals who effectively got away with £2.6 million and thumbed their noses at the police. Mercifully, this particular myth is slowly giving up the ghost.

Next, there is the school of thought that suggests that even though the job was meticulously planned, it was just bad luck that the robbers were caught. There are truths and half-truths in this theory. This job *was* meticulously planned, in many cases down to the finest detail by the small nucleus of those who ran the job but, in the end, the majority of the train gang were arrested because of their own stupidity and indiscipline.

Some police officers will still say that they had 'heard a whisper' about 'the big one' that was going to be pulled. That could, to a certain extent, be true, because several injudicious remarks had been dropped by certain of the gang members themselves. But the police had no idea whatsoever that it was the Mail Train that was going to be robbed. Had they known, the mail sorters would have been replaced with Flying Squad detectives and the Train Gang would have received the shock of their lives.

Then there is the assumption that the police – mainly the Flying Squad, who made the majority of the arrests – fitted up the train robbers in order to get them convicted. This line of argument was started by the gang. It was not true. If it had been true, every member of the gang would have been convicted, because, although almost everyone who took part in the planning of the raid or the raid itself was arrested, not all of them were found guilty. There is a school of thought that three gang members were not charged or even arrested for the job. Over the years, I have compiled the names of those who I believe were the missing three men. This is not because I have been told the names by informants, or by police officers who worked on the investigation, because I have not. I have simply come up with those names because they had the ability and the reputation to take part in such an enterprise, and they were at liberty at the time the job was pulled. Perhaps one day I shall have a glass with Bob Robinson who was responsible for 'housing' Bruce Reynolds, the gang's mastermind, which brought about his belated arrest after five years on the run. Perhaps I shall casually drop my three names into the conversation to judge his reaction. And perhaps he'll tell me whether I'm right or not.

Because one of the men I fancied for the Train Job was one I shall refer to as Barry Thompson.

At the time of our conversation, nearly a quarter of a century ago, Thompson and I were seated at a table, drinking tea. That doesn't fit the description of a hardened, first-division robber, I know; just accept that it was the case. After a successful blagging, Thompson might modestly celebrate his and his team's success with a glass of 1976 vintage Bollinger champagne. Just one glass, mind; and possibly he wouldn't even finish it. No, Thompson was a consummate professional. He hardly drank, didn't smoke and kept himself in such tip-top physical condition that his training routine would have put an Olympic athlete to shame. He dressed smartly but not pretentiously; his watch was a stainless steel Rolex but he wore no other jewellery. He lived in a smart, well appointed but unostentatious house and he drove an immaculately maintained and well-polished three-year-old Jaguar. He did not give parties, nor attend them. His neighbours thought that he was 'something in the city' and he did not attempt to disillusion them. The minute planning of blaggings was carried out at his house or at one of his accomplices' houses and anybody seeing any of them arrive or leave would have been excused for thinking that a group of businessmen were attending (or had just successfully concluded) a high-power meeting involving the acquisition or re-distribution of large amounts of money which, come to think of it, was quite correct. When neighbours, restraurateurs or hoteliers spoke to him, they would remark afterwards on his quiet, courteous demeanour.

Out on a job, Thompson was a very different kettle of fish. At six foot one, weighing just over thirteen stone, he was physically impressive enough. On a blagging he looked even more bulky and menacing, given that under his boiler suit, he was wearing a well-fitting suit, collar and tie. The boiler suit and stocking mask would be discarded in the back of the first of the three or even possibly four getaway cars. Anybody spotting him in the last of the getaway vehicles would see a calm, immaculately dressed gentleman, meticulously obeying every aspect of the Road Traffic Act. And the man who, during the blagging, would be screaming nonsensical demands to disorientate and control the terrified victims, who would be punching, elbowing, clubbing, shooting or, on at least two occasions, pouring petrol over them, would have been the complete antithesis of the person who had spoken so courteously to his neighbours. If anybody had suggested to the neighbours that the screaming, vicious, out-of-control blagger and the man who lived next door were one and the same, they would, with considerable justification, have laughed.

I could not be considered to be his next-door neighbour and Barry Thompson and I were certainly on opposite sides of the fence but we laughed, joked and drank our tea before I considered it an opportune moment to say, 'By the way Barry, what was your share from the Train Job?'

I really don't know what I expected him to say. I certainly didn't expect him to say, 'Oh, y'know, Dick, about a hundred and fifty grand, same as everybody else,' and he didn't. I suppose I half-expected him to give one of his scoffing laughs and retort, 'Fuckin' hell, I wish I had!' or something similar.

Instead, the smile came off his face as though he'd been slapped. There was something else in his expression, too. What was it? Fear? No. Perhaps a look of betrayal, as if to say, 'Who's been talking to you?' But he didn't say that. In fact, he didn't say anything at all. His mouth set in a thin, obstinate line, he sat back and folded his arms and he said nothing at all. This didn't bode well. I wanted him talking and the fact was I'd touched a nerve, really I suppose, to massage my own vanity so that I could say, 'There you are – I knew it was you!'

So I forgot the Great Train Robbery. We had another cup of tea. I talked about inconsequential matters. And after a bit, when he saw I wasn't going to pursue unacceptable and inappropriate matters which occurred on 8 August 1963, he thawed and started talking about something completely different. This is the story he told me.

*   *   *

Barry Thompson had just been released from prison after serving a nine year sentence for armed robbery. Naturally, he wanted to start going across the pavement once again and as soon as possible. He had already sorted out a nice piece of work which required the assistance of one other person; the only thing that was missing was an accomplice. Therefore his next port of call was to pay a visit to Alf Griffiths who, coincidentally, was Man Number One on my private list of unaccounted-for Great Train Robbers.

It was a hot summer's day and Griffiths greeted Thompson on the terrace of his Surrey mansion which commanded a panoramic view over the North Downs as they swept down to the Weald. He laughed and shook his head at Thompson's offer as he poured a bottle of tonic water into a glass which he handed to him. 'Sorry, Baz, I'm out.' Griffiths turned and looked at the view. 'All this is too much to lose. Besides, I'm too well known in blagging circles.'

Thompson frowned as he sipped his drink but said nothing. He really had been relying on Alf Griffiths for some assistance. 'No, I'm doing a little importing and exporting,' grinned Griffiths. 'Most of the time, I don't even see the consignment. The stuff comes in and the money goes out; straight into a nice little off-shore bank.' He paused. 'Want me to put you in?'

Thompson shook his head. He had no particular moral views on the importation of drugs; it was that he would simply have felt like a fish out of water. Far better to stick with what he was good at. He swallowed the rest of his drink and held out his hand, to bid goodbye to his former accomplice.

But Griffiths, deep in thought, ignored the outstretched hand and turned away. 'Just a moment,' he muttered. 'There is one bloke that you could make one with. I ain't worked with him but Kenny Baker has and he reckons he's a good 'un. Says he's got a lot of bottle and what's more, he's never been caught. Name's Gerry Harding. I've got his phone number, somewhere. Interested?'

And that was how Barry Thompson and Gerry Harding teamed up. Their first job was almost their last.

It was one that Thompson had spent a considerable amount of time researching and the beauty of it was that it was tailor made for a two-handed team. The prize was a security van. The delivery took place at the Municipal Offices, situated at Wansey Street, Southwark. The security van parked in Ethel Street at the rear of the premises at the bottom of a cul-de-sac. Across the road from Larcom Street was St John's Church and, from behind a wall, the security van and the two guards making the delivery could be seen quite plainly. Thompson's plan was to surprise the guards, knock them into unconsciousness, grab the money bags and then race across Larcom Street and hop over the wall and into the churchyard. There, in some bushes, would be hidden two stolen motorcycles. The money bags would be shoved into two rucksacks and with these on their backs, their faces disguised by the motorcycle helmets, they would drive to the church entrance, split up and drive separately to a predetermined place. The plan had dash, determination and it was simple.

Thompson and Harding crouched behind the churchyard wall. They had seen the delivery (Harding for the first time) and as the van drove off, they got to their feet. 'See?' said Thompson, as they walked back to where the motorcycles had been stashed. 'A piece of cake.'

'Dunno why we didn't hit it there and then, Baz,' said Harding, morosely. 'Because this is the first time you've been here,' replied Thompson, patiently. 'I wanted you to get the feel of the place and I wanted you to get used to the route you're going to take when we do it, see?' Harding grunted and with that they reached the bushes and Thompson started to pull the motorbike from the undergrowth.

'So *you're* the one who did it!' exclaimed a loud, angry voice and Thompson turned to see the furious, middle-aged church verger approaching them. 'How dare you! Don't you realize this is consecrated ground?'

In an instant, Thompson knew the job was over – that was certain. His next thought was not to let the verger see his face and he quickly donned his motorcycle helmet.

'Sorry, Guv'nor,' he muttered. 'Didn't realize – stupid thing to do – won't happen again – we'll be off, now. Sorry about that,' but as he began to swing his leg over the motorcycle, he realized that Harding had not joined him. Turning, he saw that he had grabbed hold of the astonished verger.

'You fucking slag!' shouted Harding. 'Fucking tell me what to do? I'll fucking stripe you, you—' and with that, Thompson pulled him away, pushed him towards his motorcycle and snapped, 'Get going!' They roared away and they kept in convoy until Thompson found a spot far enough and secluded enough from the scene of the churchyard.

'Blimey, Baz, that fucking priest was well out of—' and that was as far as Harding got, before he collected a right hook in his eye. As he sprawled on the ground, Thompson stood ready to go for him again. 'YOU CUNT!' he roared, really losing his temper. He was so angry he found it difficult to choose the right words. 'I must've been fucking mad – putting my lot in with a cunt like you! Crazy! You've got no more idea than— Right. Your bike – get fucking rid of it. And you, you stupid bastard – I don't want to see or hear from you again. Got it?'

'Sure, Baz, sure,' muttered Harding, tenderly rubbing his eye which had already started to swell and getting unsteadily to his feet. By the time he had done so, Thompson had kicked his machine into life and was gone.

And all might have been well if Thompson, at Alf Griffiths' insistence, hadn't decided to give Gerry Harding 'one more chance'. It really was not in his nature to do so. But he did and the two of them went on to carry out some spectacular raids which netted them enormous sums of money, money which, if prudently invested, would have provided both of them with comfortable lifestyles until the end of their days.

But of course, a blagger's life's not like that. As insecure as any actor, as soon as they finish one job of work, they begin to fret, wondering if they will ever achieve success again. So they go on and on until, inevitably, the wheel comes off. Once again, it was Harding who made a catastrophic error of judgement which led the police right to their door and a serious amount of porridge for both of them. Both of them were later released but, after a short period of liberty, both of them were inevitably imprisoned again and, in Harding's case, it is highly unlikely that he will ever be released.

Barry Thompson? Just the other day at lunch when I was in rather – er – mixed company, I was approached by someone who murmured, 'Know him?' and slid a piece of paper into my hand. On it was written Barry Thompson's correct particulars.

Expressionless, I handed back the piece of paper and shrugged in a non-committal sort of way. 'Maybe.'

Thompson had finally taken his friend Alf Griffith's advice and had gone into the import and export business; Customs and Excise had relieved him of his importation and his liberty before his recompense could be exported to a nice, safe off-shore bank account. Now, well into his seventies, Thompson faces a bleak future.

So was he or was he not the Third Man in my private list of Great Train Robbery participants? If you ever bump into him, don't bother to ask. Somehow, I think you'll meet with the same lack of success as I did.

Trouble in Store

Upminster is situated twenty miles east of London at the end of the District Line. Thanks to the stupidity of Havering Borough Council in acceding to just about every application for new pubs and fast food shops, it is fast degenerating into a dump. At night, groups of sullen, hooded youngsters fill themselves with greasy hamburgers and then wander off to the off-licence before, packs of lager in hand, they dominate the large park in Corbets Tey Road. Due to the insipid policing, buses are set on fire and there are no-go areas, so that with rival groups drifting into the area to clash with the home-grown variety of scum, it is a reckless, decent person indeed who walks the streets, alone. It's a pity that the parish councillors did not heed the words of John Buchan who, almost ninety years ago, wrote, 'If you don't exercise constant care, the jungle, in the shape of the slums, will break in.'

But the story that follows occurred in Upminster forty years ago, when it was a desirable place to live and it was a leafy suburb, instead of being referred to, as it is now, as being 'the East End of London'. There were then many fine shops, one of which was Roomes Stores, which still exists and is still properly regarded as upmarket. At the time of this story, Roomes was situated in Station Road and the two aspects of the premises – the Department and the Furnishing Store – were sited on either side of Branfill Road. The current warehouse had just been built, which was situated at the rear of the Furnishing Store, on the north side of Branfill Road, as was the extended car park. Then, because the store's takings were so substantial (and because they were usually in cash) it was considered too risky for the money to be banked and therefore it was collected by one of the security company's vans, which were becoming more and more popular. Especially with the blaggers.

During the sixties, there was probably something like fifty men in the Greater London Area who were responsible for armed blaggings on banks, Post Offices and cash in transit vehicles. But with the abolition of the death penalty, the numbers grew proportionally larger and coshes and ammonia sprays were being replaced with firearms, especially the simple to get hold of, straightforward to convert and easy to conceal sawn-off shotgun. The brothers John and Alan Morgan had experienced no trouble at all in acquiring two of these devastatingly lethal weapons.

The Morgans hailed from Dagenham and, although both had a history of petty (and not so petty) crime, neither had any convictions for blagging, although they had participated in a number of raids. John was the cleverer of the two, Alan provided the muscle. The raids which they had carried out had been in all different parts of London and each one had been meticulously planned. They had received help from an early age, having listened to Jimmy Woods, a relative on their mother's side of the family, who, with his brother George had participated in the ill-fated London Airport Robbery of 1948 and who had accordingly drawn nine years' imprisonment. Although the botched robbery had been the brainchild of Jack Spot, Woods also told the brothers about the ability of Spot's great rival, Billy Hill, who had perfected the use of the three- and sometimes four-car change-over, following smash and grab raids, during the 1930s and 1940s.

They also unwittingly received help from the police, because at that time there was little collation of crimes, each area commander thinking that each blagging committed by the Morgans was the work of separate teams.

And now, John Morgan thought it high time to hit Roomes Stores, just as the week's takings were being collected on a Friday afternoon.

He spread out a map of the area on the dining room table of their council house. 'This is the way I see it,' he told his brother. He stabbed his finger at Branfill Road. 'This is Roomes, right? Just along here on the left is the car park. You and me, with Arthur driving the van, pull up in the car park. From there, we can see the security wagon come into Branfill Road and into the loading bay, right?'

Alan Morgan nodded. 'Just the way we see 'em do it over the past three weeks, right, John?'

'Right. And they never take less than three minutes to bring the dough out and no more than four. So after the van arrives, we give 'em a couple of minutes, walk down the road, grab the guard as he comes out, get the dough, back to the van and away.'

Alan Morgan nodded. 'Yeah, that's right. We've been through all this before.'

'Now, what we do is sort out the getaway,' said John. 'The night before the raid, we put down three motors. The first is down here,' and he pointed to Champion Road, close to the junction with St Mary's Lane. 'When we get in the van, Arthur drives us down the road, then pulls the van across the road. It's narrow there and if anyone comes after us, they won't be able to get by. Then into the motor and out into St Mary's Lane and down towards Hornchurch.'

Alan frowned. 'Yeah, I don't like that bit, John. See, by then they'll have phoned Old Bill and they'll be coming straight at us, from Hornchurch nick.'

'They would, except they ain't going to see us,' replied his brother. 'Just before Upminster Bridge station, we turn left and then right.' Now, his finger pointed at Aldborough Road. 'That's where the next motor is going to be put down. See, it's even narrower than Champion Road. Arthur pulls the first motor across the road, we get into the next one and off we go. Along the route back here, we could always have another motor, plotted-up, just in case. What d'you think?'

'It looks all right,' replied Alan, a shade doubtfully. So they went over the plan again and again. Regarding the finer details, it would be Arthur's job to nick the van and the three cars. They would be cleaned and be filled with sufficient petrol before the three cars were laid down with ignition keys placed under the sun visors. As soon as the three men got into the van, gloves would be worn and would not be removed until after the robbery when the guns and money were stashed in the garage, rented in a fictitious name, and the stocking masks, donkey jackets and gloves were dumped in a convenient dustbin. Back indoors, their sister would have spent all afternoon watching television. In the event of an alibi being needed, all of them would be able to quote sizeable chunks of the programmes which she had watched.

It was a good plan, in fact, a very good plan indeed and one worthy of the genius of a Billy Hill. Unfortunately, there was a flaw in it. Every aspect of the operation was already known to the police.

The Morgan brothers' sister, Joyce, was a garrulous creature in bed and she was so enormously proud of her brothers' expertize that she murmured the whole plan to her current boyfriend. That would not have been so bad if he had not mentioned it to *his* brother, who was on bail to the Flying Squad for receiving a lorry load of goods. He was facing the almost inevitable prospect of drawing two years' imprisonment, unless, of course he could provide information so attractive as to practically guarantee a suspended sentence. And now he could.

Since it appeared that, on the information the police had been given, there was no inside agent involved, four Squad men would secrete themselves in the loading bay. This meant taking the management of Roomes into their confidence (as well as some of the staff) but this was considered to be a small, acceptable risk.

In Howard Road, opposite to the junction with Branfill Road, a Squad car would be parked up, tucked right out of sight, with another car in Upminster Railway Station's car park.

In Roomes' car park would be an observation van to monitor the movements of the robbers' van and that of the robbers themselves.

In Gridiron Place, south of the junction with St Mary's Lane, and more or less opposite to Champion Road, another Squad vehicle would be parked up.

At the junction with Howard Road and Station Road, there would be a spotter, high up in a flat, with an uninterrupted view of Roomes' loading bay. He would be in possession of a portable R/T set which would link him with the Flying Squad vehicles.

As the Morgan brothers went to attack the custodian, so the spotter in the flat would alert the officers in all of the Squad vehicles. They would not be able to warn the four Squad officers in the loading bay, but the officers themselves would be in a position to see the blaggers. As the spotter gave the attack, the four Squad men would rush out and grab the brothers; at the same time, the occupants of the nondescript van would detain the driver of the blaggers' van. The two Squad cars, parked up in Howard Road and the station car park would drive into Branfill Road if necessary to assist and to provide conveyance for the prisoners.

In a worst case scenario, the Squad vehicle in Gridiron Place was there should the robbers' van actually get away. Whether the driver tried to change over vehicles by the side of the school or not, they would be in a position to halt the getaway vehicle's progress, either by blocking or ramming it. In addition, should there have been a change of heart and the getaway van turned into Champion Road and then right into Highview Gardens and use that, or Cranbourne Gardens, to exit into St Mary's Lane, the Squad car would still be able to intercept it.

'What happens,' nervously asked a junior detective (destined never to stay very long with the Flying Squad), 'if they manage to break through and do the change over in Aldborough Road?'

The detective inspector in charge sighed and closed his eyes. He resolved to get this little prick off his team at the earliest possible opportunity. 'In that case, son,' he replied, wearily, 'they'll fucking deserve to get away!'

Just before half-past four, the spotter in the flat saw the blue van drive past the railway station and turn right into Branfill Road and he alerted the other units. The van drove slowly down the road, turned left into Champion Road and out of sight. Next, it was picked up by the unit in Gridiron Place. It had paused by a Zephyr Zodiac (the first of the three getaway cars) before turning left out of the road and down to the traffic lights at the junction with Station Road. As the lights changed, the van drove straight across the junction; it was clear that they were reconnoitring the plot. It meant that they would turn left, either at Garbutt Road or Aylett Road and then drive down Howard Road, looking for any kind of police presence. In Howard Road, they would have spotted the three Squadmen in the car instantly, except the driver noted the emergence of the van from Garbutt Road, in his wing mirror. As the van drove down Howard Road towards them, the driver gave a warning to his crew. They instantly ducked down, out of sight and the driver calmly got out of the car and knocked on the front door of a convenient house.

The van drifted by and the occupants did not give the driver, who was talking drivel to a rather surprised housewife, nor the Squad car, which was one of many parked up in the street, a second glance.

As the van reached the junction with Station Road, right underneath the spotter, so he was able to inform the other units that it had driven straight across the junction and had once again entered Branfill Road. Obviously satisfied, the van drove down to Roomes' car park, turned in and parked up. The occupants of the nondescript van received this message on their radio and acknowledged the transmission but because it was late on a Friday afternoon and the car park was jam-packed, they were unable to actually see the van. Not that this particularly mattered. When the time came and they were out of the nondescript vehicle, they would be able to easily spot the van.

And then the Squad radios crackled into life again. 'All units stand by,' said the spotter. 'Blue moneybox entering the B Road, now.' All spotters spoke in this fashion, in case the villains were somehow listening in. The Morgan brothers were not, but they had seen the arrival of the security van. The sawn-offs were hidden underneath their donkey jackets. The stocking masks were in their pockets. Just two minutes to go.

'Suspects one and two into the B Road and towards the

moneybox,' transmitted the spotter, hardly able to keep the excitement out of his voice. Within two seconds of each other, the three Squad cars' engines were switched on and ticked quietly over. The two Squadmen in the back of the observation van slowly pulled down the door handles at the rear of the van.

Just then, the security van's custodian emerged from the warehouse, holding Roomes Stores' takings. The spotter did not see this but he did see the Morgan brothers pull stocking masks over their heads and rush forward, reaching inside their jackets as they did so. 'All units, go! Go! Go!' shouted the spotter. Whilst the Squad car in Gridiron Place crept up to the junction, the other two Squad cars in Howard Road and the station car park roared into Branfill Road. From both sides of the security van dashed two Squad officers. All of them were on the large side, but one, who had narrowly missed a bronze medal for wrestling in the heavyweight division in the 1960 Olympic Games, was *massive*.

Robbers, when caught 'going across the pavement' or, in blaggers' parlance, 'on a ready-eye' have a choice of fight, flight or simply giving up. The Morgan brothers had never been caught in this fashion and they froze – then they decided to fight. It was an unwise move. John Morgan was punched in the face by the frustrated Olympic champion so hard that he literally, as he later admitted, 'saw stars'. Alan Morgan who was rather more the aggressive of the two, provided more resistance and suffered accordingly. They were relieved of their shotguns, loaded, naturally and dragged to their feet. They still offered resistance and were enthusiastically bashed.

Meanwhile, the two Squad officers had slipped out of the observation van and quickly looked round the car park; there was the blue van. They ran lightly across to it and then pulled open the driver's door. 'What's your fucking game!' roared the driver and despite being firmly grabbed, still managed to plant a hefty punch on the side of the leading Squadman's head. The officers decided that was quite enough of *that* and dragged him from the van, punching and kicking him until they were quite out of breath.

Over the years it has been the contention of many officers that Upminster police station, the furthest eastern outpost of the Metropolitan Police, was very much like a geriatric hospital. It was thought, perhaps unfairly, that those police officers who were posted in that sleepy hollow consisted of the sick, the lame and the dying.

That certainly appeared to be the case that Friday afternoon. The desk sergeant was appalled as the Squad dragged in the three bedraggled prisoners and goodness knows what the cleaner would say when she saw the blood all over the lovely clean charge room floor. Apart from that, he was furious. The first three hours of his shift had passed in a gloomy vacuum of sloth and idleness and he had had every confidence that the next five hours would drift by in the same uneventful manner. Now it had been catastrophically disrupted. Still, it was time for some decisive action.

'Edwards!' he snapped, to a particularly gormless-looking constable, who stood, scratching his balding head and staring with his mouth agape at the procession of some of the largest men in the world. 'Clear the cells out!'

Edwards spun on his heel and stared at the sergeant with something akin to panic in his eyes. 'The cells, Sarge?' he gasped. 'But I've only just started over-wintering the station's geraniums in there!'

'Just do it, and don't answer back!' shouted the sergeant, adding, 'And mind those terracotta pots!'

The brothers Morgan had never been so frightened in their

lives before. They started talking and once they'd started, they were unable to stop. 'All right, Guv'nor,' gasped John, 'you've got us cold with the shooters and everything!'

'Yeah,' breathlessly agreed Alan, 'we was all set to hit the guard and grab the dough, and – and . . .'

His voice trailed away, as he and John slowly turned to face the driver, who was in a shocking state, dishevelled, bruised and bleeding. Then Alan and John looked at each other, before turning to face the detectives. In unison, they both asked, 'Who the fuck is *that*?'

The battered, bloody and thoroughly confused figure in the corner stared back at them. 'I'm Geoff the plumber!' he wailed.

The explanation quickly became evident. Whilst the brothers were waiting for the van to arrive, their driver, Arthur, expressed dissatisfaction with the way the van had been positioned. None of them had expected the car park to be so full and, after the brothers had carried out the blagging and had run back to the van, with the number of vehicles that could well be leaving at closing time, it might well prove difficult to drive out of the exit, which had only a limited amount of space. Therefore, reasoned Arthur, it would be better if, once they had seen the security van arrive, he eased out of the car park and into Champion Road, just round the corner, and waited for them there. After all it was only a few extra yards for the brothers to run and it did mean a safer getaway. The brothers nodded. It made sense. So, as they saw the van arrive, they got out of the van which drove out of the car park. At that moment, the spotter in the flat had a sneezing fit and missed its departure entirely. The occupants of the observation van were so situated that they had never seen the van's arrival and in consequence, they missed its departure. It was impossible for the Squad cars in Howard Road or Gridiron

Place to see the movement of the van, because they were too far away and the Squad car in the station car park was totally reliant on the radio transmissions to take any kind of action. And while all this was going on, Geoff the Plumber drove his blue van, identical in every respect to the blaggers' van, into the car park, parked-up, sat back, lit a roll-up and started reading the *Evening News* while he waited for his wife to get off the train from London, so that they could go shopping.

'So where's your fucking van, now?' roared the detective inspector. Alan told him. The Squad car raced out of the back of the police station's yard and roared into Champion Road. There was the van and, in the driving seat, Arthur, wondering why the brothers were taking so long. He too, was dragged from the van, provisionally belted and dragged in.

'Look, mate,' said the DI to the still shaking plumber. 'We've made a bit of a bloomer, here, right?' Geoff, watching his blood drip down to the charge room floor, privately felt that the usage of 'a bit of a bloomer' was something of an understatement but, nodded dumbly.

'So we've got to put things right, OK? Now, where'd you live? Nearby?'

Geoff told him. 'I know where that is!' remarked PC Edwards, who was right in the middle of shifting terracotta pots full of geraniums. Everyone looked at him momentarily, before completely ignoring him again.

'Come on, mate,' said the DI, patting Geoff on the shoulder. 'Let's get you home.'

Geoff's wife, Maggie, had been nonplussed when she came across her husband's empty van in the car park and finally decided to walk home. As she entered their house, she could hear the sound of water running from the shower, so she went upstairs. She screamed at the sight which confronted her. Her naked husband was in the shower cabinet, his body a mass of cuts and bruises, his torn, bloodied clothes were in a heap on the floor with an overpowering stench from where he had soiled himself. Worst of all, there were two, excessively large men in their shirtsleeves, total strangers, who were busy swabbing her husband down, like a horse. One of them looked over his shoulder at her arrival. 'Afternoon, love,' he said, casually, before turning back to his task. 'Any more soap, Geoff?'

'Bathroom cabinet, bottom shelf,' groaned Geoff.

'Nice shower cabinet this, Geoff,' remarked the other Squad man. 'Wouldn't mind one of these, meself.'

Geoff replied, 'I 'spect I could get you one at cost—' before he was shrilly interrupted.

'GEOFF!' screamed his wife. 'What the hell is going on? Who the hell are—'

'It's all right, Maggie,' muttered Geoff. 'It's a bit complicated, that's all.'

'Come on, love,' smiled the second Squad officer, the admirer of the shower cabinet. 'I'll make you a nice cuppa and explain everything.'

And he did. The following day, a large bouquet of flowers arrived for Maggie and a bottle of twelve-year-old Scotch for Geoff, together with two tickets for the forthcoming Flying Squad annual dinner and dance. They were seated on the top table and Mr Millen and Mr Butler were especially charming. Geoff and Maggie became true friends of the Flying Squad and attended the dinners for many years to come.

The Morgan Brothers fared less well. The Squadmen capitalized on their loquacity and recorded every blagging which they had committed in their confessions. They copped twelve years apiece.

No one could understand why Arthur, the driver had not

driven off, given the amount of noise which had been generated further down the road as his accomplices had the living shit bashed out of them.

The reason was mentioned in court and assisted materially in mitigating his sentence, to one of four years' imprisonment. The Morgan brothers had chosen Arthur purely for his driving skills, rather than for anything else. He was profoundly deaf.

The Italian Connection

Every borough possesses at least one of them and sometimes more than one. I refer to the complete and utter nightmare family which is so dreadful that people in the community who have lived there for years, and who quietly and confidently predicted that their retirement years would be spent there, move out in droves.

Many of the residents of Beaumont Road, Collier Row, claim that they cannot remember exactly when it was that the Muldoon family arrived and the reason is probably because the council infiltrated them into their new hovel under cover of darkness, rather like secret agents on a daring mission behind enemy lines. Because, one morning, the inhabitants of Beaumont Road awoke and pulled open their bedroom curtains to discover that, like some plague bacillus, the Muldoon family had arrived.

Someone who got to know the family quite well stated that when Darwin had written *On the Origin of Species*, he had got it right that man had evolved from the apes; unfortunately in the Muldoon's case, they hadn't developed at the same speed as everybody else.

A genealogist would have traced a fascinating record of intrepid inbreeding in the *genus* Muldoon. The family matriarch was fat, bellicose Agnes Muldoon who had spawned a succession of rat-faced kids. The younger ones staggered around in urine-sodden nappies until they slipped down to their ankles and then the kids either stepped or tripped out of them. If it was the latter, this normally coincided with some part of their anatomy, usually their head, coming into smart contact with the floor and, although no permanent damage was inflicted on the child, it was enough to provoke screeching and wailing. This would be sufficient to interfere with the thought processes of Agnes Muldoon – who was endeavouring to work out even more ways to defraud social security of benefits to which she and her gruesome brood were not strictly entitled – and she would stop what she was doing to bellow blasphemous filth at them.

The house, which had initially looked quite smart, deteriorated at a rate of knots. The paint peeled on the window sills, scarcely a window frame existed which did not possess at least one broken pane of glass, and the floors were covered in excrement, both human and canine. The former was courtesy of the overflowing nappies, and the latter, due to the mad-looking lurchers who wandered in and out of the property and who could be heard coughing piteously at night, as they tried to rid their throats of the splinters of chicken bones, the remnants of a delicious repast of Kentucky Fried Chicken, which had thoughtfully been tossed to them by the family.

If, instead of bipeds, the Muldoons had been four-legged animals, the RSPCA would have had no hesitation in seizing and re-homing the lot of them. As it was, they behaved exactly how they pleased: the children all truanted (which was as well, since they were unteachable), Agnes devised plans to rip off various Government agencies, and the head of the family, Old Man Muldoon – his baptismal name was never established by the local residents – flopped in a sagging armchair and watched the racing on one of the five television sets acquired by the family, all of which had had their serial numbers sedulously filed off. Of course, it goes without saying that every member of the household was a thief.

The second eldest son, Billy, was a prolific burglar, as many of the local residents could bear witness to; not only that, but he also targeted commercial premises and could be relied upon, with rather more enthusiasm than skill, to attempt to rip the back off some of the more antiquated safes in the Havering area. But Billy was astoundingly inept as a criminal; despite his astonishing output as a thief, he could always be relied upon to be recognized leaving the scene of a crime or leaving his fingerprints – on two occasions, his blood-stained finger-prints – in compromising circumstances. He became regular sport for the local aids to CID who would arrive at the family home, on average once per fortnight, to collect Billy. And always Billy would resist arrest and always Agnes Muldoon would fill the air with screeching imprecations.

Billy was also of mixed race, which had caused Old Man Muldoon some consternation, since he was aware that at the time of Billy's conception he was serving half a stretch for relieving a church roof of a quantity of lead. He did bring this rather delicate matter to Agnes' attention one evening when she was in a state of mild intoxication. At first, she simpered horribly, attempting to muster an impersonation of Angie Dickinson, having seen her do the self-same thing on the silver screen, but when her husband persisted, she simply gave up all pretence of the imitation of an outraged *femme fatale* and screamed at him that he was 'a dirty-minded cunt' and there the matter ended.

Of course, it made no difference whatsoever to Old Man Muldoon; he held Billy in the same affection as he did the rest of the children – that is to say, none at all. But of the entire, dreadful family, at least Old Man Muldoon possessed a sense of humour.

On one of the many occasions when the house was being searched by the police, the family patriarch sat back in his shapeless armchair, surrounded by discarded chip wrappers, a dismembered motorcycle engine and the inevitable soiled nappies. He raised his half-consumed can of strong lager in greeting the CID officers.

''Scuse the mess,' he grinned, showing his blackened teeth stumps. 'I'm just doin' a spot of decoratin'!'

The person who suffered most from the excesses of this charmless bunch was Giuseppe Maniero – he was known locally as Seppe – who was their next-door neighbour. Seppe had been an Italian prisoner of war and, following the cessation of hostilities, he had stayed and married Heather, an English girl. They had been lucky enough to move into their house in Beaumont Road just after it had been built. Seppe, now a widower, spent much of his time gardening and tending to his racing pigeons. The entire Muldoon family had managed to spoil both for him. They tipped their household filth into his garden, threw bricks at the pigeons' coop and, on one occasion, sprayed the contents of an aerosol can over some of the birds, who had to be destroyed. Listening to the children's sniggering, Seppe, for the first time, was actually glad that his beloved Heather was dead, to save her this torment. And when neighbours saw the once friendly, but now perpetually scowling, Seppe walking down the street, muttering to himself, 'One day, I get-a those bastards!' they knew exactly to whom he was referring.

This brings us to Jimmy, the eldest of the clan. Jimmy had gone through the whole criminal justice system, visiting Juvenile, Magistrates' and Crown Courts. He had been the subject of fines (never paid), conditional discharges (continually breached) and probation orders (which were never complied with). Inevitably, he had been to detention centre, Borstal, had been recalled to Borstal and served short sentences of imprisonment. This had been the result of stealing, nicking cars, assaults and burglary. The local CID considered Jimmy to be the most dangerous of the Muldoon tribe. Tall and rangy, he was completely uneducated but possessed a certain degree of cunning.

The armed robbery which Jimmy and his associates carried out on the Security Express van which was delivering cash to the National Westminster Bank should have been a success. There were four main reasons that it was not.

Firstly, the bank was situated in Collier Row Road, less than a quarter of a mile from his home address.

Secondly, in his excitement at having pulled off a big job, he also pulled off his stocking mask before leaping into the getaway car and was positively identified by two local residents who were walking by at the time.

Thirdly, given his natural reluctance to walk anywhere, he abandoned the getaway car right outside the family address.

And fourthly, he had attempted to recruit so many of the local tearaways to participate in the heist, the job was common knowledge prior to it being executed. In fact, three such tearaways telephoned the local police station to say, 'That job at the Nat West, Guv'nor – I know who done it – is there a reward?'

The CID burst in on Jimmy who was in the act of counting the money. Since there were more than ten notes, this was causing him considerable difficulty. Jimmy, true to form, decided to offer resistance. The very large detective sergeant who led the raid and who was hugely disinclined to allow anybody to treat him as a human punchbag, retaliated by smashing the living shit out of him. Agnes Muldoon came rushing into the room at full screech and the sergeant who had just discovered, to his dismay, that he had stepped in a large pile of faeces, told her to shut her fat ugly gob, before *she* got some, and this did indeed have a calming effect on her.

The other members of the gang were rounded up without any difficulty; all were charged with robbery and appeared before Havering Magistrates' Court. Since the offence was so serious that it could only be tried at a Crown Court, the police asked for a remand in custody. Although Jimmy Muldoon and his associates made no application for bail, it still took the insipid Muppets on the Bench twenty agonized minutes to grant the police's request.

Two weeks went by, with Jimmy on remand at Brixton Prison. On his next appearance at Havering Magistrates' Court, it was intended to commit him for trial to the Crown Court, still, naturally, holding him in custody. But, as the van backed up to cell area at the court, Jimmy suddenly realized that the van's door was insecure and he and a fellow prisoner decided to capitalize on the heaven-sent opportunity. They burst out of the van and, before the startled guards could act, they took to their heels and ran.

Jimmy was not a sophisticated criminal by any stretch of the imagination but although the Muldoon family home was no more than a mile and a half away, he knew that would be the police's first port of call. But where to go? His companion provided the answer.

Pietro Andolini was a thief in his homeland and a thief over here. He had fled Italy after things became a little warm for him there, when he was caught red-handed in possession of a large quantity of stolen tobacco. In the United Kingdom he had fallen back on his former trade of pickpocket. He had made a rich haul at Romford Dog Track until he became a little too over-confident. When his wrist was seized by someone unhappy at having his wallet lifted, a fight started. The police arrived to find his pockets stuffed with wallets belonging to the habitués of Romford Dog Track and he, like Jimmy Muldoon, had found himself remanded in custody. Now, they were both on the run and Andolini had little trouble in persuading Muldoon that Italy was the best place for both of them. Muldoon, of course, had no idea whatsoever where Italy actually was.

That they managed to reach Dover, stealing food, money and acquiring transport, without getting arrested was nothing short of miraculous, given Muldoon's lack of intelligence, but the police were, to a certain degree, at fault as well. They could not conceive that he would try to flee the country and thought that, within days (and possibly hours), they would receive a telephone call from one of the many disgruntled neighbours to say they had seen him slinking into the family home.

It was a friendly lorry driver at a transport cafe who overcame the problem of their lack of passports by letting them hide in his vehicle, which providentially was en route to Italy. He was going to deliver a consignment of spare parts for agricultural machinery to a factory in Padua and the lorry, having disembarked at Calais, sped across France, through Lille and Reims, and down towards Châlons-sur-Marne in the southeast of the country. Within two days, they had crossed the border into Italy and, skirting Turin and Milan, they eventually arrived in Padua. The driver, having delivered his consignment, went off to telephone a freight forwarder company who could provide him with a 'backload'- a consignment that he could deliver back in the United Kingdom – and he and the two escapees parted company.

Andolini's home was in a suburb of Rome and although it

was there that he was wanted, it was, he told Muldoon, a city big enough to swallow both of them up. So it was to Rome that they intended to travel, but that was 528 miles away and now they needed money. Andolini made some enquiries and discovered the whereabouts of the area's top criminals; and then he went to work. Outside an electrical company was a lorry, fully laden and it took only a matter of minutes for Andolini to get into the cab, start up the engine and drive the twenty-odd miles to where he was sure he could find a willing purchaser.

It was in this particular area of Italy, during the 1980s, that a series of gang wars had led to many prominent Mafia gangsters being murdered. On the Riviera del Brenta, between Padua and Venice, a new group, just as deadly as any of their Mafia counterparts, came into being. The *Mala del Brenta* – it was also rather confusingly referred to as *Mafia del Brenta*, *Malavita del Brenta*, *Mala* or *Mafia del Piovese* – was formed and the members were made up of criminals from the Veneto region. Also operating in the area were members of the feared *Cosa Nostra*, *Camorra* and the *Ndranghetta*. At the same time, many Mafia groups were making inroads into white-collar crime and were also putting their money into legitimate enterprises. The Italian press called it *La Cosa Nuova* – 'the new thing' – but some things in the Mafia never change and one of them is *vendetta*.

So when Andolini and Muldoon turned up to meet the local *Capo* (or chief) of the *Mala del Brenta*, they were somewhat astounded when they did not receive either the fulsome praise or the large amount of money which they expected. Pietro Andolini did not appreciate being called 'a son of a whore' but, when it was explained to him that the lorry, the trailer and the contents, valued at several hundred million lire were the property of the *Capo*'s uncle, he understood why.

Jimmy Muldoon understood not one word of the exchange but when wild-eyed Andolini got down on his knees in front of the enraged *Capo* and started praying volubly, he did come to the conclusion that something was considerably amiss.

The trouble with the system of Mafia punishments is that they do not consist of probation orders, suspended sentences or well-meaning magistrates saying, 'Don't you dare do that again' before fining the offender a risible amount. Their form of punishment consists purely of production of a *Lupo* or sawn-off shotgun, the contents of which are discharged straight into the offender's face. The resultant corpse is left in a prominent place and the disfigurement is a salutary warning to anybody else who might be tempted to mess with the Mafia. That was the fate of Jimmy Muldoon and Pietro Andolini. Their bodies were found in the middle of Padua, on the Via Trieste, just by the bus station and although passers-by gaped and cried, '*Che sarà successo?*' ('What can have happened?') don't worry about that – they bloody well *knew* what had happened.

The *Ufficio Federale di Investigazione* – the Italian Federal Bureau of Investigation – realizing immediately that this was a Mafia hit, commenced an investigation which brought them nowhere near to the actual perpetrators. They quickly identified Andolini from his fingerprints but they had no idea that he had travelled to England, or that he was wanted, there. When Andolini had been arrested at Romford, he had given false particulars and had declined the offer of informing his country's ambassador of his arrest, since that would have alerted the English police that he was wanted in his homeland. Muldoon's fingerprints were similarly checked but, of course, since Muldoon had never been further east than Southend before, no trace of his identity was found.

And there the matter rested, until someone in the Italian system of justice, thought it might be an idea to circulate both men's fingerprints through Interpol. Since Italian police officers frequently use the word *domani* in the same way that their Spanish counterparts relish the word *mañana*, this took several months.

There was enormous consternation in the Metropolitan Police (as well as some undisguised joy) when it was discovered that Jimmy Muldoon had been the subject of a Mafia hit. The officer deputed to break the news to his mother, stood on the doorstep and suffered four complete minutes of non-stop, screaming abuse, before she ran out of steam and paused to say, 'So wot you fucking want, anyway?'

'Your Jimmy's dead,' laconically replied the officer. He turned on his heel and, as he walked away, had the satisfaction of hearing a 'thump!' as her fat body crashed to the floor of the hallway, out cold, in a dead faint.

News like this could not be contained for long; one of the CID officers had a drink with the crime reporter of the *Havering Recorder* who was tempted to impart the circumstances of her son's demise to Mrs Muldoon, who suddenly put two and two together. 'You dun this!' she screamed, pointing an accusing finger at her next door neighbour, Signor Giuseppe Maniero. She had heard his muttered threats about 'getting' her family – he was Italian, her beloved 'baby' was murdered in Italy – therefore, he must have been responsible.

Seppe raised his eyebrows. What on earth was the fat *strega* on about now? '*Che?*' he murmured. The reporter took him to one side. Did he know anything about the murder? 'Murder?' echoed Seppe. So the reporter told him what he knew and, when he saw a grin suddenly appear on Seppe's face, he started to add two and two together. Was he, Seppe, asked the reporter connected in any way with the Mafia? Seppe stared back at him. He was just about to repudiate the slur, when he stopped. He did not deny any connection with the Mafia; neither did he admit it. Instead, with that enigmatic smile still on his face, he turned and walked away.

When the story, with all of the attendant innuendoes, appeared in the *Havering Recorder*, it sent shockwaves around the community. The residents of Beaumont Road eagerly discussed the news over their garden fences. Was Seppe or was he not responsible for Jimmy's demise? He was an 'Eyetie', wasn't he? Well, there you are then. And what about his bleedin' pigeons, then? Used to pass messages, weren't they?

Seppe, who of course had no connection whatsoever with the Mafia, decided to capitalize on these circumstances. Every time he saw Agnes Muldoon and she screamed, 'Murderer!' at him, he would smile, draw his index finger across his throat and murmur softly, 'You-a next!'

The family matriarch went straight to Romford police station, told them she was in fear of her life from the Mafia, a member of which was living next door, and demanded that she and her family receive a twenty-four hour armed police presence. This was politely refused.

Next, Agnes Muldoon made a further request, this time through the family solicitor, and again the request was denied. Her next step was to call in all of the local newspapers to her address and deliver a bellicose press conference. This was conducted in the street, since all of the reporters sensibly but politely declined to enter the premises, and it was to the effect that her son had been mercilessly gunned down by foreign gangsters and now ('wot with 'im, next door'), she feared for her life and those of her 'babies'. To conclude the proceedings, she put the blame fairly and squarely on the shoulders of 'the slag filf, wot nicked my Jimmy and then let 'im escape.' The reporters prudently declined the offer of tea, skilfully evaded the attentions of the snapping lurchers who had wandered out into the street and rushed off to file their copy.

And still, the demanded twenty-four hour armed police presence did not materialize. In desperation, she now went to Havering Council, demanding that she be re-housed; in turn, the council contacted the police, stating that such action could only be taken if a possible threat could be substantiated. And all of a sudden, there was light at the end of the tunnel. The detective chief inspector at Romford police station called in a certain detective sergeant who was known for his ability to compose the most extravagant of reports. He put the problem to him; could he assist? The cunning sergeant nodded; it would take about a week, he told his superior and was told to get cracking. He spent some time in the company of an Italian lady of his acquaintance who kept abreast of the news in her homeland and then set to work on a report which many later described as being 'a work of art'.

A week later, the council's housing official was called to the office of the detective chief inspector. He was told that the report which he was going to be shown was absolutely top secret. He would not be permitted to retain a copy of it. However, the information contained in it might well be of assistance in bringing the council to a conclusion concerning the proposed re-housing of the Muldoon family. He was then handed the report, which, he was assured had been compiled with the cooperation of the competent Italian authorities. However, this was somewhat stretching the truth. This was at a time when if an English police officer wanted to trace the registered keeper of a Milan-based car from one of his Italian counterparts, the search would take four months. The information gathered in the report had been gleaned from other sources, although it was absolutely accurate. The official's eyes scanned the type-script. Yes, it had been confirmed that James Brian Muldoon had been murdered by the Mafia group known as *Mala del Brenta*. It was also known that, in the past, Mafia members had often murdered members of the dead person's family, to prevent them carrying out assassinations of their own, for revenge.

The housing official frowned and looked up from the document. 'The Muldoons are a large family, aren't they, Chief Inspector?'

The DCI nodded. 'They are indeed.'

The official thought for a moment and then his face cleared. 'However, I can hardly think that the Mafia, for goodness sake, would come all the way to England to try and find the unfortunate Mr Muldoon's family?'

The detective sergeant cleared his throat. 'Excuse me, sir but, given the considerable amount of publicity generated by Mrs Muldoon, they might not have to look very far.'

The man from the housing tut-tutted. 'Yes, but to come all the way to England? Oh, really . . .'

'They might not have to, sir.' It was the chief inspector speaking. 'Please continue reading the report.'

The official resumed reading and saw that the feared leader of the gang was one Felice 'Angel Face' Maniero. He looked up. 'Maniero? Maniero? Where have I heard that name . . . Good heavens! The next-door neighbour!'

'Of course, it may be just a coincidence,' said the DCI, soothingly.

'But – but – the finger across the throat signs that he's been making to the family!' stammered the official. 'Mrs Muldoon told me!'

'Always denied by Mr Maniero,' smoothly replied the sergeant.

'My God, this is dreadful!' squealed the man from the housing department. 'We must get them out of Beaumont Road, immediately, immediately!'

The DCI sighed. 'If you say so, sir,' he said, quietly. 'Yes, I'll take that report, sir, thank you. And now, remember – not a word about this! I'm not sure I should have shown you the report at all. I really must insist upon your absolute discretion. If word of this gets out, there could be some rather unsettling diplomatic repercussions.'

'Of course, Chief Inspector, of course!' stuttered the official, as he snatched up his briefcase. 'You can rely on me – good day!'

The Muldoons vanished as suddenly as they had arrived, all those years before. The surveyor who inspected the vacated premises came to the conclusion that the Black Death had probably commenced in an environment very similar to the house in Beaumont Road. Seppe was regarded as a local hero and thereafter never had to pay for a single drink in the local Royal British Legion Club. The detective sergeant, the composer of the flowery report, was told by the DCI that although there could be no official recognition, such as a commendation for his considerable assistance to the community, he must have incurred considerable expense in compiling his report and, therefore, when he next submitted his diary for checking, instead of claiming his usual three or four pounds for incidental, out of pocket expenses, perhaps he would submit a claim for fifty pounds, which he, the DCI would be happy to authorize.

The Muldoons' neighbour's namesake, 'Angel Face' Maniero turned police informer which resulted in the destruction of the *Mala del Brenta*. Some of the former members started a new organization, *Nuova Mafia del Brenta*, who were unsuccessful in their attempt to assassinate Maniero; they, too have now been broken up. All of which resulted in a pretty happy ending.

As Sure as Death

Villains have usually taken the death of their own seriously. William Patrick 'Billy' Blythe is not a name which comes immediately to mind nowadays but during the 1940s and 1950s his was a big name in the London underworld. It was the only thing about him which was big. Physically, he was a thin, gaunt-faced midget, and a satanic one at that. In 1945, Peter Vibart of the Flying Squad had twenty stitches inserted in his face after Blythe, a former Army deserter, slashed him with a razor. The three-year sentence he received did not prove a reformative exercise because, following his attack on Jack Spot in 1956, which required a blood transfusion, plus seventy-eight stitches to hold Spot's face together, Blythe was arrested again – coincidentally, Vibart was one of the arresting officers – and this time, he received five years' imprisonment. Blythe served just four months of his sentence before he died of a burst duodenal ulcer at the early age of thirty-nine. His funeral at Kensal Green cemetery, with twelve Rolls-Royces forming the funeral cortège and floral tributes costing over £1,500, was described in the *Daily Mirror* as being 'the biggest gangland funeral ever'.

The lives of Frederick 'Slip' Sullivan and Tommy Smithson were inextricably linked, but not their deaths. Sullivan, who was believed to have been involved in the £287,000 Eastcastle Street bullion robbery in 1952, was involved in a fight with a

Maltese, whose ear was severed. Smithson, a rather unbalanced gambler, strongarm man and former fairground boxer, was brought in to redress the balance and cut Sullivan's throat. By way of revenge, Smithson was ambushed by a dozen men who leapt out of a lorry and mercilessly attacked him. They slashed him all over his face and body, battered his head and almost severed his arm and, just to finish matters off, they reversed the lorry over him, twice, before they chucked him over a wall, into Regent's Park. He was admitted to hospital, close to death. Within four hours of receiving a five-pint blood transfusion, he was sitting up in bed and, although he was swathed in bandages, he was smoking, having consumed a four course meal. Five days later, with fifty-four stitches in his face alone and his arm still paralysed, he discharged himself from hospital, and refused to prosecute, having received anything between £500 and £1,000.

Meanwhile, 'Slip' Sullivan was sentenced to twenty-one months' imprisonment. Shortly after his release, he was stabbed to death by his girlfriend. Smithson who, during a further gangland encounter, received another twenty-two stitches in his face, followed Sullivan to the grave eighteen months later, aged only thirty-six after he was shot dead by Phillip Ellul, a Maltese gangster. The funerals of both men were described as 'spectacular'. Sullivan's supporters marked his passing with six hundred wreaths and Smithson's hearse was followed by six Rolls-Royces, accompanied by over one hundred floral tributes. The Kray Twins, who held Smithson in the highest esteem, attended the funeral, as did a club owner who rather risibly described Smithson as being 'as harmless as a day-old chick'. It was in direct contrast to Smithson's warning to his victims: 'Pay up or be cut'.

But these are men who, though well-known in their day, have vanished into the mists of obscurity. What of the ones better known to the public? Of the brothers Kray, Ronnie was the first to die, in 1995. A glass-sided hearse, drawn by six plumed black horses, conveyed his body the nine miles from Bethnal Green, on a route that was lined with 60,000 people, to the plot in Chingford cemetery which Reg Kray had purchased in 1967, originally for his first wife. It would become the final resting place for the Krays' parents and for all three brothers. There was a more modest attendance at brother Charlie's funeral, five years later, but, thousands still lined the route. Charlie had been serving a twelve-year sentence for drug smuggling when he died of a heart attack. Reg Kray attended both funerals, escorted by prison officers but, within six months, he was dead too.

This time, the crowds were lined six deep along the route. An estimated 100,000 people turned out to pay their respects and eighteen limousines conveyed family and friends to the cemetery. Over two hundred police officers were present to maintain public safety. Rather surplus to requirements were double that number of hulking shaven-headed thugs, wearing long leather coats, sunglasses and red arm bands with the letters RKF (Reg Kray Funeral), who were acting as 'security'.

Three-and-a-half years later, Tony Lambrianou died. A henchman of the Twins, he was convicted, with them for his part in the murder of Jack 'The Hat' McVitie. Far more restrained in comparison with his mentors, a modest three hundred and fifty people attended his funeral but it was in equally bad taste with the thick-necked thugs in attendance, the ludicrously worded flower tributes, and a chauffeur-driven car with the letters and numbers of the registration plate squeezed together to form the word 'GUNS'.

The most compelling subject that is aired at these funerals is the need to mitigate the deceased's misdeeds. It is simply not enough to say, 'Well, he wasn't a bad bloke, was he?' or

'He did have his good points.' No, East Enders go absolutely overboard with their acclamation for the deceased. ''E was a big fucking teddy bear, weren' 'e?' was the incredible way that one gangster, with a shocking and well-deserved reputation for mindless, spiteful violence, was described.

One criminal who was thoroughly well liked, was Charlie Wilson, one of the Great Train Robbers. His death came suddenly and violently and has never been satisfactorily resolved.

The guests had not long left the luxurious villa at Llanos de Naguelos, Marbella, where Pat and Charlie Wilson had been celebrating their thirty-fifth wedding anniversary. Late in the afternoon of Monday 23 April 1990, Charlie had been chopping a salad in the kitchen when the front doorbell rang. The caller and Charlie went out by the pool and a furious argument ensued. The visitor kicked Charlie in the groin and, as he doubled over, broke his nose and shot him twice, in the face and the neck. As Charlie lay dying, his killer shot the family dog before escaping on a yellow mountain bike.

It was popularly believed that the gunman was one Danny 'Scarface' Roff, a highly dangerous south London criminal, who had escaped from custody in 1988, whilst serving a thirteen-year sentence for burglary and possession of a firearm. Seven years after Charlie Wilson's murder, thirty-six year old Roff, who had been partially paralysed as a result of an attempt on his life, was shot dead, outside his home in Bromley.

On 10 May 1990, gangland turned out at Streatham Cemetery to pay their last respects to Charlie. Of the train gang, Bruce Reynolds was present, as was Roy James, Ronald 'Buster' Edwards, Bobby Welch and, briefly, Jimmy White. Tommy Wisby and Jim Hussey were unavoidably detained, since they were both serving long periods of imprisonment for trafficking in half a million pounds' worth of cocaine, but they sent a wreath. Absent for the same reason were Reg and Ron Kray, and at that time it would have been considered inadvisable for Ronnie Knight to have ventured back into England (though the officers investigating the £6 million Security Express robbery at Shoreditch would have been delighted to see him), but they all sent wreaths, as did many others.

So these were the dramatic funerals of the old and the bold of the criminal classes. Though the high and mighty in the underworld might once have been household names, East Enders often have notoriously short memories and it is usually only when, for one reason or another, the villains have been retained in the public eye that their funerals attract such public attention.

A name that was on everybody's lips during the 1920s was Eddie Manning, a Jamaican who was also known as 'Eddie the Villain' and 'The Worst man in London'. When he first arrived in England, he worked in a munitions factory, then as a drummer in a travelling dance band. It was then that he first discovered exactly how lucrative drug trafficking could be. His first prison sentence, in 1920, was one of sixteen months' imprisonment for shooting three men in the legs. After his release he went on to run both a highly lucrative drugs business and a string of prostitutes. In 1924, he was sentenced to three years' penal servitude for the possession of cocaine and opium; the offence was aggravated after the death of two people, both due to drugs overdoses, were linked to him. And after he was arrested in 1929 for receiving stolen property in excess of £2,000, he died in Parkhurst, in the third year of his sentence. He was, by then, largely forgotten and (with the possible exception of a few old brasses) hugely unmourned.

Charles 'Darby' Sabini was a highly feared gang leader in the 1920s and 1930s, and with very good reason. Although he looked and dressed like a peasant, was illiterate and scrupulously uneducated, he was both cunning and charismatic. He also possessed a fully-loaded automatic and a good right hook from the days when he was an up-and-coming middleweight boxer. Most importantly, he had the ability to bring together hundreds of thugs to effectively seize control of the bookmakers at racetracks all over England. Sabini, who was linked to murders and innumerable woundings, was seldom arrested. If he was, he was hardly ever charged. But on the occasions that he did face a court, he was invariably acquitted. However, during World War Two, the authorities saw this as a heaven-sent opportunity to have him interned as an enemy alien. The internment, then the death of his son, who was serving in the RAF, and finally a prison sentence for receiving stolen goods, broke Sabini's spirit. When he died in Hove, in 1951, aged only sixty-two, he was both penniless and forgotten.

And Jack Comer, also known as Jack Spot, the self-proclaimed 'King of the Underworld', who punched and slashed his way across London to run protection rackets and who also masterminded the attempted robbery of gold bullion at what became known as 'The Battle of Heathrow' in 1948, also fell from grace. He lost control of his gang, his supporters drifted away and he became bankrupt. Like Sabini, his court appearances had usually ended in acquittal. But his final conviction, thirty-two years before his death was, like Sabini, for receiving stolen goods. Instead of a prison sentence, Comer was fined a derisory £12; he had hit rock-bottom. He died a widower and penniless, one month away from what would have been his eighty-second birthday.

For someone who was nicknamed 'Dodger' for his ability to dodge out of trouble, Jack 'Dodger' Mullins was someone curiously ill-fated to be right in the forefront of confrontations of the law. He was born in the last few years of the nineteenth century and it was rumoured that he collected either the Military Medal or the Distinguished Conduct Medal (or perhaps, both) during the First World War but it is difficult to establish whether or not he actually accepted the King's shilling. Beyond doubt, he was a fighting man, war service or not, and was handy with a knife, a gun, a razor and, of course, his fists. His original trade or calling was that of a pickpocket, one that he was very good at, but he was renowned as a blackmailer of publicans and bookmakers, an offence for which he received four years' penal servitude in 1926. Although he could be a person of great charm, this was not a view shared by the governor of Dartmoor Prison when Mullins took a leading part in the 1932 mutiny. He received his fifty-first (and final) conviction in 1956, at the Inner London Sessions. He was then sixty-four years of age and he was sentenced to twelve months' imprisonment. 'Women could walk the streets in safety, in them days!' is an oft-heard cry from the old East Enders and to a degree that was quite right. It did not necessarily extend to women travelling in cars. Mullins, tiring of one recalcitrant girlfriend, pushed her out of a car which was travelling at speed and broke her back. It was said that the copper who caught up with Mullins at Epsom Downs effected his arrest by breaking his nose with a knuckleduster. When Mullins died, ten years after his last conviction, the curtain was slowly coming down on mindless thugs like Mullins & Co.

One woman who attended Reggie Kray's funeral suggested that gangstars were 'fun' and if there was fun to be found in gangsters, it extended to some of the funerals as well.

When the mother of an East-End gangster died, her son, who was on remand for a catalogue of serious offences, was permitted to attend the funeral, together with a police escort. The officer in charge of the escort had a quiet word with the gangster regarding his behaviour, and that of the other mourners, and then the funeral went ahead. It was an emotional and a very dignified affair, and afterwards, the gangster, wiping the tears from his eyes, fulsomely thanked the detective in charge of the escort. 'Thanks very much for the way you looked after things,' he said. 'You handled things just right and I'm very grateful. Actually,' he added, 'I wanted to slip you a few bob, just to show my gratitude, although I thought it best not to. Your guv'nor would probably have stuck a few more charges on me, if I had.' He was referring to the fact that when he had been arrested his address book had included the name and home telephone number of one of the detectives involved in his investigation. The officer concerned had been transferred at record-breaking speed, so the gangster might well have had a point.

The widow of one East-End hardman was a little shaky when it came to funeral protocol. When the ever-present glass-sided hearse containing her husband's coffin arrived, drawn by the usual six black horses, she was unaware that there was a limousine awaiting her presence. To the stunned silence of her fellow mourners, she climbed up next to the hearse driver. Although many who were present thought that was bad enough, others were of the opinion that she had compounded the felony by wearing a pair of white stilettos. The last straw occurred when she broke one of her heels.

The final words on death and humour must come from that game fighting man, Tommy Smithson. Having been shot, first in the arm, then in the neck by his killer – another of his assassins noted that there was 'thick blood, like liver, from his mouth' – he nevertheless chased his killers downstairs. As they leapt into their getaway car and sped off, Smithson collapsed in the street. His final words were, 'Good morning, I'm dying.'

Death may be the great leveller, but humour runs it a close second.

A Robber Unmasked

In the late 1960s, situated at the junction of New Road and Ballards Road in Dagenham was a bowling alley which was known as 'The Princess Bowl'. Above the entrance in cursive neon script was the name of the establishment, except that the neon lighting had failed on the first four letters of the second word. Therefore, the illuminated sign which no Ford worker, emerging from Kent Avenue opposite, could possibly miss, read 'The cess Bowl.' That, more than anything else perfectly epitomized Dagenham.

Few of Dagenham's villains possessed wit or charm and Terry Wiseman, who had gone off the rails to a serious degree shortly after leaving school at fourteen, was not one of the exceptions. Before leaving school he had engaged in a little petty larceny which had brought him to the attention of the courts, but afterwards he quickly came to the notice of the local CID after driving a stolen Vauxhall straight through a jeweller's grilled window and snatching what the outraged proprietor described as being three thousand pounds' worth of stock. Wiseman, a tough, blond-haired young tearaway would have disputed this, knowing full well that the total value of the goods was no more than £750, as he had totalled up the price tags of the stolen watches, rings and brooches before selling them to a receiver in Bow. Since he was to deny any knowledge of the raid when questioned by the CID at

Dagenham, this hardly seemed a prudent course of action. The denial actually suited his questioners, because what they knew (and Wiseman did not) was that he had carelessly left an accusing fingerprint in the stolen car. It perfectly matched one of the impressions of his prints which were kept on file at C3 (or Fingerprint) Branch, New Scotland Yard.

It is possible that Wiseman might have had the wit to have satisfactorily explained this away, except that in his eagerness to relieve the shop-owner of his entire stock, he had nicked his finger on a shard of broken glass and had left a second, and this time, bloodstained print on the inside of the shop window. The detectives did their work well. As a juvenile, Wiseman should have been questioned in the presence of his parents or a responsible adult. However, since Wiseman had been spotted by a patrolling 'Q' Car and had been hoiked off the street, no adult was aware of his predicament. This alone would not have disbarred him from being interviewed in the presence of an appropriate person, unless the juvenile did not wish this course of action to be taken. The wily old detective sergeant (second class) had little difficulty in persuading him that 'he was a big lad now' and that the involvement of his mum or dad was not strictly necessary. Wiseman, his chest swelling with pride at his new found maturity, had no difficulty at all in agreeing with him. Taking him into the yard at Dagenham police station, the detective sergeant pointed out the stolen Vauxhall which had been used during the raid on the jeweller's and which was now under cover. 'Ever seen that car before, lad?'

'Not me,' asserted Wiseman.

'Ever been in a car like it?' pursued the detective. 'Ever sat in one?'

'Never,' replied Wiseman, decisively.

Then he was taken to the jeweller's. 'Look, son,' said the

cunning old detective, confidentially, 'I've had the word that you did the smash and grab here. Your name's been stuck up, so that's why I've got to ask all these questions, see?'

'Oh, yeah,' replied Wiseman, confidently. 'Got your job to do, ain't yer?'

'So look me in the eye, lad, and tell me. Were you involved in any way with the raid on that jeweller's, across the street over there, last Tuesday fortnight, when that stolen Vauxhall was driven straight into the window and three thousand quids' worth of jewellery was taken? Were you involved?'

Wiseman looked the old detective steadily in the eye. 'No,' he replied, disingenuously. 'I wasn't. I swear it on me mother's life.'

'Right-oh, old son,' said the detective, smiling at him in an avuncular fashion. 'Come on – back to the nick. Just a few formalities and then it's all done.'

Which was how Terry Wiseman volunteered a statement under caution. In it, he stated that not only had he never been in the Vauxhall which he had been shown in Dagenham's station yard, he had never set foot in a Vauxhall of any description. Moreover, he had not participated in the smash and grab at Simpson's Jeweller's and indeed, he had never been within half a mile of the premises.

'I don't see how you can charge me with this,' said Terry indignantly, as the sergeant took his fingerprints. 'It ain't as though I've admitted anything.'

'I expect it'll come to you, later,' murmured the sergeant, as he passed him an evil-smelling rag. 'Wipe your fingers with that, son. That's it. Now sign there, just to say they're your dabs. Lovely. Right, come on, you soppy little wanker.'

It was the sort of offence, said the judge at the North-East London Quarter Sessions that would normally merit a long custodial sentence for an adult. Since Wiseman was but fifteen years of age, he received what the judge said was the next best thing, which was a period of Borstal Training.

Wiseman graduated from this seat of further education at the age of seventeen and decided never to do a bit of work again without wearing a pair of gloves. For the next four years, he adhered to a larcenous career and, although he was pulled in once or twice, there was always insufficient evidence with which to charge him.

The trouble with felonious young men who continually get away with their crimes is that they tend to get cocky. The trouble with zealous CID officers of that period was that they tended to get miffed at such inappropriate behaviour.

Emboldened by his success, Wiseman finally overstepped the mark when he decided to turn to street robbery as an even more lucrative way of accumulating wealth. Selecting an elderly rent collector as a suitable victim, Wiseman kept his route and habits under observation for two weeks before the attack. The rent collector had made his last collection of the evening at a house in Lullington Road. As he headed towards Hedgemans Road and the comparative safety of his Ford Consul, Wiseman struck, dragging his victim to the ground, savagely coshing him and making off with £350.

This time, there was no forensic evidence to link him with the crime and, thanks to his stocking mask, neither the unfortunate rent collector nor anybody else could identify him. Wiseman did make the mistake of bragging to a small circle of admirers in the Eastbrook public house of his latest misdeed. Unfortunately, one of the group was on bail to the newly formed Regional Crime Squad and, being desperate for a result, he informed his arresting officer of his drinking companion's boastfulness. They came for Wiseman early the following morning. He might have been able to satisfactorily explain away the £285 which the detectives discovered taped to the back of a bureau drawer but, alas, he was hung over from the night before. Far from offering an acceptable explanation, Wiseman openly mocked the detectives and dared them to do their worst. It was an imprudent move, because they did. The rent collector positively picked him out on an identification parade, something that outraged Wiseman, given that he and the rent collector both knew that he was wearing a stocking mask at the time. It was not something, however, that he could challenge in court without implicating himself. He could, and he did, bellow from the dock that he had been severely maltreated with a telephone directory and that his confession had been concocted by the detectives but it did him no good at all at the Essex Assizes. Following a two day trial, after which the detectives were congratulated for their perspicacity and skill at recovering £150 of the stolen money, the trial judge sentenced Wiseman to thirty months' imprisonment.

And yet, following his release, Wiseman had still not come to accept that the CID was a force to be reckoned with. There was a fight in the Heathway one evening which was nothing at all to do with Wiseman, save that he was purely an interested onlooker. By the time the police sirens could be heard in the distance, the scuffle had already run its course, the combatants had separated and the audience had started to disperse. The wireless car pulled up, the R/T Operator and the observer got out but neither they nor the rapidly dissolving crowd were seeking confrontation and that would have been that, if only the division's Q car had not arrived. Even then, if Wiseman had followed the crowd, all would have been well, except that the detective constable and the aid to CID who were crewing the car got out and Wiseman stopped because he recognized them. In a moment of madness, he decided upon a little police-baiting.

Facing them, his hands in his pockets, Wiseman threw down

his challenge. 'Can't nick me, can yer? Got me 'ands in me pockets, ain't I?'

The detective constable raised his eyebrows. 'What?' he enquired, politely.

'Wot I said,' replied Wiseman patiently, 'was that you can't nick me, 'cos I ain't done nothing.'

The detective calmly regarded Wiseman, in the same way that an experienced psychiatric nurse considers a lunatic in full rant. 'Get in the car,' he said, quietly.

In the charge room at Dagenham police station was a very young, inexperienced uniform sergeant, the whiteness of the three chevrons on the sleeve of his tunic bearing mute testimony to its owner's recent promotion.

'Right, turn your pockets out,' said the sergeant, briskly.

Wiseman affected a loud sigh to display his boredom at the proceedings. As he laboriously emptied his pockets, he loudly identified each item. 'Right – comb.' With that, the comb was placed on the charge room desk. 'Handkerchief.' That too, joined the comb. 'Let's see – seven shillings and fourpence ha'penny. Check that, will you?' This to the sergeant, who did just that. 'Three keys on a ring. Flick-knife – YOU BASTARD!' With that, Wiseman flung the offending article, which he had never seen before, under the charge room table.

'I saw that!' cried the sergeant and, turning to the detective constable, he added, 'I'll be a witness!'

The following morning at Barking Magistrates' Court, the detective had a quiet word with Wiseman before going into court. 'Well, Terry? What's happening this morning?'

'What's happening?' snorted Wiseman. 'I'm fucking pleading not guilty, ain't I? Fighting it every inch of the way.'

'Are you?' replied the detective. 'Well, Terry, I've got to tell you something. When you've been planted by me, you've been planted by the best. Understand? And we've just about had enough of a cocky little cunt like you. Know what I mean? So you take a tip from me, old son. You plead guilty this morning and after that, you move right out of the area. Got it? Because if you don't, I'll give you three guesses as to what's going to happen to you.'

The magistrate declared that the flick-knife was a 'fearsome-looking weapon' and, acknowledging Wiseman's guilty plea, sentenced him to two months' imprisonment. But, happily, his conviction did him quite a bit of good. Following his release and believing that he had no chance whatsoever against Old Bill as tricky as that, Wiseman did move out of the area and became a reformed character. He met a local girl at a dance, married her and was accepted into the family's business, which was the running of a general store. Eschewing his former lawless ways, in time he prospered and acquired a corner shop of his own.

Bert's Human Chessboard

The actor Wilfred Brambell was one of those people who never looked any younger than he did when he expired at the age of seventy-two, in 1985. During his career in films and television, he was inevitably cast as a tramp, an old man, a drunk or, on one occasion, a 'thin prisoner'. He is, of course, best known for his role as Albert Steptoe in the popular, long-running series, *Steptoe and Son*. I mention this, purely because in describing the inappropriately named Bert Pope, I have to rely to a certain degree on Wilfred Brambell's physiognomy.

Pope had lived a hard life, which explains the fact that, whilst he did not appear to look a day over seventy, at the time when this tale is recounted, Bert Pope was just a few weeks short of his forty-third birthday. Short, scrawny, a permanent leer on his face, which had the appearance of a building's façade which has been sandblasted, and not a single, sound tooth in his mouth, Pope cut a repellent figure. A social worker, of the type who is desperate to find some sort of redeeming feature in one so cruelly afflicted by fate, said that there was undoubtedly some seam of decency and integrity in him which had hitherto been untapped, but a kindly colleague told her, quite accurately, that she was talking out of her arse. Pope was rotten through and through.

Bert Pope saw himself as a mastermind of crime but not in the same mould as, for instance, Billy Hill who, during the

1940s and 1950s, planned and carried out raids of enormous sophistication, which paid out tremendous rewards and who, following his death on the last day of 1983, left a substantial fortune. No. Pope was a reincarnation of Jonathan Wild, the corrupt receiver of stolen property who informed on those who refused to go out burgling for him as well as those who did. His crimes eventually caught up with him and Wild was hanged in 1725.

Pope, who was highly vindictive and extremely manipulative, decided to capitalize on his ability to move people around his human chessboard, a game in which he was invariably the winner, when he was approached by a member of the Foam-up Gang.

This team of assorted half-wits had been making a reasonably lucrative living around north London by targeting newsagents. In the dead of night, they would squirt expanding builder's foam into the shop's audio alarm system, creeping away until the foam had set hard and then, safe in the knowledge that the alarm would be unable to betray their presence, returning to sledge-hammer open the door and steal as many cigarettes and other resaleable commodities as they could lay their hands on. Since the noise of the sledgehammer was prone to excite attention, usually from the owners of the shop who invariably lived above the premises, this was an operation that was not without risk. However, so far, the gang had got away scot-free.

Their undoing was to offer a load of stolen cigarettes to Bert Pope. Pope immediately recognized the gang as a bunch of dopes and saw that he would be able to do himself a great deal of good. He discovered pretty well everything about the identities of the gang, including the registration number of the vehicle that they habitually used, before offering them a sum of money for the goods which was so ridiculously low that the gang left Pope's presence in disgust.

Pope's next action was to inform his contact at Edmonton police station and give him all of the pertinent information regarding the Foam-up Gang. This set the wheels of police surveillance into motion, since this particular little bunch was becoming more and more of a thorn in their sides. It was just a matter of days later that the driver of the vehicle left his address at midnight, picked up his associates at their various addresses and all of them, quite unaware of the van, the car and the motorcycle which were following them, went straight to a tobacconist's in Bounds Green Road, Wood Green. The officers were so close to the premises that they could quite clearly hear the 'hiss!' of the foam entering the shop's alarm, as they could the nervous giggling of the gang as they crept away. Half an hour later, as the gang returned and swung the sledgehammer at the door, they were mightily surprised to find themselves grabbed, flung to the ground and handcuffed. It would have been difficult indeed for the gang to suggest that this venture had been an imprudent 'one-off' on their part, what with the further six cans of expanding builder's foam which was found in their car, nor did they even try. They admitted all of the offences which they had carried out, were remanded in custody and subsequently received sentences ranging from two years' probation to fifteen months' imprisonment, none of them having the slightest idea of how they had come to be arrested.

Their ultimate fate was of no concern to Bert Pope; it was time to further capitalize on the rest of his plan. First, he accepted his reward from the police Informants' Fund and then a further one from the insurance company. Next, with the opposition out of the way, the Foam-up burglaries could continue; this time with Pope's own team of burglars, one of whom was Gary Curtis.

'Gary, do yourself a bit of good,' murmured Detective

Constable Bob Marshall. 'Stick up that slag Pope for me; there'll be a nice safe drink in it for you, plus you do need a bit of help at court.'

Gary Curtis shuddered, momentarily shut his eyes, as though the gates of hell had opened to give him a glimpse of what lay beyond and shook his head. DC Marshall was quite right. Curtis did need a leg-up at court. The offence for which he was currently on bail to the officer was only one of taking and driving away but unfortunately most of his other previous had been for the same type of offence. It was therefore a strong possibility that this could just be the one, if the officer in the case could not be prompted to express a few benign words to the beak, which could propel him in the direction of a custodial sentence.

'I couldn't do that, Mr Marshall,' he replied, shakily. 'No.' He nervously stirred his tea in the little cafe off Turnpike Lane. 'No offence, Mr Marshall, but you have no idea of the sort of person you're talking about.'

A less mature officer would have rather unkindly told Gary Curtis 'to stop talking like a prick,' but Marshall was an experienced officer, so he contented himself by raising his eyebrows. 'Really?'

Curtis leant across the spotted tabletop and as he did so, glanced at the nearby tables, like a stage conspirator. 'This is between you and me, right?' he muttered. 'That Pope – well, he's a top police informant, see? Knows half the brains at Scotland Yard, he does. See, what he said to me was if I ever get into trouble, he could look after me.'

'How's he going to do that, Gary?' asked Marshall, extending a pack of cigarettes across the table.

Seizing the offered cigarette seemed to give Curtis more courage. 'What he said to me was, if I could give him information about jobs which I'd heard had been pulled or ones that were coming off, he could let the Old Bill know and they'd go to my credit. See?'

Marshall sighed. He quite liked Gary Curtis, who had married at seventeen and now had two kids and a heavily pregnant wife. Curtis had already propped up various bits and pieces of information to him which had resulted in the arrest of a couple of burglars and a car thief but Marshall would be the first to admit that Curtis was not the sharpest knife in the rack and his incredible assertion regarding Bert Pope's beneficence baffled comprehension. 'Gary, don't you see he's using you like a mug?' said Marshall, quietly. 'All he's doing is milking you for your information, then passing it on to the police and copping the reward for himself. There is no sort of – what – credit balance? There's nothing like that. The police don't work that way.'

'Sorry, Mr Marshall, but you're wrong,' replied Curtis, firmly. 'That Pope, he's got the Yard well squared up, don't you worry. It'd be more than my life's worth to give you anything about him.' He stood up to go.

'You take it easy, Gary,' said Marshall, 'but remember, your court date's coming up. You're going to have to pull something out of the hat to save you from going away.'

Curtis shuffled out of the cafe – shuffling was one of his less endearing traits – and Marshall sat down again. He knew that someone was handling Pope and, what was more, he knew who, and he couldn't have cared less. As far as he was concerned, Pope was a highly dangerous, manipulative bastard, as treacherous to the police as to those he was informing against, and it was his intention to nick him as soon as possible, milk him for every bit of intelligence he possessed and then charge him.

But things never quite work out the way that one would wish. They worked out quite differently for Curtis, for Marshall and, ultimately, for Pope.

Within a few days of Curtis' meeting with his handler, Pope, by his usual mesmeric skill, persuaded him to participate in a burglary with an accomplice, provided, naturally, by Pope. The target was a warehouse on an Edmonton trading estate and Pope's information was that the premises contained high-value hi-fi equipment and that the security was non-existent.

At one o'clock in the morning, Curtis and his assistant were busy, trying to jemmy open the rear door to the warehouse, without success. What was needed was a far larger case opener, an item that neither Curtis nor his partner possessed. So Curtis wandered off to a telephone box and dialled a number which was engraved upon his heart.

'Oh – er – Mr Pope – sorry, like—' stammered Gary Curtis, before he managed to impart the reason for the call.

'Oh, Christ,' muttered Pope. 'Right – fifteen minutes.'

Pope dropped off the much larger case opener to the intrepid duo and, with the curt command 'Right – get on with it!', he got back into his car and returned home.

The rear door of the warehouse finally yielded to the superior jemmy but to Curtis' dismay, there was very little inside that warranted nicking. Back to the telephone kiosk he went and informed Pope of the current state of events, plus the desire to know what he should do next. Pope had not the slightest intention of getting out of his sagging bed twice in one night, especially when there was nothing worth stealing but, true to form, a typical mischievous Pope plan was rapidly forming in his cold, calculating mind.

'Just go on back to the warehouse, Gary,' he said, 'hide yourself inside and wait for me. It could be there's something you've missed. I'll come down and check it out but if there's still nothing,' he added soothingly, 'well, don't worry. You'll get a nice drink anyway, for your trouble.'

Gary Curtis was actually rubbing his hands together as he headed back to the warehouse, and so was Bert Pope. He picked up the telephone again, dialled the number for Edmonton police station, informed the operator that he was a certain detective sergeant's top informant and gave them the address of a warehouse where two known criminals were breaking in – right now! That was the first part of the plan disposed of.

In the darkness of the warehouse, Gary Curtis heard the sound of the car pulling up outside and he started to walk towards the sagging door; then he stopped. Since when had Mr Pope owned a dog? He must have, since who else could be responsible for all that barking? As the second, then the third car screeched to a halt, Curtis was beginning to realize that matters might have gone seriously amiss.

Pope duly received his reward from the Informants' Fund, the judge told Gary Curtis that the very least sentence he could give him was Borstal Training, adding that had he been older than nineteen it would have been considerably more and Detective Constable Bob Marshall was furious, absolutely hopping mad.

He now privately resolved to nick that slimy bastard Pope as quickly as possible. When Marshall was told that he was being posted to the Flying Squad, he was utterly delighted. Now, he would have the time and the back-up to give Pope the nicking of his life.

Not so. On 10 July 1978, much of the Flying Squad personnel were devolved to four area offices around London, for the purpose of combatting armed robbery, to the exclusion of everything else. That was what Marshall was unequivocally told by the officer in charge of the Walthamstow office and any plans he had for the much merited nicking of Bert Pope would have to be put on hold until such time as he, Marshall, completed his posting on the Squad and returned to division which might or might not be in the Edmonton area. But, in the event, Marshall never did nick Bert Pope. Neither did anybody else.

Pope's body was found at the bottom of the stairwell of the gruesome tenement where he lived. The pathologist who carried out the autopsy decided that the cause of death was Pope's broken neck and the amount of bruising on his body, plus the amount of alcohol he had consumed, was consistent with a fall, down five flights of stairs. The coroner declared a verdict of 'death by misadventure', one or two of the Pope family gave an unconvincing display of grief and a detective sergeant was deprived of his top informant.

In fact, Pope's demise coincided with Gary Curtis' release from Borstal and, in fact, it is possible that Pope's passing was linked with the second part of his plan regarding Curtis.

Because the day following Gary Curtis' arrest and after he had appeared at Tottenham Magistrates' Court and had been remanded in custody, Bert Pope arrived at Curtis' flat, where he saw Mrs Curtis, heavily pregnant with her third child. Expressing sorrow at her husband's incarceration, and being fully aware that any young mother in her situation could do with more money, he offered, with a winning, black-toothed smile, to supply these extra funds to her. Loosening the cord on his stained, shell suit bottoms, which fell around his skinny ankles, he grasped hold of his grubby and flaccid member and invited Mrs Curtis to perform what is collo-quially known as a 'blow-job' when all these promised riches would be hers.

Mrs Curtis acted with wisdom and dignity not normally associated with a young woman of her age and background and firmly informed Bert Pope that she would willingly shove red-hot needles into her eyes, and laugh whilst she was doing so, before her lips came into anything near contact with his shrivelled todger. This information was imparted to her husband during her first visit at Rochester Borstal, so Gary Curtis had a long time to stew over matters.

Several weeks passed following the death of Bert Pope and the release of Gary Curtis and Detective Constable Bob Marshall was being driven in a Flying Squad car through Muswell Hill Broadway. He had been on leave and he had not heard of Pope's fate but as the car turned into Muswell Hill, he saw a familiar face. It was Gary Curtis and his wife, who was pushing a double pushchair containing their two younger offspring, and they had all just emerged from Alexandra Park. Curtis was carrying their eldest child and he had said something which had made his wife laugh. Then the car passed the young family and they disappeared from view, but Marshall had noticed something different about Curtis. He wasn't shuffling any longer. He wondered what had happened to put a spring in his step. It must have been the birth of the kid, thought Marshall idly; it couldn't be anything else.

Up in Smoke

Arsonists may not automatically spring to mind as being villains but of course they are.

The best known fire-raiser was probably Leopold Harris, who knew exactly what he was doing because he was also an insurance assessor. He was the head of a gang of arsonists who made their living by buying up, over-insuring and then setting fire to properties. Harris set up the Franco-Italian Silk Company, where the stock was worth £3,000. Since he was also the assessor to the company who had insured the property, Harris was able to secure a payout of £15,000. His false claims totalled anything between one quarter and half a million pounds and at his trial in 1933, forty-year-old Harris was sentenced to fourteen years' imprisonment. He grassed up everybody he could think of, including London's Salvage Corps officers, many of whom Harris grandly claimed 'he had in his pocket'. One of them was Captain Brymore Eric Miles who had distinguished himself during the First World War, winning the Military Cross. He fell from grace after it was discovered that he had been receiving £25 per month for turning a blind eye to Harris' spectacular run of arsons. For corruption and conspiring to pervert the administration of justice, Miles was sentenced to four years' imprisonment.

And one of Britain's most prolific serial killers pleaded guilty in 1981 to twenty-six cases of manslaughter and arsons in dwelling houses. Bruce George Peter Lee – his baptismal name was Peter Dinsdale but he changed it to be associated with his hero, Bruce Lee – set fire to the properties over a seven year period, simply because he 'loved fire'. Aged twenty-one at the time of sentencing, Lee, who had pleaded guilty to killing more people than the Yorkshire Ripper, the Black Panther and the Moors Murderers put together – the youngest was six months old, the oldest, ninety-five – was quite understandably described by the judge at Leeds Crown Court as a 'psychopath' and was ordered to be detained indefinitely under the Mental Health Act. He was sent to Rampton, where he remains to this day.

The flames of religious hatred are often fanned into arson attacks; during a nine-month period in 1965, thirteen synagogues were set on fire in Stoke Newington by members of a Neo-Nazi group, ten of whom later received prison sentences. And following the 7 July 2005 bomb attacks in Central London, mosques in Leeds, Belvedere, Telford and Birkenhead were subjected to arson attacks.

But on the other hand, take Derek Kelsey, who initially used to set fire to rubbish bins and then telephone the Fire Brigade, just to see them turn up. Not many people would regard that as an act of villainy but then he graduated to commercial premises and finally, houses, just for the pure joy of seeing the flames roaring skywards and hearing the noise of the fire engines arrive, which almost drowned out the screams of the unfortunate people still trapped inside the house. Some people might think that what Derek was doing was uttering a cry for help. I hope he gets it, in the secure unit where he's incarcerated so that he never gets out, and goes back to his old habit of sticking his grubby, bitten forefinger on to the number 'nine' button on a public telephone and prodding it three times.

Perhaps Derek could, to some extent, be excused on the

grounds that all he wanted to see was the flames and the arrival of the fire engines, rather than put people in danger but that certainly wasn't the case of Harry Banks, who when his amorous advances towards a barmaid in a Manor Park pub were rejected, did no more than return to the pub in the early hours of the morning, douse it in petrol and set fire to it.

And then there was the case of Terry Norrish who smashed a window to break into a west London shop. Precisely why he considered it necessary to set fire to the premises prior to leaving is unclear but he did and it killed the man sleeping in the flat above. Norrish was brought in and denied having anything to do with the break-in or the fire. He was physically examined and strange scratches were found running vertically down his back, for which he was unable to account. They were explained after the detective in charge had the broken window from the shop removed and brought to the police station. He pulled the carcass of a pig through it and the striations on the carcass caused by the jagged glass were a perfect match with the scratches on Norrish's back.

What else? Well, there was Geoff Allen who insured and set fire to buildings for profit and he *was* a villain, no error there, because he followed right in the footsteps of Leopold Harris, who died in 1974, the year before Allen's demise. Then there was the case of poor, crazy George Murphy who set fire to a Victorian house in Holloway, with him in it and, in his fervent desire to reduce himself to ashes, almost took me with him.*

And now we turn to the case of Michael Wilson, who not only immediately confessed to his misdeeds but was 'hungry'

* For fuller accounts of both Messrs Allen and Murphy, see *You're Nicked!* (Constable & Robinson, 2007)

to do so. When Wilson collected his winnings from his local betting shop, he discovered that they were £1.40 light. The betting shop manager refused to rectify the omission. 'Right, you cheating bastard,' Wilson promptly replied, 'tonight, I'll burn this fucking place to the ground and we'll see who's the winner, then.'

Late the same evening, Wilson walked down to the local garage with a can, which he filled with a gallon of petrol. Then it was back to the betting shop, where he tipped most of the can's contents over the façade of the building which he then ignited. With the betting shop a roaring inferno, he returned home, together with the almost empty can. The detective who paid him a call the following morning noted that the jeans and trainers which Wilson had been wearing the previous night reeked of petrol and mildly commented that it was fortunate that Wilson had not incinerated himself as well as the betting shop.

Wilson made a full confession and, after appearing at the local Magistrates' Court, he was remanded in custody at Chelmsford Prison. At his next appearance, the Bench informed him that he would further be remanded in custody in order that committal papers might be prepared so that he could be tried at the Crown Court. Asked if he had any questions, Wilson leaned nonchalantly forward in the dock and replied, 'Look, I can't be doing with all this fucking about. Would you please give me four years in Chelmsford today? That's what I want.'

The amazed Chairman of the Bench eventually found his voice. 'Why on earth would you want such a sentence?'

'Sir, the food in Chelmsford is fantastic,' earnestly replied Wilson, adding, rather tactlessly, 'far better than me mum gives me.' Warming to his theme, he continued, 'You get a cooked breakfast, a choice of three meals at lunchtime and another choice in the evening. Supper is up to you, but I always have it anyway. So, like I said, I want four years – starting today.'

Regretfully, the Bench was unable to accede to Wilson's strange request, since their limited powers precluded such a course of action, but he refused to give up. Wilson requested that the officer in the case visit him in the cells, where he told him that if he could swing it for an immediate four-year sentence in Chelmsford Prison, he would grass up everyone he could possibly think of.

The detective shook his head in bewilderment. He really doubted the accuracy of the information concerning the criminality of anyone whom Wilson was prepared to stick up. He was also questioning Wilson's sanity. Chelmsford nick was noted at that time for a very tough regime, housing some of England's hardest criminals and although he acknowledged that Michael Wilson's mum was no great shakes as a cook, her culinary dishes were a million times better than the *haute cuisine* served up in Chelmsford.

This brings us, lastly, to the exploits of Thomas Hambling, a particularly unsavoury character who had his fingers severely burnt by really pushing his luck once too often.

Hambling was a very unpleasant con artist who was responsible for setting a number of buildings on fire. After a period of weeks, or sometimes months, he would go into the police station in the area where the fire had occurred and shamefacedly confess to it. Since he knew as much about the circumstances of the fire as the investigating officer, the written confession that he made would be packed with authenticity.

After being charged, he would invariably be remanded in custody until his trial at the Old Bailey where he would plead not guilty. He would offer what would appear to be a cast-iron alibi as to his whereabouts at the time of the fire, and tearfully inform the court that the police were so keen to clear up the crime, they had beaten the confession out of him. Since the police knew about every aspect of the arson, said Hambling, it was easy for them to dictate the admissions to him and threaten him with even further violence if he did not willingly sign the statement.

On every occasion, he was acquitted and on at least one of those occasions, the trial judge had some very harsh remarks to make regarding the integrity of the police officers in the case. Hambling's next port of call would be to a firm of solicitors to instruct them to bring a civil action of unlawful arrest and malicious prosecution against the police. Only once did the police defend the action; they lost, and lost heavily. The other cases were settled out of court, resulting in substantial winnings for Hambling.

And then, like many criminals who, flushed with their own success, get a little too confident, Hambling strolled into a police station to confess to another arson.

According to your principles, it's for you to decide whether Detective Inspector Bernard Jepson was merely astute or as tricky as a barrel-load of monkeys. This is a summary of his statement:

'I visited the scene of the fire and, at the fire's seat, I took a sample of the debris which I placed in an envelope and which I produce as Exhibit BJ/1. Later, I saw the defendant, Thomas Hambling at the police station. I introduced myself, cautioned him and I said, "I understand that you wish to admit starting the fire which I am investigating." He replied, "Yes sir, that's right and I should like you to take a statement from me, saying so." I then took a statement from him, which I produce as Exhibit BJ/2. At the conclusion, I emptied the contents of the turn-ups in Hambling's trousers into an envelope, which I produce as Exhibit BJ/3. I caused Exhibits BJ/1 and BJ/3 to be conveyed to the Metropolitan Police Forensic Science Laboratory for analysis and comparison.'

Despite his earnest denial of the charge at the Old Bailey, Hambling was sentenced to seven years' imprisonment. To nobody's surprise, least of all Thomas Hambling's, his cunning, manipulative ways stopped then and there.

The Square Mile

The eight-hundred-year-old City of London is a city within a city. Known as the Square Mile, it houses the Guildhall, the Bank of England and is responsible for the Lord Mayor's Show. Best of all it is famed for its businesses and its finance houses. But ask a member of the Square Mile to explain exactly what is meant by a van dragger and he or she would undoubtedly look at you goggle-eyed. You would probably get the same reaction if you were to demand the meaning of a joey, what was meant by being 'at the creep' or to discuss the activities of a jump-up gang. To be fair, it would be understandable. These are crimes which have largely gone out of fashion in the City but, not so long ago, they were rife and those responsible earned a good living from the Square Mile.

The City of London is encircled with areas known to be the haunts of thieves; Camden to the north-west, Islington and Hackney to the north, Aldgate and Tower Hamlets to the east. Just north of Hackney Road is the little known area of Haggerston. In the seventeenth century it was the residence of the gentry but times change. In more recent times, Haggerston has been a place that many villains and ne'er-do-wells have been pleased to call home. It was from their base that van draggers and jump-up artists went to work in the City.

Van draggers – the gangs who stole vans or lorries and their contents – tended to wait outside the warehouses and factories on the outskirts of the City and then follow a delivery van full of expensive and resaleable commodities, such as cigarettes, spirits and women's dresses. The theft would then be effected with or without the assistance of the driver. With the former, the driver and the gang would arrange for a stop to be made outside an agreed cafe and whilst the driver was inside, taking his meal, the van would be taken by the thieves and the contents would be unloaded at record speed. By the time the driver had finished his meal, 'discovered' his van had gone and loudly raised the alarm, his vehicle would have been abandoned several streets away. In fairness, in the austere post-war years, it would have been difficult for many drivers to have resisted the chance of an extra few bob.

Whether or not the lorry, loaded with electrical goods valued at £2,200, which was stolen from Bow in 1947 was taken with or without the connivance of the driver is now unknown. Unfortunately for my Uncle Bill, who was one of the five-man gang responsible, he and his accomplices were fingered by a Ghost Squad nark; rather quickly, too. The lorry hadn't quite reached the Mile End Road before a Flying Squad Railton pulled across its bows and Uncle Bill went off to quod; and not for the first time, either. It appears that dear old Uncle Bill was the ringleader, because he copped the most porridge, a richly deserved pontoon – or twenty-one months' imprisonment.

In the event that a driver could not be persuaded to be venal, the van draggers would follow the van for several weeks in order to spot weaknesses in the driver's personal security. When the time was right, the gang would jump out of their vehicle, attack the van from both sides, drag out and overpower the driver, sling him into the back of their own vehicle and take the van to their slaughter. After the van had been relieved of its load, the tied-up and blindfolded driver would be inserted into the back of his own van, driven to a convenient spot and then the soft-hearted gang would telephone the police to let them know the location of the van. They were not as considerate as all that, though; if the driver had suffered a heart attack from being left tied up or gagged for too long, the gang could have been tried for murder, since the driver would be a victim who died in furtherance of a robbery and for this, the whole gang could swing.

Jump-ups had been fashionable since the nineteenth century – perhaps 'more fashionable' would be a more appropriate term, because this offence had been practised long before that – and this would be perpetrated by a van following a vehicle making deliveries. When the van stopped to make a delivery and was unattended, one of the gang would literally 'jump up' into the back of the van. Whilst two of the gang would keep look-out – they were known as 'crows' – the first gang member would throw down parcels – known as 'joeys' – to another of the gang, who would sling them into their own vehicle. Usually, according to their weight, five or six such joeys could be shifted during one hit. The same number could be lifted when the target vehicle stopped at traffic lights; as the lights changed, the delivery vehicle would go in one direction, the jump-up artists in another and the loss would only be discovered at the next stop. Of course, these offences were often opportunistic; one never knew what the prize was going to be.

This is what Jimmy Douglas discovered to his cost. Douglas, who hailed from Haggerston, had always been a thief, mainly a van dragger. He and his team had made a respectable living at it until, one day, he and his team had nicked a joey which was later found to contain the ebonite ends of billiard cues.

The general merriment which resulted inevitably reached the ears of the Flying Squad who felt duty-bound to collect Douglas. When he was released from his resultant stretch, it coincided with the arrival of World War Two. Douglas was one of the two million men and women called up for active service on 1 January 1940 but sadly he displayed little enthusiasm and most of his service was tarnished with trips to the glasshouse, each time of longer and longer duration. Eventually, it was decided that he and the Royal Army Service Corps should part company. Douglas did say this was on medical grounds, which was not entirely untruthful: he had severely injured his back falling off the NAAFI roof whilst attempting to gain unlawful entry. His brief spell in hospital was followed by a somewhat longer spell in the glasshouse.

In post-war London, any further aspirations to being the lead man in a jump-up team went right out of the window because of his dodgy back and so Douglas looked around for pastures new. He found what he was looking for at Liverpool Street main line station. The prize, this time, was luggage. Every morning and every evening, commuters were bustling in and out of the station, families with bulging suit-cases, bowler-hatted businessmen with gleaming briefcases, commercial travellers with sample cases.

Douglas would hang around telephone boxes, the bars, the kiosks selling newspapers and refreshments and best of all the ticket counters; all places where, at any given time, the trav-eller would put down his or her piece of luggage whilst their mind was on something else. Douglas would stroll by at an angle to them, then – whoosh! – the luggage was gone and so had Douglas, straight into a bustling crowd or down the Unders. In time, he was able to instinctively tell just by the look of a person what sort of prize their luggage would contain and, in fairness, he was seldom wrong. Also in time, his face became known to the Line Bogies and on several occasions, Douglas was ignominiously given a Sus and this was not without its dangers. Although a Sus carried a maximum three months at the Magistrates' Court – uncomfortable enough – there was always the danger that he could be sent to the Sessions for being 'an incorrigible rogue' and this carried a sentence of twelve months' imprisonment.

So Douglas eschewed Liverpool Street as a means of income – in any case, his back had started giving him a twinge whenever he bent down to swipe a suitcase and some of them were heavy – so he contented himself by trading on bits and pieces of crooked gear on his home manor. It was time, thought Douglas, to take things easy and let his son carry on the family business.

During the years that followed, Jimmy Douglas was fond of saying, 'That boy of mine – my Mark – 'e done it all hisself. Never needed a shove from me. 'E took to being at the creep as though 'e was born to it.'

Mark Douglas was indeed a talented performer of being at the creep – more commonly known as entering a large communal building, full of offices, and stealing property whilst they were unattended, usually at lunchtime. This offence – it was also known as 'stair jumping' – was quite lucrative. Mark Douglas dressed himself in the type of natty suiting beloved of other workers in the Square Mile and it only needed a little *savoir faire* to get past the doorman – there were no swipe cards in those days – and it was amazing the items that were left in jackets on the back of chairs, in overcoats hung from a hook or on and in desks. If no one was in the reception area on the way in, Douglas would get a little bolder and walk out of the building with a typewriter under his arm. So that was lunchtime taken care of; and then the rest of the afternoon would be spent in Soho, where, in and around the Berwick Street area, anything and everything could be disposed of. It was also ideal to meet new acquaintances and renew old ones.

So when Douglas met up with Beryl, a bold-eyed divorcée, and it transpired that she was working as a cleaner for a major blue-chip company in the City, it appeared that their meeting had been guided by providence. This was confirmed when, over a couple of drinks, Beryl casually mentioned that when she cleaned the accounts department of the company, cheques were left all over the place. 'You can't believe it, Mark,' said Beryl, eying him shrewdly. 'Cheques made out for thousands of pounds. Just left on people's desks.' She sighed. 'I mean, anyone could nick 'em,' and she was not particularly surprised to see the gleam appear in Douglas' eye.

'Do you think you could?' asked Douglas, with an attempt at nonchalance. 'Lift one, I mean?' He had deliberately framed the question in that way, so that if she suddenly took umbrage and screamed, 'How dare you!' he could easily laugh the whole thing off as a tasteless joke.

But she didn't. 'Reckon I could,' she murmured and held up her empty glass. 'Any chance of another drink?'

Two days later, Beryl slid an envelope across the table to Douglas, in the same bar in D'Arblay Street. He flicked the flap open to discover it contained a cheque, drawn on the National Westminster Bank, in favour of Watterstone Letterheads & Co. Ltd. The payment came to just over £10,000.

'It was attached to an invoice, all ready for payment,' whispered Beryl, excitedly. 'I tore off the invoice and burnt it. When they can't find it, they'll think it's been posted off to these Watterstone people.'

'Bloody-well done,' breathed Douglas and kissed her; but it was a pyrrhic victory, because he simply did not know what he was going to do with it. He started making enquiries amongst the kiters who had been making a decent living from passing stolen cheques for years but these cheques were usually blank, waiting to be filled in – by the kiter, naturally. No, all of them said the same thing. This cheque was useless unless he was the person or company shown as payee on the cheque, which Douglas most certainly was not. The only way round it, said one of the kiters, would be if the payee's name could somehow be bleached out and his name (or a suitable alias) inserted. Other than that . . . well, it was just a worthless scrap of paper.

This was completely out of his league and Douglas got to his feet. 'Well, thanks anyway, boys,' he said. 'I'll be on my way, then.'

'Hold up,' said one of the kiters. 'There is a geezer . . . Kiss they call him. I don't use him meself, never had to, but he's good at that sort of thing, I hear. Tommy knows him. You know Tommy don't you? Tommy Galpin?'

Douglas nodded. 'Sure.'

And then, right on cue, Tommy Galpin walked into the bar. After a long conversation over a couple of drinks, Tommy agreed to broker an introduction between Douglas and Kiss. All Douglas had to do was to open a bank account in a dodgy name and Tommy sold him a set of stolen documents which allowed him to do just that. The following Monday, the two men met. The man known as Kiss was tall, heavily built, in his late forties with fair hair, and a wispy moustache. He was also the owner of a marked, mid-European accent. 'Give me cheque,' said Kiss, in his heavily accented English. 'In one week, I will give you back cheque, identical to this made out in a name which you will tell me. It will be for £10,000 – I will want £2,000 for arranging it – cash on delivery.'

Douglas hesitated only a moment. Well, why not? Even if this bloke rooked him, he wouldn't be any worse off; it wasn't as though he could do anything with this cheque in its present state. 'Right,' he said, and passed the cheque over. He scribbled down his alias to be inserted on the cheque and telephone number on the envelope. 'Give us a call when it's ready.'

For the next week, Douglas carried on at what he was good at – getting at the creep – and practically forgot about Kiss and the cheque which he had pretty much written off as a bad debt. So he was startled when he heard the thickly accented voice on the telephone. 'We meet tomorrow, twelve noon, same place as before,' said Kiss abruptly, before hanging up.

The following day, Douglas carefully examined the cheque which Kiss passed him. It looked the same in every respect as the original cheque he had handed over, except that it was made payable to 'Michael Singleton', his chosen alias. Douglas pushed over two grand in tens and twenties to Kiss. 'You pay cheque in, no problem' said Kiss and so it proved to be. Douglas went to the Palmers Green branch of Barclays Bank, where he had opened the bogus account and paid it in, telling the cashier that it was his redundancy money. Four days later, he forti- fied himself with a large Scotch before, as nonchalantly as possible, strolling into the bank and asking if the cheque had cleared. There was no hint of duplicity in the teller's eyes as he assured him that it had, although he was a little surprised when 'Mr Singleton' asked for it all to be withdrawn in cash, preferably tens and twenties. As he sauntered out of the bank, as casually, he hoped, as he had entered it, he was half expecting a hand on his shoulder or a sudden shout – but his exit was quite uneventful.

Beryl was delighted when Douglas pushed an envelope under the table to her, which, he told her, contained a grand. Another cheque? A bigger one, this time? Beryl was delighted to agree.

In the meantime, Douglas decided that the 'Michael Singleton' account was no longer any good, since he figured that when the cheque was remitted to the drawer's account, the balloon would go up. In fact, he probably could have got away with using the bogus account on several more occasions without incident, since accounting departments are notoriously slow at putting two and two together. But he met up with Tommy Galpin again and arranged the sale of another bogus identity, which became another dodgy bank account in the name of Jeffrey Wilkinson. Within two days, Beryl came up with the goods. Another cheque which had been attached to an invoice as payment for another company – this one was made out in the sum of £50,000.

Kiss took possession of the cheque and Douglas' new bogus details as they sat at a table on the pavement outside an open-air cafe in Dean Street. He told Douglas that the cheque would be ready in about ten days' time – this time his fee would be £10,000. Douglas shrugged his shoulders. Why not? No point in being greedy. He had seven grand from the previous deal; some spirited work in the City's offices and a loan from dad secured the balance.

The call came just nine days later. 'We meet outside French Protestant Church tomorrow, at nine in the morning, yes?' That was no problem for Douglas; although he had never been acquainted with the interior of the church, he knew where it was – just off Soho Square.

The following day, which was 13 August 1976, saw Douglas just walking out of Soho Square towards the church and he could see Kiss in the distance. He hurried his pace and as the two men met up, Douglas said, 'Hello, mate, how're you—' and that was as far as he got before four men seemed to step out of nowhere. Two of them grabbed hold of Kiss, one of them snatching the thin envelope out of his hand, the envelope which Kiss was just about to hand over to Douglas, saying, 'I'll have that.' The other two men grabbed hold of Douglas and one of them said, 'Serious Crime Squad – you're nicked.'

'What d'you mean I'm nicked?' blustered Douglas and started to struggle, which caused one of the men to punch him, hard, in the ribs. At that moment, two cars pulled up by the men and Kiss was placed in the back of one of them, with Douglas in the other.

On the way to Limehouse police station, Douglas' thoughts were racing. He knew he was nicked for having a dodgy cheque but that was all; he didn't know the half of it.

For months, the Serious Crime Squad had been investigating the activities of a gang known as 'The Hungarian Circle'.* This organization had been active for twenty-five years carrying out frauds all over the world. They possessed not only great con men and women; they also had the backing of the finest forgers, one of whom was Stephen Kisfaludy, who was known as Kiss. The gang had a top-of-the-range printing press and quite a lot more, besides. They had stolen cheques – those stolen by Beryl added to their stock – plus bank drafts from which they were able to obtain the correct paper and typesettings and a machine for printing in the amounts for the drafts. When Kisfaludy received the stolen cheques from Douglas, he had not altered them; he had simply beautifully forged an exact duplicate, inserting the amount and the name of the payee. They also forged travellers' cheques, currency and passports. During the investigation, the Serious Crime Squad had used surveillance, both human and electronic, photographs – there were 5,000 of them alone – and had taped conversations between several of the conspirators in public places, using 'boom' style microphones.

Most of the conspirators had been arrested at six o'clock that morning. Kisfaludy was not at his address when the police

* For a full account of the investigation into the activities of 'The Hungarian Circle', see *You're Nicked!* (Constable & Robinson, 2007).

called but they knew where he would be at nine o'clock that morning, together with a not unimportant associate, thanks to a telephone call which had been intercepted the previous day.

Much, much later in the day, Douglas was taken from his cell to an interview room. Present was a detective inspector and a detective constable. 'Sit down lad,' said the inspector genially.

'Look, I ain't saying nothing, right?' said Douglas, as he sat down.

'Good, lad, that's fine. I hope you won't say anything, because that'll make my job so much easier,' replied the DI.

Douglas frowned. This was not the sort of treatment he was expecting.

'Y'see, son, if you did decide to say something, it'd be bollocks, wouldn't it?' said the inspector. 'It'd be a pack of lies, right? But because I'm a copper, I'd have to check out everything you told me. That'd take a lot of time. And I got up early this morning, and now I'm tired and I want to go home. So instead, you just stay quiet, listen to what I've got to say and then you can be charged and go back to the cells, all right?'

He then gave Douglas a brief outline of the gang's activities, before tossing down a number of photographs, one at a time. The first showed him and Kiss together in the pub; the next, taken in the same pub, showed Kiss both handing over the first forged cheque and receiving the two grand. Both photographs had been taken by a policewoman, sitting at another table, using a handbag camera.

The next showed Douglas receiving the £10,000 cash across the counter in Barclays Bank. This had been taken by someone, not a customer of the bank, using a briefcase camera. The last photograph, was of Kiss and Douglas sitting outside the cafe and had been taken from across the street by the photographer who was in the back of a van which untruthfully stated that it was the property of 'Poppies Flowers'. And then the inspector put a tape recorder on the desk and pressed the 'start' button. Douglas heard the conversation between him and Kiss which had been recorded by the Scotland Yard technician, who had also been in the back of the van. Last of all, the inspector tossed the ten grand, in tens and twenties on to the desk, together with the forged cheque for £50,000, made payable to 'Jeffrey Wilkinson'.

'See what I mean, son?' It was the detective inspector, again. 'Not much you can say, is there? Only that you're involved with this little lot way over your bollocks – and what's more, they've got an excuse because they're foreigners. But you're not, are you? English born and bred, aren't you? Yep, ought to know better. So you'll go and draw the same as them. Nines and tens, I'd say.'

Douglas' mind was in uproar. Of course, he could not know that, in due course, a representative from the Chase Manhattan Bank (City of London Branch) would tell a jam-packed courtroom at the Old Bailey, 'They had the ability to bankrupt a small European country,' but what he did know was that he had suddenly graduated from being at the creep, big-time.

'Er – wait a minute, Guv'nor,' he said, nervously. 'I think I'd better make a statement. You see, this tart I know, well it was all her idea . . .'

145

'They Can Always Get You
on your Diary . . .'

It is not known who was actually responsible for the hijacking of the lorry-load of Scotch nor, as far as the story is concerned, is it important. Suffice it to say, the lorry was headed for Felixstowe Docks and when the driver pulled in to a cafe and left his cab to answer a call of nature, he was seized, knocked unconscious, bundled into the cab which was then driven off, in a direction far different from its intended destination. When he awoke, the load had been separated from the cab and he was obliged to answer a number of cogent questions from a number of disbelieving detectives.

The load found its way into the possession of three villainous south London brothers named Saunders; Ernie, Billy and John. The crates were unloaded and hidden; the trailer was removed. Due to the size of the shipment, it was necessary to enlist a little assistance and sometimes the help is not always as reliable or as loyal as one might hope . . .

'It's all there, Mr Jenkins!' excitedly exclaimed Harry Mitchell into the telephone. 'It's at the Saunders' place right now – and it's going to be moved sometime tomorrow!'

'Nice one, Harry,' grunted Detective Sergeant Cyril Jenkins of the Regional Crime Squad. 'I'll catch you later,' and with that, he put the phone down.

Both Harry Mitchell and Cyril Jenkins had been drinking,

not to render either of them paralytic you understand, but sufficient to cause errors of judgement. Mitchell had stated that the stolen Scotch was at 'the Saunders' place' and Jenkins knew that the villainous Saunders brothers had a smallholding on the borders of Kent and the Metropolitan Police District; *ergo*, that's where Mitchell meant when he said that that was the location of the property. But Mitchell didn't mean that at all. When he said 'the Saunders' place' what he actually meant was the brothers' slaughter, or run-in, which was situated many miles from their main residence. He was under the impression that Sergeant Jenkins was aware of the location of the slaughter; but Jenkins was not. Which just goes to show the peril of taking strong drink; something which was going to rebound on just about everybody concerned in this little drama.

Jenkins acquired a search warrant from an obliging magistrate, and then phoned round for the other members of his team to meet him in the office for a six o'clock start the following morning. Then, as an afterthought, he telephoned his detective inspector.

The detective inspector's name was Dave Watmough and, really and truly, the Regional Crime Squad was not the best posting for him. Detective inspectors on the RCS needed to be rather dynamic figures, able to go out and drag in a case or information to present to their team but Watmough tended to be happy enough to let his team acquire their own work and keep him up to date on how the enquiries progressed. Thus it was that Watmough was told that his team intended to raid a receiver's establishment, one that was controlled by a well-known and very villainous south London family, and was asked if he would care to accompany them. Watmough thought for a moment and then realized that, to avert a scolding from his olive-skinned Mediterranean wife, some much required decorating needed to be completed in his kitchen the following morning, so he refused the offer. The next afternoon, Watmough turned up at the office. 'How'd that raid go on the receiver's place?'

The senior detective sergeant on his team, Cyril Jenkins, mournfully shook his head. 'Nothing, Guv, a right blow-out. Fucking snout, it's him who needs nicking!'

Watmough chuckled. 'OK, show me down as going along.' The reason for this falsehood was simply that when a board for the rank of detective chief inspector presented itself to him, Watmough could point out that he was always in the fore-front of his team's activities. It was a small point but, for the board, an important one; it showed leadership, something which was much needed in the rank of detective chief inspector and one which was singularly lacking in Watmough's make-up. So his details were added to the names of the other officers on the search form and Watmough entered the details in his official diary.

Jenkins had been right, at least as far as the non-discovery of the hijacked Scotch was concerned; the job had been a blow-out. The Saunders brothers had been predictably furious about their smallholding being searched which made the detectives all the more clumsy in the way in which they conducted their business. After nothing was found in the outbuildings, the detectives turned their attention to the brothers' bungalow. They did not really expect to find crates and crates of stolen Scotch in there but many thieves and receivers find it irresistible to 'cream off' some of their spoils for their own consumption; it has been the downfall of many a crook. But not this time. Not a bottle was found and the RCS officers left, as far as they were concerned, empty-handed.

As the last of their three cars drove away from the small-holding, the eldest brother, Ernie, was fuming. All right, so they hadn't found the Scotch but he'd been grassed-up and those bastards had taken a right fucking liberty. However, one thing at a time. Picking up the telephone, he dialled the number for New Scotland Yard. 'I wanna make an official complaint,' he growled. 'Some of your Regional Crime Squad blokes have turned me over and they've nicked a grand off me!'

CID officers, unlike their uniform counterparts, were obliged to keep an official diary. On the left-hand pages were recorded their day-to-day duties; when they came on and off duty, what they did, where they went and with whom, who they met, whom they arrested and for what, their meal-times and the names of licensed premises that they entered. On the right-hand side, details of the expenses which they incurred and also claims for mileage, if they were authorized to use their own car on duty. At the rear of the diary, fuller details of the arrests they made. These entries were usually made every day and submitted for checking every week. The diaries were inevitably the focus of attention when misconduct on the part of the officer was alleged at court. Usually, the hysterical braying for the diary's production in court was no more than a fishing trip. But when an internal investigation was carried out by the Complaints Department, the diaries were always seized and scrutinized for any evidence, no matter how slight, of wrongdoing. It was a fortunate officer indeed who walked away completely unscathed from such an investigation. There was an old saying in those days: 'If they want to get you, they can always get you on your diary.'

So when Complaints Department came along to the Regional Crime Squad office, they seized everyone's diary and served Forms 163 (the official complaints form) on all of the officers who had gone on the raid and interviewed them. Watmough was initially bemused; he knew nothing about the matter and then, just before he was about to be interviewed, he realized that he couldn't say that he hadn't been to the premises, because of the entry in his diary, saying that he had. Making a false entry in one's diary was a serious disciplinary offence and one that, in a best case scenario, could lead to a massive fine and demotion and, in a worst case one, dismissal from the Force.

So, swallowing a very large lump in his throat, Watmough was interviewed under caution and signed a totally untruthful statement, in which he averred that he had indeed been at the receivers' premises and that nothing untoward had happened. And that, prayed Watmough, would be the end of the matter.

It was not. Some money, totalling almost one thousand pounds, which could not be accounted for was found in the possession of a number of the search team. A report was submitted to the Director of Public Prosecutions who came to the conclusion that if some of the RCS officers were involved in the theft, the rest *must* be. All of the officers, including Watmough, were suspended from duty, then charged and were committed to stand their trial at the Old Bailey.

In the meantime, Ernie Saunders dealt with the second of his considerations; someone had grassed him, a matter which needed to be addressed and accounted for in full. He and his brothers entered a certain south London pub, right in the middle of the lunch-time drinking session. Their entrance was enough to ensure that silence suddenly fell upon the clientele. There, sitting together, were the three men who had helped unload the stolen Scotch and the Saunders brothers arrival made the heart of one Harry Mitchell beat very much faster. 'Fuckin' grass!' growled Ernie Saunders and, by pure coincidence, grabbed hold of Mitchell. As tables overturned in the customers' haste to vacate the premises, the eldest Saunders brother drew an open razor from his pocket and Mitchell squealed as it flashed in his direction. It was not a deep cut but it produced a 'V' shaped cut from the corner of his mouth; the mark of a grass. Of course, it was not really clear if Harry Mitchell had been the grass but, quite obviously, it was one of the three helpers who had bubbled them. Therefore, in true democratic fashion, brothers Billy and John also produced open razors from their pockets and striped helpers numbers two and three. This was not really considered to be unfair; it demonstrated that the brothers Saunders were not to be trifled with.

In fact, one of the helpers did complain to the police; and although the investigating officers did manage to trace six of the fifty-one customers who were actually in the pub at the time, it transpired that, at the time of the attack, all of them were simultaneously voiding their bladders in the pub's very cramped urinal and had heard and seen nothing or nobody.

Something which went down in criminal folklore was that when the senior investigating officer asked Ernie Saunders where he was and what he was doing at the time of the attack, he laconically replied, 'I was cutting the grass' and brothers Billy and John almost had a seizure trying not to laugh.

But in Number One Court at the Old Bailey, Watmough was in the middle of a nightmare. The villainous family each took their turn in the witness box and loudly vilified the various officers. Then the brothers turned to Watmough and each in turn faltered. 'I don't remember that little geezer at the end being there,' each of them truthfully stated.

And Watmough who was gripping the brass rail of the dock so tightly that it was in imminent danger of becoming concave and who certainly knew that he had been nowhere near the premises, had to go into the witness box and state, with the sweat running down his face, that he had.

The jury were out for over a day before they returned verdicts of not guilty in respect of all of the officers. It was the end of the line for Watmough. The tremendous strain of having to compromise himself, knowing all the time he had done nothing wrong (apart from making a false statement and committing perjury) proved too much. With his health in tatters, he was reinstated just long enough for him to be invalided out of the Force.

On the island of Crete, about ten miles south-east of the town of Georgioupolis is the village of Asi Gonia, which means 'at the corner'. There is a man who lives there, a small man, as deeply tanned as any of the other villagers and what remains of his hair is now deeply grey. It is his blue eyes which suggest that he might not have originated from these parts. Every day, he makes his way to the *kahfehneeo* (or coffee house) and acknowledges the greetings from the other villagers – *Γειά συς!* – either in the same language or with a nod of his head. And there he sits, sipping his coffee with the attendant glass of water, saying nothing. He has a habit of blinking, quite a lot. Sometimes – it is not very often, because Asi Gonia is off the beaten track – tourists arrive and, if they see the small man in the coffee house reading a *Daily Telegraph* which is at least three days old, they might engage him in conversation. They learn very little, save that he is English, that many years ago he married a Cretan girl from this village and when he retired they came to look after her ageing parents. But that is all. Suddenly, he gets up, wondering if he has said too much, shakes hands with the visitors and leaves. The tourists are always impressed with the strength of his handshake; but his grip is nowhere near as powerful as the pressure he exerted, so many years previously, on the brass rail in the dock of the Old Bailey.

'For Services to the Public . . .'

There are con men and there are con men. At the upper end of the scale was the self-styled Count Victor Lustig who, during the early part of the twentieth century, toured the world, gambling, fornicating and making a substantial living fleecing mugs who wanted to turn a quick, dishonest buck. Having kept one step ahead of the law in the United States, the Czechoslovakian-born fraudster returned to Paris in 1925 from whence he had fled three years previously. Now, the interest which various law enforcement agencies had shown in him had died down.

As he sat at a pavement cafe, in the shadow of the Eiffel Tower, he glanced at a newspaper. In it was an article about the tower which had been constructed in 1889 for the Paris *exposition* at a cost of £260,000. However . . . the Eiffel Tower had never been intended to be a permanent structure and now it was in need of a great deal of repair. Indeed, stated the article, the Government was wondering if it might be better to pull the entire structure down, rather than actually repair it. A smile creased Lustig's scarred, thin face. The article had set out the blueprint which would permit him to perpetuate one of the greatest confidence tricks of all time.

He had a counterfeiter create Government stationery which declared him to be the Deputy Director General of the *Ministère de Postes et Télégraphes*. Next, using these letter-headings, he wrote to five scrap-metal dealers, asking them, in fairly vague terms, to call on him at his suite in the Hotel Crillon. When, one by one, they arrived, Lustig, who spoke French fluently, swore them to secrecy and informed them that the government intended to sell the Eiffel Tower for scrap – all 7,000 tons of it. This, he stressed would have to be carried out with complete confidentiality, because the Parisians would be furious if the news of the intended sale of their beloved monument was to leak out. He invited the five men to submit their bids within a week, but Lustig had already sorted out the dupe. André Poisson was a prosperous and successful scrap-metal dealer but he had an inferiority complex; because he came from the country, he knew his Parisian counterparts looked down their noses at him, regarding him as a bumpkin. Knowing this, Lustig also knew that Poisson would be unable to resist the chance to snub them. So it was almost inevitable that Poisson would cough up 250,000 francs – well over £500,000 by today's standards – plus a substantial bribe for Lustig, in his guise as a corrupt government official. As soon as he had handed over an impressive-looking receipt, acknowledging that Monsieur André Poisson was now the accredited owner of the Eiffel Tower, upon which demolition could start immediately, Lustig beat a hasty retreat to Vienna. During the following champagne-filled week in Austria's capital, Lustig studied the French newspapers on a daily basis but when no news of the swindle appeared, he realized he had underestimated his dupe's inferiority complex; rather than look a bigger fool than he actually was, Poisson had uttered not one word of complaint and had quietly retreated to the country. Nothing, thought Lustig, could top that; except, of course, returning to Paris and selling it all over again. And that was exactly what he did, sending his imposing letter-headings out to five different scrap metal dealers. This time things went badly wrong after the victim realized that he'd been fleeced. He reported the matter to the police, the crime hit the headlines of newspapers right around the world and Lustig escaped once more, again to America. There, the American Secret Service got on his trail for passing counterfeit currency and, in 1934, he was arrested. The following year, Lustig was sentenced to twenty years' imprisonment; twelve years into his sentence he died in Alcatraz.

At round about the time that Count Lustig was escaping back to the United States, the Charity Organisation Society had started making enquiries into the appeals for donations in respect of St Thomas's Church, Kennington, south London. The society simply could not understand how the vicar of St Thomas's, the portly, bespectacled, thirty-eight year old Reverend Harry Clapham, could afford a series of expensive cars, including an American Studebaker, or pay for long, expensive holidays in Germany, Austria, Palestine, America and Canada or a cruise to the West Indies with his wife and two children on a stipend of £400 per year. These were paid for by gifts from well-wishers, airily explained Clapham. Although suspicions still remained and expanded, it took another fifteen years before Clapham was caught.

The investigation revealed that just one percent of the £117,000 which Clapham had received had gone to charity. Money had been donated from all over the country, sometimes just pennies from achingly poor people, and had found its way into Clapham's ninety-seven bank accounts and had paid for his nine houses. Following his three-week trial at the Old Bailey in June 1941, on twenty-one counts of fraudulent conversion and falsification of accounts, Clapham was sentenced to three years' penal servitude.

It is difficult to place Lustig and Clapham in the same category of dishonesty; the former dashing and adventurous, the latter, slimy and pocketing the hard-earned money of those who could barely afford to part with it. Perhaps right in the middle of them was Abe Solokoff. Not for Abe the thrilling complexities of selling the Eiffel Tower, nor stooping so low as to take the money out of poor people's pockets; he worked the corner game and, what was more, he was good at it.

In recent years, the corner game, much like jump-ups, seems to have faded from the scene but, at one time, it was immensely popular with con men. It had been used with great success during and just after World War Two when commodities were very scarce if, indeed, they could be obtained at all. So when the fraudster approached a retailer with the offer of cartons of cigarettes or crates of whisky which were obviously stolen, it was an offer which was irresistible. A convincing-looking carton would be produced by the con man and it would be clandestinely handed over to the mug who would pass the fraudster the money. It was only when the mug opened the carton that he would discover that he had purchased a very expensive box of sawdust; by then, the con man had vanished 'round the corner' – hence the name of the scam. Often, if the promised prize was a lorry-load of goods, the con man had to speak and move very quickly indeed, to persuade the mug to part with his money before he had even seen the goods which did not exist, either in cartons or not. It was this latter variation of the corner game of which Abe Solokoff was a master.

Abe was tall, slim with a headful of grey, wavy hair. He exuded confidence, willing people to like and trust him. It was Abe's proud boast that he was able to spot a mug at one hundred yards so when he overheard Jim Francis in conversation in an East End pub, it soon became clear that Francis was a plumber's mate and that his employer had been badly let down on a consignment of spares. After Francis' companion had left, it was with consummate ease that Abe struck up a conversation with him; after all, Abe, now in his sixties, had been in the con game for over forty years. Abe explained that from what he had overheard of the conversation, he believed that he would be able to assist Francis' employer with the accessories for his company and if he, Francis, would broker an introduction to his employer which resulted in a successful transaction, he, Abe, would be delighted to award young Mr Francis a commission of fifty pounds.

A further meeting was arranged for the following day, between the three of them: Abe, Jim Francis and his employer, Pete Murrell. Then Jim went off to speak to his employer; Abe went to carry out a quick course in plumbing accessories.

The next day the three of them met up in the same pub. After Abe had purchased a round of drinks, he took a sheaf of typed papers out of his inside pocket. 'Take a look at that,' he said as he slid the papers over to Murrell.

Murrell's eyes widened as he saw what was written on the manifest. Yes, there were massive amounts of copper tubing but also there were vast quantities of everything else that he needed; stopcocks, gate valves, drain cocks and servicing valves. Then there were the taps: Pillar taps, high-neck taps and Bib taps as well as taps with handwheel handles and lever handles as well as kitchen mixers, bath and basin mixers, bath and shower mixers, monobloc mixers. Murrell actually licked his lips as he turned the page and when he saw what was listed his eyes positively gleamed; none of which was lost on Abe. Yes, there were sinks and lavatory suites but there were also dozens of different ball-valves: Portsmouth, Equilibrium, Diaphragm and Servo-diaphragm. He didn't bother to complete his reading of the list; everything and more that he wanted was there. He looked up sharply at Abe. 'How much?'

Abe, who already knew that such a parcel of goods would come to six grand, trade, replied, 'Fifteen hundred.'

Murrell, who, on the basis of what he had seen, had privately totted-up a total of at least five grand was delighted. Leaning back in his chair, he murmured, 'I suppose you could say that they're – er – a bit hot?'

'No,' replied Abe, reasonably, 'I'd say that they're nicked. So if you want them, the deal needs to be done quickly.'

Murrell certainly wanted them, so it was arranged that he and Francis would meet Abe outside the pub on the following day at twelve noon, sharp, and would bring with them the cash and a lorry big enough to transport the very reasonably priced plumbing equipment.

As it turned out, Murrell was unable to attend the meet the next day. A crisis had arisen in his office, one that needed his immediate and constant attention, so he dispatched Jim Francis with the lorry, with the reminder that he was not to part with the cash until he was in possession of the goods.

Just after midday, Francis brought the lorry to a halt outside the pub, where Abe was already waiting. He expressed initial surprise at Murrell's non-attendance but knowing what was going to occur, the employer's absence suited him. With Francis driving, Abe issued rapid instructions as to the route they should take and after half an hour of twists and turns, Francis, who came from south London and was confused when he was north of the river at the best of times, was completely lost. In fact, they had been going round in circles and were no more than a quarter of a mile from where they had started their journey. They were in the car park of a disused warehouse. 'Right, Jim, the lorry with the gear on board is just round the corner.' Francis noted that Abe was perspiring. 'Be glad to get rid of it, I can tell you; I had a phone call this morning to say I should expect a visit from Old Bill. Now, we've got to move fast. Get the tail down on the lorry; I'll go and get my lorry round here and the lads and I will give you a hand to load up. Oh, and by the way, here's the fifty quid I owe you; much obliged.' Abe went to get out of the cab and then paused and turned. 'Just give me the dough will you, Jim? It'll save time later. Come on, quick! I ain't got time to hang around!'

Francis hesitated just for a moment; Murrell had said that he shouldn't part with the money until the gear was on board . . . still, this bloke had been straight with him, he'd given him his fifty quid, hadn't he? 'Cheers, Jim,' smiled Abe. 'Five minutes.'

With that, he climbed out of the cab and trotted off to the corner and vanished. Around the corner, instead of the promised lorry full to the gunwales with dodgy gear, was Abe's Mark X Jaguar. He got in, pressed the ignition and drove off, in the direction of Buckhurst Hill and home. And as he drove, he chuckled to himself. He was fourteen hundred and fifty quid better off and Murrell would be hard-pressed to go to the law and tell them he'd been rooked on a dodgy deal, trying to purchase a consignment of stolen goods. Unfortunately, he had reckoned without Jim Francis's finely honed sense of survival.

After waiting the required five minutes which turned into ten and then fifteen, Jim Francis ran to the corner to discover, with the bile rising in his gorge, that he'd been conned. Eventually finding his bearings, he made his way back to his employer with a ready-made story. There was no lorry-load of gear, he told the furious Pete Murrell. As soon as they had got to the rendezvous, he said, Abe had pulled a gun and had robbed him of the fifteen hundred pounds. And this gave Murrell the confidence to report the matter to the police.

Detective Constable Geoff Tanner took a long, detailed statement from both men. Privately, he thought that Murrell had been the victim of the corner game and he didn't trust shifty-looking

Jim Francis by half. He took both men to the photographic albums section of C11 Department at the Yard and, one at a time, they looked through the various books containing photographs of known con men, all of whom were aged in their sixties. Francis spotted Abe Solokoff's photograph straight away, but gave no indication of doing so; eventually, he closed the last album, stating with every indication of regret that he was unable to identify anybody. Murrell, on the other hand, made a very positive identification of Abe. Tanner thanked both men, who then left the building, and wondered why it was that Francis, who had spent far more time in Abe's company, had failed to identify him. Still, he walked down one flight of stairs to Criminal Records Office on the third floor and picked up and signed for Abe's very bulky CRO file.

By the time that DC Tanner knocked on the front door of Abe Solokoff's neat semi-detached house in Buckhurst Hill, he had read Abe's file from cover to cover. Abe had been arrested time and again for fraud offences, mostly for the corner game variety of fraud. Now and then, he had been acquitted but, nevertheless, he had built up an impressive number of convictions. It was Abe who answered his knock and Tanner was subjected to an overwhelming display of charm. He must come in immediately and have some tea or, of course, coffee if he preferred it. A search warrant? What nonsense! Mr Tanner was quite welcome to search anywhere he pleased; there was no need for a search warrant. Ruth, my dear (this to his dignified, long-suffering wife) this is Inspector Tanner from the Flying Squad. Oh, DC Tanner? Well, well, it was only a matter of time before his talents were properly recognized. And from City Road police station? The Flying Squad needed men of his calibre. And there was much more of the same before Abe was requested to accompany Tanner to the police station. Abe injected so much enthusiasm into his acceptance that an onlooker would have thought that Abe had been waiting for such an invitation all his life.

Abe received the shock of his life at the police station when Tanner put the whole allegation to him. A gun? Robbery? The blood drained from his face. 'Mr Tanner, I swear to you, robbery is not my game!' he wailed, piteously.

Tanner shrugged, unsympathetically. 'There's a first time for everything, Abe.'

Abe was deep in thought. Finally, he said, 'Can you give me ten minutes to myself?'

Tanner nodded and locked him in a cell. After fifteen minutes, knowing that he was in an impossible position, Abe fully admitted the corner game offence, to the prejudice of Messrs Francis and Murrell but vehemently denied the use of a firearm. Tanner was inclined to give him the benefit of the doubt. This was based on the fact that (a) during the whole of his criminal career, Abe had never resorted to violence or the use of firearms and (b) by telephoning Pete Murrell, he discovered that Francis had not turned up for work and was nowhere to be found. Prudently keeping the last of these considerations to himself, Tanner interviewed Abe, who, realizing he was being let off the firearms charge, started talking out of sheer relief and, for the rest of the day, kept Geoff Tanner hugely amused with the tales of his assorted con tricks over the years. Abe was eventually charged with the plumbing gear corner game offence, plus one or two others and was released on bail. He strongly hinted to Tanner that he might be in a position to supply him with information, although he never did, but when he appeared at the Old Bailey, he pleaded guilty to the charges and asked the court to take quite a list of similar offences into consideration.

In the witness box, Tanner passed a copy of Abe's long list of convictions to the judge and read out his last three. He agreed that Abe had been fully cooperative and had admitted his guilt at the earliest opportunity; indeed, Tanner mentioned to the judge that many of the offences admitted by Abe had never been reported.

After hearing an eloquent plea for clemency from Abe's barrister, the judge acknowledged Abe's plea of guilty, his age and his obvious remorse but felt that, given his appalling number of convictions over a period of some forty years, the minimum sentence he could pass was one of four years' imprisonment. Immediately, there was an urgent, whispered conference between Abe and his barrister and as the judge was about to rise, thereby signalling the finish of the proceedings, Abe's counsel said, 'I know this is irregular, My Lord but the prisoner wishes to address you.'

The judge frowned. 'Not only is it irregular, Mr Blenkinshaw but since the prisoner has been sentenced, it is quite improper.' He paused. 'However . . . well, very well, Mr Solokoff. What is it you wish to address me about?'

Abe stood up in the dock. 'My Lord, given my plea of guilty to these offences, I do feel, with the greatest possible respect, that a sentence of four years is unduly harsh. I am now sixty-two years of age, My Lord, and at a time of my life when I feel I should be spending time with my grandchildren.'

'Even if you possessed any grandchildren, Mr Solokoff, which you quite clearly do not,' quietly remarked the judge, 'that is something which you really should have reflected upon, before committing this series of thoroughly dishonest offences.'

'Quite so, My Lord; I was about to add to Your Lordship, "if I had any"' hastily interjected Abe, quickly abandoning Plan A and implementing Plan B. 'But, implausible though it may seem at first sight, I would like to point out to Your Lordship, that I have, in fact, been carrying out a public service.'

The judge's eyebrows assumed the shape of crescent moons. '*What?*'

'Oh, yes,' confidently replied Abe, warming to his theme. 'You see, My Lord, when I've given someone fifty quid, as I did on this occasion and then con them out of fifteen hundred quid, they'll realize how criminal they've been in attempting to buy a load of dodgy gear and they'll never do it again!'

The judge allowed himself a wintry smile at Abe's desperate, twisted logic, before telling him that the four year sentence stood.

Outside the court, Geoff Tanner bumped into Mrs Ruth Solokoff and her daughter, Lucy, who very courteously thanked him for the fair way in which he had spoken up for Abe. A couple of years went by and Tanner received a telephone call from Mrs Solokoff. It was to tell him that Abe had died suddenly in prison and she asked if he would care to attend the funeral. Tanner did so. It was a beautifully conducted service and the refreshments were served afterwards in an atmosphere of dignity and friendliness.

Ten years later and Geoff Tanner had achieved Abe's high expectations of him and was now a detective inspector on the Flying Squad. He had just finished obtaining an important statement in a robbery case and had gone in to a pub in one of the City of London's winding streets for a lunchtime pie and a pint when he heard his name called. Turning, he discovered it was Lucy, Abe and Ruth Solokoff's daughter. Tanner bought her a drink and enquired after her health and the health of her mother.

Lucy's face clouded over and she explained that her mother was dead. After Abe had died, Ruth, who had been married to Abe for many years and had endured the good times and the bad and was devoted to him, had gone into a decline.

One of her oddest eccentricities was to lock herself away

in her bedroom twice a year with a copy of the *Daily Telegraph*, a newspaper which she did not normally read. This would happen at the end of June and the beginning of the year and following each occasion, her depression would be far more profound.

Just before she died of a heart attack, Lucy discovered the reason for her twice-yearly obsession with that newspaper. Abe's conning ways had reached out to her from the grave. In her befuddled state, she now believed every word that Abe had said to the judge regarding his public service, and on the occasion of the Queen's Birthday and New Year's Honours, she would frantically search the lists of OBEs and MBEs, to see if Abe's services to the public had finally been recognized.

The Unkindest Cut of All

Some people who shine at various occupations are let down by their lack of social skills.

Gordon More, for example, was very good at what he did, which was breaking into commercial premises. At the time of this story, More was twenty-seven years of age, of average height and slimly built. The building did not exist that he could not climb. As agile as a monkey, More would scamper up the side of a building, calling on the aid of a drainpipe, if one existed, but utilizing any convenient handhold if one did not. He did not possess an impressive array of burglars' tools; if a window possessed a catch or some other means of opening it, More's skilful use of an old kitchen knife or perhaps a chisel would more than suffice for him to gain access. If the window was a fixed pane, it would usually only require the use of brown paper, liberally spread with jam, to be placed on the glass – the operation was known as 'dressing the front' – together with the accompaniment of a sharp tap. The window would shatter, with all of the sharp shards of glass adhering to the jam. Burglar alarms were his speciality; More seemed to possess a sixth sense as to whether or not an alarm existed and, if it did, how to neutralize it. So More was a serial, professional burglar and, as such, he made a reasonable living out of it. He had his outlets, so that the stolen property only remained in his possession for a limited period and he worked alone.

That being so, it would be reasonable to assume that he was never caught. That assumption would be wrong. The reason why he worked alone was because few other screwsmen would work with him. Despite his acknowledged expertize as a burglar, he was prone to make stupid, unforgivable and totally unprofessional mistakes such as the time when he barged into a pub, swaggered up to the bar and loudly informed the barmaid that he'd just had it off at a snouters and how'd she like to come out to a night club? A sudden silence descended over the bar, quite a number of the clientele began to express an almost impertinent interest in him and the barmaid mutely pointed to the sign which was displayed on the door, which stated in large block capitals:

STRICTLY PRIVATE PARTY
STOKE NEWINGON CID

Gordon More's social skills were not great. In consequence, a number of More's meticulously planned burglaries resulted in him spending a not inconsiderable time behind bars.

There was another reason for his larcenous solitude. A number of his peers had noticed that it would often take very little for his temper to spiral frighteningly out of control. Whilst they were quite prepared to take risks, they preferred not to do so in the company of someone whom they privately regarded as being as mad as a bag of bollocks. And because none of his would-be accomplices were trained psychiatrists, they could not possibly be aware that not too deeply hidden in More's personality was the growing desire for self-harm.

It had just turned midnight as Police Constables Bedson and Richie strolled up Holloway Road towards Archway. They should, of course, not have been walking together at all but they were on adjoining beats and it was a quiet night. If the section sergeant crept up on them, Bedson was ready with the excuse that Richie had called him over to his beat because he thought that he had seen a suspicious movement in an alleyway, they had investigated it and when he (the section sergeant) had arrived, Bedson had been just about to return to his own beat. It was the sort of excuse that had fooled not one section sergeant in the history of the Metropolitan Police but it was difficult to disprove. So the two young officers ambled along, discussing women and the current fortunes of Arsenal, when Gordon More walked out of Marlborough Road, and into the Holloway Road, ahead of them. He was carrying a large holdall, which was really necessary since it was full up with perfumes and men's toiletries from a chemist's shop which he had just broken into. The shop had been situated in Hornsey Road, which runs parallel to Holloway Road, and it had been More's intention to turn right, cross the Holloway Road and then enter Pemberton Gardens, turn into Junction Road and go home. However, to take that route would undoubtedly have excited the officers' suspicions and, therefore, More turned left, and strolled down towards the approaching constables.

'Hello,' said Bedson. 'Look at chummy. Where'd he come from?'

'Marlborough Road, I think,' replied Richie, adding doubtfully, 'or it might have been Davenant Road. What's that he's carrying?'

'Sports bag,' answered Bedson. 'Probably just come from the gym. Look, he's crossing over towards us.'

It is now impossible to try to determine the plan of action that More had formulated. Undeniably, it was with an incredible presence of mind that he had walked right up to the officers and, perhaps his initial thought was to try the biggest bluff of his career. Certainly, as the conversation commenced,

More was as cool as a cucumber. He gave a cheery grin and nodded. 'Evenin', gents.'

PC Bedson returned the smile. 'Evening. Been down the gym?'

More followed his gaze, down to the sports bag. 'What this? Oh, no. Why? Want to see what's in it?'

'Wouldn't mind,' said PC Richie. Everybody was completely relaxed.

More put the bag down on the pavement. 'Done meself a right bit of good,' he said. 'Managed to buy a job lot from a pharmacy that's gone out of business.' He pulled open the zip. 'Not bad, eh?'

'Not bad at all,' replied Bedson, admiringly, looking at the products by Old Spice and Elizabeth Arden, which were very popular at that time.

PC Richie thought that it was very odd that this bloke should be humping this little lot around with him at that time of night, so he asked, 'Got a receipt, have you?'

More straightened up. 'Sure,' he replied. 'Got it right here,' and he put his hand into the inside pocket of his jacket. 'Got it here, somewhere.' He frowned as he rummaged around and then he smiled. 'Ah! Here it is.'

And as PC Bedson stepped forward to examine the receipt, More pulled out an open razor with a serrated edge and hacked the officer's face wide open. It was so unexpected that both officers froze; then PC Richie darted forward and did the only thing he could think of; he grasped hold of both sides of the wound, from which blood was fountaining and pressed them together, to stop his colleague's face from falling apart. And with one swift movement, More lunged at him and cut open his calf; a wound designed to disable Richie and force him to release his grip on Bedson's face. Leaving the scene of carnage, plus the incriminating holdall behind him, More raced off towards the sanctuary of Junction Road.

Had it not have been for the passing taxi driver who, seeing the plight of the officers, bundled them, and the holdall, into his cab and set off to the Whittington Hospital, PC Bedson's name would certainly have been included in the Roll of Honour, situated just inside the reception area at New Scotland Yard. Even so, it was touch and go. As fast as blood transfusions were being pumped into PC Bedson, so it appeared that they were pouring out. Eventually, his condition stabilized and the long, slow road to recovery began.

Meanwhile, the night-duty CID – a detective sergeant (second class) and two aids to CID – had been informed. The bag containing the stolen property was searched. More had done it again. The bag was his. And in case it was ever mislaid, he had helpfully written his name and address inside.

More had been fast asleep at the kitchen table when the aids crashed through his front door. The noise brought him immediately awake. He looked round wildly for the razor which he needed to hide. As he reached out for it on the table, so the aids tore into the kitchen and believing, not unreasonably, that More was grabbing the razor to dish out a similar attack on them as he had upon their uniform colleagues, the closest of the aids punched him, with one ham-like fist, in the eye so forcefully that he knocked him right out of his chair. And *that* would be the very least of More's depredations.

Back at Holloway police station, Detective Sergeant (Second Class) Derek Goddard, the third member of the N Division CID, was waiting for the return of the aids with their prisoner. It was not through any lack of resolution that he had failed to accompany the aids – his bravery had been acknowledged on many previous occasions – it was because he had informed the detective chief superintendent of the division that there was a strong possibility that PC Bedson might die and so he stayed close to hand in case it became necessary for him to take a dying deposition from the officer. Now it appeared that Bedson was out of immediate danger.

Derek Goddard was highly respected and well liked, not only by his contemporaries but also by the public, both straight and criminal. He did not suffer fools gladly – in fact he did not suffer them at all – but he was very fair and straightforward. It was thought by his senior officers (with considerable justification) that he would go far in the Metropolitan Police. Several elderly ladies had written to his chief superintendent (and one to the commissioner) acknowledging his tact and kindness when he investigated their burglaries. The thieves and receivers whom he dealt with compassionately at court queued-up to give him information. He dealt with everyone with kindness and good humour. That is, almost everyone.

What was not generally known was that Derek Goddard was the son of an equally well-respected police officer who had been killed during the Blitz, while attempting to stop the car of a smash and grab team. Goddard had been brought up in the police orphanage and he had two abiding passions. One was to join the Metropolitan Police, of which he was extremely proud, at the earliest possible opportunity. The second was an overriding loathing of violent criminals. His philosophy was that if people wished to commit crime, then it was his job to catch them, if he could. But if they used violence during the commission of an offence, then the gloves were off. Even where a victim was threatened was enough for Goddard to use quite disproportionate violence when effecting an arrest. This had shocked a very few of his contemporaries – he never worked with *them* again – who voiced their concern and were promptly told to mind their own fucking business.

The aids to CID who carried out More's arrest were

fortunately made of sterner stuff. It was just as well. They were about to witness Goddard at his worst.

More was dragged into the charge room. The station officer was unusually absent. The only other person present, behind the charge room desk, was Sergeant Goddard. 'Found this, Sarge,' said the meaty aid, whose fist had caused an uncomfortable swelling to appear on More's face, and handed over the razor. Goddard nodded, curtly. 'I understand you cut one of my officers,' he said, mildly.

More simply looked at him. Once again, his communication skills had failed him. He made no reply.

Goddard looked at him dispassionately, as if he was a bag of garbage which has fallen from an overflowing dustbin. 'Bring him over here.'

The aids pulled More over to the charge room table and Goddard leant across the table towards him. 'I'm going to teach you a lesson you'll never forget,' said Goddard, softly, 'so that you'll never lay a finger on another police officer, ever again.' To the aids, he said, 'Put his hand on the desk.'

The aids placed More's hand, palm upwards on the charge room desk. Goddard opened the razor, pressed down with all his weight and all but severed the first joints of More's fore, middle and ring fingers. As the blood spurted, More shrieked and passed out. The meaty aid looked on in horror. His partner noisily retched. Neither of them had seen a fellow officer act in such a barbaric fashion and they never would again.

A few hours later, More appeared in the dock at Highbury Corner Magistrates' Court. In the witness box, Sergeant Goddard requested a remand in custody, in order that committal papers could be prepared on a charge of attempted murder. He had set out the circumstances of the burglary at the chemist's shop, followed by the completely unprovoked assault on the two officers. The Stipendiary Magistrate, Mr Bodenham, was suitably horrified at Goddard's harrowing description of the attack and ignored More's whimperings from the dock. Goddard stated that if More was released on bail, he feared he would abscond (having already done so) and that he felt that he would commit further offences (as he had in the past).

'What about this?' suddenly screamed More, holding up his bandaged hand, through which blood was seeping.

'I was about to add,' said Goddard, smoothly, 'that the defendant also has suicidal tendencies. After he was brought to the police station, he snatched the razor – the same one, Your Worship, which he used to such a devastating effect on PC Bedson – and attempted to slash his wrists. It was only with great difficulty that I managed to stop him, which regrettably resulted in some injuries to his fingertips.'

Mr Bodenham sniffed, disapprovingly. 'Superficial, I'm sure,' he remarked before remanding More in custody.

Several months later, an exquisitely stupid jury accepted More's improbable story that he had not wished to kill PC Bedson and instead he was found guilty of inflicting grievous bodily harm, with intent to resist arrest on both officers. For those offences, plus the burglary, he was sentenced to seven years' imprisonment.

All this occurred prior to ex-gratia payments being made available from the Criminal Injury Compensation Board and therefore PC Bedson's only memento of the whole, sorry business was a horrifically scarred face, which no amount of cosmetic surgery could improve.

The years went by, Derek Goddard climbed the ladder of success via the Flying Squad (where *nobody* questioned the way in which he effected arrests), More was released from prison, married, produced a son and went straight back to his larcenous ways.

Police Constable Barney Lomax was driving his Panda car along Vicarage Lane, West Ham at one o'clock in the morning, when, as he approached the junction of Ham Park Road, a Transit van suddenly shot out of that turning, causing him to brake sharply. The van tore down to the junction with Portway and made a shuddering left-hand turn. With PC Lomax in hot pursuit, the van flew across the junction with Upton Lane and in to Plashet Road. As PC Lomax endeavoured to both steer the Panda car and give a running commentary on his personal radio, the van slowed momentarily as it reached the junction with Green Street, before swerving right, then almost immediately left into Plashet Grove.

The Forest Gate area car, alerted by Lomax's radio commentary, thundered across the junction with Katherine Road and headed straight for the van on a collision course. The van driver's nerve gave out and, swerving to the nearside, he crashed the van into a lamppost and leapt out. With the area car in front of him and PC Lomax, who had abandoned his car and was running towards him, Gordon More had nowhere to go. He flung his arms in the air and shouted to PC Lomax, 'No violence! No violence!'

Lomax, who had been a promising lightweight contender for the Lafone Cup but nevertheless had no intention of bashing More, misread his frenzied statement. He had thought that More was begging him not to ill-treat him. In fact, in his inarticulate way, it was More who was endeavouring to inform him that he had no desire to attack PC Lomax.

More was handed over to the CID at Forest Gate police station who, not knowing anything of More's antecedents at that time, were slightly surprised at the alacrity with which he stuck his hands up to stealing the van and packing the back with the dresses which had been the proceeds of him breaking into a clothing factory. Because the total of the stolen property amounted to several thousand pounds, Newham (West) Magistrates' Court decided that it did not have the jurisdiction to deal with him and committed him in custody, to await trial at the Crown Court.

And this is where I make an entrance into the whole sorry saga of Gordon More's life. I had never met him, knew nothing about him, nor did I hear the whole story until many years later.

I received a phone call from the Department of Social Security, who occupied a very tall building in the Romford Road. I was informed that a woman was detained there, having made a spurious application for benefits. I drove along to the building, went up to the top floor in the lift where I met the investigator, and the woman in question who was accompanied by a boy of about four. I arrested the woman and took her and the child to the police station. The boy was in the back of the car and was climbing about all over the place. 'Keep your kid still, will you?' I said, irritably.

'He's always into mischief,' she replied carelessly, as though that was a sufficient way of instilling a little discipline into him. 'Climbs everywhere.'

He continued climbing into and on to everything in the CID office, so much so that I got a motherly-looking WPC to keep an eye on him whilst I took the mother's statement. She admitted the offence and added that she had committed the fraud because her husband was on remand in prison. I asked his name and she told me – Gordon More. It meant nothing to me. I charged and then bailed her and was glad to see the last of that squirming, agile little brute.

That afternoon, I received another call; again it was from the Department of Social Security and, in fact, it was from the same investigator with whom I had had brief dealings that morning. 'Mr Kirby, I can't believe it; that wretched woman that you arrested this morning? She's back, with that rotten kid of hers and she's trying it on all over again. Bloody cheek! I can tell you—' All of a sudden there was a lot of noise in the background – confused shouting, some screaming.

'What's going on?' I demanded.

'I don't know – something's happened . . .' There was some more confused shouting, before she screamed, 'WHAT! Jesus Christ, the kid's gone out the bloody window!'

The Mores' child had got into mischief once too often. Climbing out on to a window sill, he'd overbalanced and plunged one hundred and thirty feet, straight into the Romford Road, killing himself instantly.

Prison Liaison at the Yard very kindly gave me the job of arranging security at the church where the child was buried and where a weeping Gordon More attended, securely handcuffed to a prison officer. It was a beautiful and moving service and the words of the vicar moved me to tears.

It proved a bit too much for Gordon More as well. Before he could come to trial, he was found dead in his cell. Once again, and for the last time, More's communicative skills had let him down. He expressed himself in the only way he knew how; a bloodied razor blade was found in his mutilated fingers.

Full of Holes

Former Detective Chief Inspector Tom Halsey is an urbane sort of fellow; nothing ever fazed him as a serving police officer and the years of retirement have not clouded his smooth disposition. So when he opens this book and reads the names Gordon Lowe, Keith Sumner and Henry Selby, his eyes may momentarily narrow, because villains so seldom escaped Tom Halsey's net, but that's all the emotion he will register. And when he discovers for the first time that the Post Office Tower at Euston was Messrs Lowe, Sumner & Selby's target for an armed raid, all those years ago, he will not act in the way that some ridiculously inadequate police officers behave. After looking profoundly gobsmacked at a piece of sensational news, about which they had not the slightest inkling, they smirk, tap the side of their noses with their index finger and remark, 'Yes, I heard a whisper about that,' a statement which is complete bollocks.

No, Tom Halsey was so successful he doesn't need to behave in such a silly, blustering fashion. He will put down the book, look me in the eye and say, 'Ah.' After a couple of seconds, he will probably mutter, 'Bugger!' And then, his equanimity completely restored, he'll say, 'Another drink, old boy?'

The Post Officer Tower – it is now officially known as BT Telecom Tower – was officially opened in 1965 and, measuring six hundred and twenty feet from top to bottom, it was, at the time, the tallest building in London. The public were delighted to discover that the restaurant on the thirty-fourth floor rotated a complete three hundred and sixty degrees every twenty-two minutes but the reason for the construction of the tower was rather more practical; it was built to cater for the rising telecommunication requirements and to transmit high-frequency radio waves.

The Tower is situated at 60 Cleveland Street, London, W1. Just to the north is the A501 – Euston Road to the east, Marylebone Road to the west – and more or less straight ahead is Albany Street. In short, plenty of escape routes.

Messrs Lowe & Co were career armed robbers who had individually and collectively carried out successful raids with some of the characters who became known as the Wembley Bank Robbery Gang. Fortunately, they had parted company with them, prior to the arrival of Derek Creighton Smalls. In getting the best deal afforded to any Supergrass, 'Bertie' Smalls walked free after grassing everyone he could think of in respect of twenty-one raids, which netted a total of £1,288,051 and 308 years' imprisonment for those concerned.

'There's a load of dough being delivered by Securicor,' Lowe told his associates, 'and we've got to move fast. As soon as the van pulls up and the moneybags come out, we've got to hit the guards there and then – no pissing about.'

'Why can't we have someone inside the lobby, to hit them both ways?' asked Keith Sumner. 'That way, the guards won't know if they're coming or going.'

'Because there isn't a lobby,' replied Lowe. 'You can only get in by using one of two hi-powered lifts that move like shit off a shovel.' Lowe's information was correct; the lifts travelled at twenty feet per second, taking just thirty seconds to reach the top storey.

Henry Selby nodded. 'See what you mean. We're just going to have the one shot at it.'

'Speaking of which,' added Lowe, 'we'll all have shooters and we're not going to take any shit from the guards – right?'

The other two nodded. Since the abolition of the death penalty, more and more blaggers were carrying firearms, something they seldom did before.

With the plan evolved, it still required weeks of further research and planning. The timing of the wages van was logged, and the getaway route carefully planned. All would have doubtless gone completely to plan, had it not have been for Keith Sumner's sexual urges.

Sumner had a very strong sex drive, which was usually more than adequately catered for by his equally strongly-sexed wife, Phyllis. Except that the night before the raid, Phyllis had unexpectedly been called away to look after her ailing mother who lived in Kent and would not be returning until the following day. This was more than the horny Sumner could contend with; before a raid, as he heatedly reminded his wife, he had to have a shag, to release the built-up tension. However, as Phyllis pointed out, frustration was one thing and a sick mum another.

Left to his own devices, Sumner made his way up to Soho and paid a visit to a brothel he had used before, situated in Great Peter Street and run by one Fat Tony Micallef, a left-over from the infamous Messina Gang of the forties and fifties and also a fully paid up member of the Maltese Syndicate. Happily humping away in the sack with Françoise de Montgelard – a name her customers found rather more exotic than her baptismal one of Gladys Hopkins – Sumner made a classic mistake after Mlle de Montgelard complimented him on his tremendous performance and expressed her enormous gratification; he boasted. True, he had taken a drink or two before his tremendous sexual assault, but that was no excuse. Although he did not give away every dot and comma of the intended raid, he said quite enough to put him and his associates on a collision course with Scotland Yard.

After Sumner had left, the girl excitedly informed Fat Tony of what she had learnt. He did not exactly advertise the fact that he was a vociferous snitch to the Flying Squad but Mlle de Montgelard knew that she would be a fiver the richer for imparting the information to him. Fat Tony had seen the punter enter the premises and he questioned the girl closely, extracting every available morsel of information from her until he was satisfied and then he patted her cheek and pushed a soiled five pound note into her cleavage before reminding her that other customers were waiting and to stop slacking. His capital outlay of £5 would be fully justified after he collected rather more from the Yard's Informants Fund, courtesy of his friend Chief Inspector Halsey.

The following morning, Fat Tony overslept, so it was not until almost twelve noon that he telephoned the Snouts' Line of the Flying Squad and breathlessly asked to be connected to Tom Halsey.

'Mister Tom? You know who this is. Listen. There goin' to be a robbery today. No, I don't know where. No, I don't know who, either. But listen. Three bad bastards are going to do the job. They all got shooters, yeah, they say if the guards fuck 'em about, they goin' to fill them full of holes. What I do know is that the three of them is goin' to meet up in the Cambridge Arms before they do the raid. Round about one. I see one of them last night. What I do, I meet you in the pub. When I see the geezer, I show out to you, we go in the bog, I mark your cards, I make myself scarce, yes?'

Halsey thoughtfully put the telephone down. He glanced at his watch. Christ, just an hour to go; he'd better get things moving, fast. 'Dave James!' he shouted down the corridor.

Detective Sergeant James usually worked with Halsey and now he came trotting into his office.

'There's a three-handed blag going off today. Don't know where, but the team are meeting up in the Cambridge Arms in about an hour from now. Get a surveillance team together, as many as you can, quick, and get the lads shootered-up. We'll bottle 'em off and nick 'em on a ready-eye.'

James scratched his curly head. 'Guv'nor, I don't know as I can. Just about everybody's at the Derby, today.'

Halsey cursed; having no interest in the sport of kings, he had completely forgotten about the race meeting. 'And then most of the rest of the blokes are either on leave or at the Bailey on the Streatham wages snatch job,' continued James. 'All in all, Guv, I don't reckon we can scrape together more than half a dozen of us.'

Halsey sat down at his desk. 'Right, get hold of everybody you can. Phone the police room at the Bailey; tell the blokes that if they're not wanted to make their way back here, pronto. Phone the drivers' room; tell them all to stand by and not to go out – tell them to get a bite to eat now.'

As James bustled off down the corridor towards the communications room, Halsey was thinking furiously. Even if he did contact the troops at the Derby, they could never get back in time. And with just half a dozen troops, how the hell could they carry out surveillance on three wicked, armed bastards, who, after they left the pub, would have eyes in their arses? Try tailing them off and, if they tumbled that they were being followed, there could be a shoot-out in the packed, lunchtime London streets. He had no idea how they were going to travel to the robbery plot, individually on public transport perhaps or together in a car. How could they plot up the venue of the robbery when he didn't know where it was? No. It was looking more and more as though they would have to be taken in the pub, while they were relaxed and hope to Christ that they had the shooters on them, instead of them being in the boot of some unknown car, parked in an unknown street. It was not, considered Halsey with masterly understatement, the most desirable of circumstances.

Just after one o'clock, Halsey entered the Cambridge Arms from one door and Dave James from another. The bar was utterly jam-packed and Halsey who, of necessity, spent much of his working hours collecting information inside licensed premises could not remember a time when he had seen a bar so full. But he did see Fat Tony at the other end of the bar, who nodded agitatedly at him and headed for the Gents. Seconds later, Halsey joined him; mercifully, for such a full bar, they were alone. 'At a table, just to the left of you, Mr Tom,' gasped the snitch. 'The geezer I see last night, he got a brown jacket on, the other two, blue suit and a grey one. Three right bastards. Can't miss 'em. Been in here about ten minutes.'

'Right-oh, Tony,' replied Halsey quietly and pushed two £10 notes into his breast pocket. 'We'll speak later.'

As Halsey left the lavatory, he spotted the three men at the table. They were drinking, chatting and they appeared completely at ease. Halsey pushed his way through the throng to where Dave James was standing. 'Dave, get the troops in,' he murmured. 'Two in from each door. We'll take them at the table. Right?'

James nodded and made his way to the exit. As he did so, Halsey edged closer to the three men at the table. From the corner of his eye, he could see the Squad men making their way across the bar. And then they were there, they encircled the table and Halsey quietly told the three men they were under arrest.

Lowe, Sumner and Selby were utterly shocked. As they got

to their feet, they were searched and Halsey breathed a sigh of relief when he discovered that they were all in possession of loaded pistols. The three men were so stunned they did not attempt to struggle. They were relieved of their armoury, handcuffed and escorted outside. It was a very slick arrest. In fact, it was so smoothly effected that, despite the fullness of the bar, not one other person had noticed what had happened. It was, as Halsey later commented, over a congratulatory drink, almost supernatural.

Of course, the three robbers were consummate professionals and said not one word to incriminate themselves. There was nothing in their possession or in their homes, when they were later turned over, to suggest the whereabouts of the venue of the robbery. Lowe and Sumner both had car ignition keys in their possession but these were found to fit their own cars which were at their home addresses, which saved the Squad officers (and their uniform counterparts) from trying to fit the keys in the locks of all the vehicles parked in the streets and the cars parks around the vicinity of the Cambridge Arms. Because two of the Squad officers were sure they had overheard a conversation in the cell passageway at Cannon Row police station to the effect that 'the guards were lucky they weren't shot full of holes', the three were charged with conspiracy to rob a person or persons unknown, which was a bit thin. Much stronger, of course, was the charge of possessing firearms with intent to commit an indictable offence.

The trio's solicitors, who had been promised 'a right good drink' for a decent result, got to work with a will. At the Old Bailey, the prosecution's case was howled down by the predictable type of left-wing barrister who appeared for the three blaggers. His closing speech to the jury was a tour de force.

'Members of the jury, you have heard these Flying Squad officers giving evidence which is frankly incredible. You are asked to believe that three armed men were arrested in a crowded public house, during a busy lunch hour, that they were disarmed, handcuffed and led out through the crowd in the bar – and no one noticed? The whole episode strains credibility and flies in the face of the common sense which, members of the jury you all possess in full measure. "Lucky the guards weren't shot full of holes" as two of the defendants were alleged to have uttered? Members of the jury, you may agree with me that the only thing shot full of holes is the prosecution's case, a case, mark you which is as full of holes as any housewife's colander. I ask you, can any credence whatever be placed on this story or any of the officers' evidence? If not, and I am sure you agree with me, my clients are entitled to your verdict that they are not guilty.'

And that was the verdict reached by the jury. 'Let them be discharged,' muttered the judge, who was furious at the verdict and was looking forward to handing out twelves and thirteens. Grinning and winking, the trio swaggered out of court and that was that.

Although, not quite. About a year later, Tom Halsey was strolling along Regent Street when who should he bump into but Gordon Lowe.

'Hello, Mr Halsey!' exclaimed Lowe. 'Remember me? No hard feelings I hope – come and have a drink.'

And Halsey, fully aware of the threat made in respect of the unknown guards at an unknown venue and also unsure of what might be concealed under Gordon Lowe's natty suiting, demonstrated what was consistently said about him by his aide, Dave James, which was that he was 'as smooth as a cucumber's cod-piece'.

'No thank you, Mr Lowe,' he replied, courteously. 'I want no more holes in me than God intended.'

'Over the Wall We Go . . .'

Few offences in the criminal calendar excite the attention of a section of the public so much as when someone escapes from prison. Why? Probably because they see the villains thumbing their nose at authority, something they'd quite like to do. The interest accelerates when the person who's 'gone over the wall' is someone associated with a famous crime or someone who is a household name.

When Charlie Wilson escaped from Winson Green Prison on 12 August 1964, just four months after having been sentenced to a total of thirty years' imprisonment for his part in the Great Train Robbery, he was held in great esteem by quite a number of the population, especially since a lot of people felt the sentence was one which was manifestly excessive. It was a spectacular escape by any stretch of the imagination.

A three-man team scaled the twenty-foot wall of the maximum security prison at three o'clock in the morning, knocked the night security officer unconscious, bound him and used his key to unlock Wilson's cell door on the second landing. With Wilson out of his cell, re-locking the doors as they went, the four men climbed a rope ladder over the perimeter wall and clambered inside the hinged flap of a petrol tanker. In less than an hour, Wilson was on board a small plane at a deserted airfield and en route to France. It was the beginning of three and a half years of freedom for

Wilson which was brought to an end after Detective Chief Superintendent Tommy Butler, the head of the Flying Squad and the officer in charge of the Great Train Robbery investigation, arranged a cunningly staged 'car accident' at Mountain View, Rigaud, Quebec Province, Canada. A very surprised Ronald Alloway, alias Charlie Wilson, was once again, back in the boob.

Just eleven months after Wilson's unofficial parole, it was the turn of his associate in the Great Train Robbery, one Ronald Arthur Biggs. A red pantechnicon with the roof cut away and a scaffolding tower inside was parked outside the perimeter wall of Wandsworth Prison. A rope ladder was thrown over the wall, one of the escape team brandished a shotgun and Biggs and a fellow prisoner, Eric Flower, scaled the ladder and escaped in two stolen cars which were waiting nearby. Biggs was on the run for over thirty-five years in Australia and South America and it is likely that it would have been longer, had ill-health not forced him to return voluntarily to England, old, sick and worn-out. He was immediately incarcerated in Belmarsh, Britain's top-security prison.

One of the most prolific escapers was Walter 'Angel Face' Probyn. Apart from escaping, Probyn also had a love of firearms and a hatred of police officers. Probyn escaped from custody on almost twenty occasions and fourteen of these were from Approved School, between the ages of nine and fourteen. After he had pleaded guilty to stabbing a police officer with a knife, the judge at the Old Bailey declared that he was too young to be sent to Borstal, and sentenced him to be detained for four years; on a previous occasion before the courts, Probyn had been convicted of attacking a police officer with the jagged edge of a sardine can, before attempting to hit him with an axe.

Years of long custodial sentences for serious offences

followed, interspersed with escapes until 24 August 1964. Probyn, who was serving a five year sentence for shopbreaking and larceny, escaped from a working party from Dartmoor Prison. Six weeks later, the police had received a tip-off that Probyn and his wife, Beryl, would be in Burdett Road, Bow and an ambush was set up. After they arrived and got out of a hire car, with the sixth sense given to all persistent criminals, Probyn realized that something was wrong and he and his wife tried to make an escape across a flat roof, hotly pursued by the police. Probyn pulled out a .22 Star target pistol and fired the first of nine shots at his pursuers. That nobody was killed was nothing short of a miracle. It was clear from the direction of travel that the Probyns were making for their hire car and even after being hit with a broom and being brought down by a rugby tackle, Probyn struggled to his feet and kept going, firing as he went. By now, police cars had hemmed in the hire car; Beryl, who had been exhorting her husband to shoot their pursuers, had been arrested but Probyn had still managed to get into the car. One of the officers smashed the windscreen with a broom; Probyn dived right through the broken glass and landed on the pavement on all fours. He pistol-whipped one officer, then two other police officers tackled him but still he fought his way loose, fired another shot and ran off. He was chased and overpowered in the back garden of a nearby house; sadly, he suffered the loss of two teeth, a broken arm and several broken ribs during the course of his arrest.

The Probyns pleaded not guilty to a whole range of offences but they were convicted and Wally Probyn was sentenced to twelve years' imprisonment, to commence at the conclusion of the five-year sentence which he had interrupted. Beryl Probyn was sentenced to five years' imprisonment for aiding and abetting her husband. During the whole episode she had displayed considerable determination, not to mention strength.

When she was arrested, her handbag was discovered to contain one hundred and seventy-four rounds of ammunition.

The term 'escaper' cannot be used without mentioning Alfie Hinds. Born in 1917, in Newington Butts, Alfred George Hinds came from a family of thieves; his mother was a shoplifter, his father was sentenced to seven years for a bank robbery; a punishment which was accompanied by a 'bashing' – ten strokes of the cat o' nine tails.

Alfie Hinds had eight previous convictions, some of which were for safeblowing. He also had made a number of escapes, including one when he was serving in the Royal Tank Corps. He deserted in 1941 and remained on the run until the end of the war; recaptured, he escaped again. But, by 1953, it appeared that he was living a blameless life, working with his brother in a building and demolition business. In September of that year, the safe at Maples Department Store, Tottenham Court Road, was blown and cash and jewellery valued at £38,000 was stolen.

Detective Superintendent Bert 'Iron Man' Sparks – a very tough character indeed – was in charge of the investigation and a number of arrests were made, including one man who arrived at Hinds' house and was in possession of four watches, stolen from Maples. Hinds was arrested too. He had insisted on following Sparks around his house, telling him, rather tactlessly that he wanted to ensure that Sparks would not plant anything. 'What?' retorted Sparks. 'Do you think I'm a fucking benevolent society?'

At any event, Hinds was charged. The prosecution evidence consisted of Hinds being in possession of traces of fuse and debris from the safe and one of the co-accused gave evidence against him. He was sentenced to twelve years' preventative detention.

Hinds was adamant that he was innocent of the charge. He tried all the legal avenues to get his case overturned without success and in November 1955 escaped from Nottingham Prison. He was on the run for two hundred and forty-five days before being caught in Dublin. He tried to take legal action, on the grounds that his re-arrest had been unlawful, without success and in June 1957 he escaped again, this time from the Law Courts, in order to have his case heard in Dublin, which he thought would be more sympathetic than an English Court. He was arrested as he attempted to board a plane at Bristol Airport.

In June 1958, Hinds escaped again, this time from Chelmsford Prison and he eventually got to Ireland. But he didn't pursue his case through the Irish courts; instead he smuggled cars across the border, saying later that he 'didn't regard smuggling as a crime'. After twenty months of freedom, he was caught, attempted to escape from the customs office, was remanded to Crumlin Road Prison and offered five hundred pounds to a fellow prisoner to help him escape. Sentenced to a total of twelve months' imprisonment for smuggling, Hinds unsuccessfully tried every trick in the legal book to prevent being returned to the mainland. He issued writs and attempted to sue anybody who tried to stop him; and in this, he was finally successful.

When Bert Sparks retired from the Police Force, he had his memoirs serialized in the *Sunday Pictorial*. In it, Sparks named Hinds as being the brains behind the Maples safeblowing and Hinds sued for libel and won £1,300 in damages and costs. Even so, the Court of Appeal still rejected his claim that he was innocent.

Hinds was eventually released. He wrote an account of his sufferings, aptly entitled *Contempt of Court*, lectured at polytechnics, at the National Council for Civil Liberties and appeared on television. Later he went to live in Jersey where, with an IQ of 150, he became secretary of the Channel Islands MENSA society and it was there that he died, aged seventy-three.

He never stopped insisting that Sparks had fitted him up for the Maples safeblowing, however, there is very little doubt that Hinds was indeed guilty as charged.

It would be quite wrong if I failed to include Zoe Progl, the first woman to escape from Holloway Prison. She was born Zoe Tyldesley in 1928 and grew up in Limehouse. The daughter of an alcoholic, violent father, it was not long before she immersed herself in the world of crime. She married a US serviceman when she was eighteen and stole cars, broke into factories, flats, Post Offices and houses. She was part of a shoplifting team, used a variety of disguises whilst passing stolen cheques, rolled drunks, stole jewellery, and was part of a lorry theft gang. At the age of twenty-two, Progl had two children, and the father of one of them was that ill-fated gangster Tommy Smithson. Progl had six illegal abortions carried out; she also was involved in drug taking, lesbianism and prostitution. Her custodial sentences were relatively light and did not reflect the successes she had achieved as a criminal; three years' Borstal Detention for forging savings books (she was lucky not to also be convicted of harbouring an escaped prisoner), then fifteen months' imprisonment for breaking into a chemist's and receiving a stolen safe.

When a friend was sentenced to seven years' imprisonment for a robbery which he stated he had never committed, Progl helped arrange his escape. It would stand her in good stead for her own escape.

She was sentenced to a total of two and a half years' imprisonment for larceny and housebreaking and on 24 July 1960, with some outside assistance, she went over the wall at Holloway Prison by means of a rope ladder. She had forty days of freedom before the Flying Squad tracked her down and she had another eighteen months' imprisonment added on to her sentence.

And yet, six months after her release, she remarried and vanished from public view and the world of crime . . . It is hard to imagine a woman as hardened to a lifetime of crime as Zoe Progl going straight after twenty years of crime. But, of course, you have not yet been introduced to the Bobbed-haired bandit.

She was born Lillian Rose Kendall in 1903. When she married, she became Lillian Goldstein, but to the public she was known as the Bobbed-haired Bandit. At a time when few women possessed a driving licence, Goldstein was a brilliant and daring driver of fast cars. When she met up with Charles J. 'Ruby' Sparks, it seemed like a marriage made in heaven.

Sparks had been born in Tiger Yard, Bermondsey in 1894. His mother was a receiver of stolen property, his father was a bare-knuckle fighter and his Uncle Frank a burglar. Unsurprisingly, Sparks took to thieving like a duck to water and, before long, he was making a lucrative living from stealing registered letters from trains after his accomplices loaded him on board, concealed in a hamper as part of the luggage. After his associates were caught, Sparks turned to breaking and entering and acquired his nickname after breaking into a house in Park Lane, the London address of an Indian maharajah. He discovered a packet of large red stones but, believing them to be worthless, he gave them away to friends. The following day, the friends were doubtless delighted and Sparks mortified after the red, worthless stones turned out to be forty thousand pounds' worth of uncut rubies – hence his nickname.

Turning to smash and grab, he teamed up with Goldstein and they enjoyed a lot of success, with Sparks smashing jewellers' shop windows and the daring Goldstein driving the getaway car with considerable skill and élan. After five successful years, Goldstein was just twenty-four when she and Sparks were caught, following a country house burglary; she was acquitted and Sparks was sentenced to three years' penal servitude.

Imprisoned at Strangeways, he sawed through his cell bars and went over the wall but was caught within a couple of days. Sparks had not long been released from his sentence before he was arrested again and this time he was sentenced to five years' penal servitude, to be followed by another five years' preventative detention. Following an active role in the Dartmoor mutiny, he was sentenced to an additional four years' imprisonment and although he was able to successfully argue, that given the additional sentence, the preventative detention sentence was unlawful, not long after his release he was again arrested for burglary. At Kingston Assizes on 10 February 1939, he was sentenced to five years' penal servitude.

Just eleven months to the day after being sentenced, Sparks, using duplicate keys, escaped from Dartmoor with two associates. He was on the run for five months and sixteen days, a record at the time. His days were not spent in idleness; he teamed up with Billy Hill and carried out a series of smash and grabs, which only came to a halt after Hill was caught in April 1940. Sparks' nights were spent with Goldstein at her Wembley Park home but the police, too, had not been idle and when it was discovered that Sparks was going to the Ritz cinema, Neasden, a large-scale surveillance operation was carried out.

The street suddenly erupted with police officers and Sparks, a rubber-faced master of disguise, wearing dark glasses and sporting an impressive sun-tan, was grabbed, refused to admit his identity and attempted to bluff his way out of this undeniably tricky situation. The accounts of his arrest are as confusing as they are diverse.

Peter Beveridge, the head of the Flying Squad, played a safe hand and said that when Sparks was arrested, he grinned and accepted the situation philosophically.

Sparks, on the other hand, stated that he had almost managed to fool just about everybody and he had nearly got a passing constable to arrest the Flying Squad personnel for being a gang of kidnappers. During the entire arrest, detention and trial, Sparks insisted he kept up a non-relenting stream of saucy, cheerful, cheeky remarks to police and judge alike.

Detective Sergeant Bob Higgins told of a long surveillance operation on Goldstein and after he grabbed Sparks (although versions here differ; other accounts say it was Detective Sergeants Duncan Crerar or Matthew Brinnand who nabbed him) he took him over to Detective Inspector Ted Greeno, who positively identified him.

Greeno, on the other hand, stated that when Higgins brought Sparks, who had an identity card in the name of Johnson, over to him, he still refused to admit he was Sparks and it was not until he was taken to Willesden Green police station that Sparks, doubtless with a rueful grin, said, 'Well, Guv'nor, you can't blame me, can you? I was nearly away with it but when you came along, I knew it was all up.'

In fact, it was almost certainly Matthew Brinnand, who had been in court when Sparks had been sentenced, who positively identified him. The waters became even more muddied when, fifty years after the event, Bob Higgins recalled that when he was arrested, Sparks cried, 'No violence, Guv'nor! I've had the cat once – I don't want it again!'

Ah, well. The law does not concern itself with trifles.

At the Old Bailey, a thoroughly humane Recorder of London, Sir Gerald Dodson, sentenced Sparks to twelve months' hard labour, to run concurrently with his existing sentence. For harbouring him, Goldstein was sentenced to six months' hard labour, but she served little of it. Calling her back to court, the Recorder varied the sentence to one of being bound over in her own recognizance to be of good behaviour for a period of three years – 'A leniency she does not deserve,' sourly commented Detective Superintendent Bell of the Yard.

After his release, Sparks foreswore a life of crime (apart from being arrested for a little black marketeering) met a nice girl, had a nice family and settled down. He died in 1972.

Goldstein, too, drifted into obscurity and respectability, and died within a few years of her former lover with whom she had enjoyed exciting times. But their relationship had started to pall, even at the time of his Dartmoor escape. No more was she 'a girl bandit, with dark bobbed hair, a small innocent-looking face' as the newspapers had once described her. Her hair was now grey, her face lined and when she looked at Sparks, she had a way of screwing up her eyes which prompted him to ask if she had started wearing spectacles.

'Yes, sometimes,' she replied, uncomfortably, 'but only for reading.'

Trade-off

It appears to be stating the bleeding, blinding obvious when I say that informants are people who inform police about criminals. However, not everything is as clear-cut as might originally be thought.

First, there is the person who might just be a nosy neighbour who mentions to the beat bobby that the chap next door is always blocking the pavement outside his house with different cars; investigation reveals that they're all stolen.

Then there's the person with a keen civic responsibility who sees the horrible little yob of the son of the family who lives opposite furtively exchanging packages for money with other low-lifes of the area; an observation nets an up-and-coming drugs dealer.

The best known informant is one who moves in criminal circles, hears snippets of information and informs the police about those who have committed a crime or who are about to commit one.

Two aids to criminal detection which brought the Flying Squad into disrepute were 'participating informants' and 'mugs'. The former consisted of an informant not only telling police about an offence which was going to occur but also participating in it. Usually, the offence would be a robbery and the blaggers would normally be arrested following an ambush whilst the informant would escape. This was not without peril to the inside man; usually the dimmest of blaggers would realize that something was amiss when one of their number escaped, despite the fact that the number of police officers present would have been sufficient to subdue the most hostile Notting Hill Carnival riot. The usage of 'mugs' was where a lorry-load of goods had been stolen and the investigating police officers reached an agreement with the thieves whereby the lorry, together with a quarter of its load, would be left at an agreed location and where, at a certain time, someone would arrive to drive the lorry away. It was clear to everybody concerned that the intellectual capabilities of this 'someone' – the 'mug' referred to –precluded him from involvement in such a serious offence. But he would nevertheless be arrested, the crime would be cleared-up, the mug would probably cop a couple of years and a financial settlement between the thieves and the investigating officers would be reached.

This dubious practice was knocked right on the head when, in June 1961, Ernie Millen CBE became head of the Flying Squad. 'It is the 1960s,' growled Millen, 'and this has got to stop!'

And then there were 'trade-offs' which came in different guises. Really, a trade-off was for one person to inform on another because that person was causing disruption in their lives. Therefore, a battered wife might inform that her brutal partner was about to participate in an armed robbery, to free her of the toils of being a human punch-bag. A drugs dealer would inform on a rival, so that he could corner the drugs market in his area. Yes, 'trade-offs' came in all different forms where just about everyone benefited, except of course for the victim; but then again, it was usually the consensus of opinion that the person concerned was a thorough-going shit who deserved everything he got. And this was certainly the case in respect of Chrissie Daniels.

*   *   *

Sid Goldblum lived the life of a respectable citizen. Every morning, he would drive his gleaming blue Triumph 2000 down the driveway of his prestigious house in Gidea Park before turning to wave goodbye to his beloved daughter, Rose. Cutting through Romford, then Dagenham, Goldblum would reach the A13 and drive to Canning Town, and thence to his stall in Rathbone Street market. There he sold dresses, which provided a good income. Goldblum was well-liked in the market and was tolerated by his snooty neighbours who thought him a nice enough little fellow – for a Jew, of course – but there was a side to him that was not completely obvious to the casual onlooker. To start with, many years before, he had been an up and coming welterweight boxer in the East End where, fighting under the name of Sid Gold, he had been talented enough to force a draw during a bout with the Whitechapel Whirlwind, Jack 'Kid' Berg. But he had fallen into bad company and, after a few court appearances, he had delved into the big-time and following a lorry hijacking where the driver had been badly injured, Goldblum had been stuck up by a Ghost Squad nark and had been sentenced to six years' imprisonment. The vast majority of his jail time had been spent in Dartmoor and Goldblum had loathed every second of it. Upon his release he might well have drifted back into his old ways but he was rescued by his younger brother, Alfie, who had just started up a sweat-shop in Brick Lane where he manufactured dresses. His sibling managed to acquire the licence for a stall in the Rathbone Street market. Sid Goldblum had married Esther just prior to his sentence and Rose, their only child, had been born whilst he was inside and he was determined never to return to prison. It is true, he had since dabbled in the re-distribution of some stolen property and had received a visit or two from the police, but he had not been charged or even arrested. Esther, with a piercing glance, assured him that things had better stay that way. But then Esther had been taken from him by cancer and it was just him and Rose. She was a girl who was not overburdened with brains but she was pretty and loyal and Goldblum fervently hoped that one day soon she would meet a nice Jewish boy, a solicitor or perhaps an accountant, whom she would marry and provide him with lots of grandchildren on whom he would dote.

That is, until Chrissie Daniels came along.

To many people, it was a mystery as to why Chrissie Daniels was attractive to women. At just under six feet, he was tall enough and was sturdily built, and he possessed regular features, but his long hair was always unkempt and dirty, he was not noted for his personal hygiene and his slightly protruding teeth were yellowing. But he certainly had a good line in chat and it was not always used to charm young women. Daniels was a thief, although not a brilliant one, and not many good thieves would work with him; they considered him too flash and too unreliable. But although Daniels was arrested time and time again, he was seldom convicted. For one thing, he always lodged a complaint of police misconduct; later, he would get associates to also complain about the officer and, on several occasions, he got women to make accusations that the arresting officer had sexually molested them. Then, when the case got to court, Daniels always defended himself, rather than call upon the services of a solicitor. In doing so, he received far more leeway than most prisoners in the dock. He would vilify the officers in court, demanding to know if they were currently under investigation for rape and, even though the accusation was utterly spurious, the officer had to agree that such an investigation had commenced.

His closing address to either a gullible Magistrates' Bench or an equally susceptible jury would be along these lines:

'Look, I know the police 'ave got their job to do and this is a serious crime they've got on their books, so it's got to be cleared up, ain't it? They've got to 'ave someone for it, ain't they? But why's it got to be me? All I can tell yer is, it weren't me, but you've got to make up yer own minds on who's telling the truth, ain't yer? Me, or some crooked copper who goes round raping women. Up to you.'

Inevitably, the case would be thrown out. And, just as inevitably, the CID at Plaistow police station loathed Daniels and dreamed of ways in which to bring about his downfall. They were not helped by the detective inspector who was collectively regarded by the entire CID office as being 'as weak as piss'. Daniels had made so many damaging allegations against so many of his staff, he was terrified that this would adversely affect his future advancement and he therefore decreed that Daniels would henceforth be left strictly alone. And as the CID office, as well as the aids to CID, sat and quietly fumed, so Chrissie Daniels took Rose Goldblum out on their first date.

Sid Goldblum was furious when he discovered his daughter's liaison with Daniels. He was aware of his highly dubious reputation with women and the very thought of Daniels sullying his beloved daughter filled him with disgust. But what could he do? It was a highly charged scenario. What he wanted to do was to smash Daniels' face in, but even if he could achieve this highly desirable state of affairs what would it achieve? He was aware of Daniels' manipulative ability and this would only attract Rose to him even more, as a victim. Buy him off? An offensive thought, paying out money to a slag like Daniels and was this a viable proposition? He would probably accept and then come back for more. Worse, he could propose marriage and Rose might accept; oh, fearful thought! The very thought of them married, with Rose churning out Daniels look-alike little slags, whilst Daniels went looking for gratification elsewhere. What would be the alternative? To have him fitted up? Easy enough to do but silly Rose would regard him as a martyr, someone to be slavishly visited at HM Prison Wandsworth, someone who was a victim of police corruption, someone to be worshiped even more. So what else? To top him? But who could he rely upon to do it? Himself? At his age? Somebody else? Someone he would have to pay to carry out the dirty deed and therefore someone who could betray him at a later date? And at that time, the death penalty still existed for murder. If he were to be topped, who would there be to look after Rose, Rose who might be impregnated with that bastard Daniels' brat? Not even the cheery bonhomie of Harry Pudney, the licensee of the Ordnance Arms in the Barking Road could cure him of his depression. He sat at a table, nursing his double Scotch, deep in thought until he heard a voice behind him. 'Hello, Sid,' said Detective Inspector Ted Warriner. 'Long time no see!'

Ted Warriner had, until recently, been the well-respected detective inspector of the Flying Squad's Five Squad, where he had achieved notable successes. He was now in his nineteenth year of service with the Metropolitan police and it had been a career which had been crowned with success. He had earned the approbation both of his peers and the criminal fraternity. He had been commended by the commissioner on no less than twenty-three occasions and most recently had received the Queen's Commendation for brave conduct after single-handedly unarming a gunman during the course of an armed burglary. And now, he had been posted to Plaistow police station, there to replace the lack-lustre incumbent DI who had been posted to C2 (or Correspondence Department) at the Yard where, his superiors reasoned, he could do less harm than he had perpetuated at Plaistow. (In fact, he did little harm at all; in time he would be suspended over a major corruption enquiry and would be obliged to take a very premature retirement.)

Warriner had arrived at Plaistow to discover a CID office which was robbed of morale and this, he resolved, would receive a turn-around, sooner rather than later. He set out on a pub crawl of the manor to find out who and what was what. At his second stop of the evening, he discovered the means of curing the despondency at his police station.

Ted Warriner had met Sid Goldblum previously when he had been investigating a series of lorry hijackings. More than once, Goldblum's name had come into the frame as a receiver and Warriner had paid Goldblum a visit at his Gidea Park address. There, he had been courteously received, Esther had provided tea and matters had been dealt with in a very civilized way. But Warriner, with the utmost civility, had put his point of view across and Goldblum had been left in no doubt that if he stepped out of line, Warriner would be on him like a ton of hot horse shit and there the matter ended. Esther was politely thanked for her tea, Rose was complimented on her prettiness and Sid Goldblum was left thinking that Ted Warriner was one very tricky Old Bill with whom, if one had any future dealings with him, one would need to be extremely circum-spect.

'I was sorry to hear about Esther, Sid,' said Warriner, sincerely. 'A very classy lady, that.'

'Thanks, Mr Warriner,' replied Goldblum, pleased that the detective had troubled to remember his late wife's name. 'Let me get you a drink.'

And he did. Several drinks. And after a short period of reminiscences, he told Warriner about his current troubles.

Warriner had already heard about Chrissie Daniels and had privately determined that the cause of so much aggravation and despondency at Plaistow police station should be resolved without delay. He had, however, been unaware of Daniels' liaison with Sid Goldblum's daughter. He swiftly decided that the root cause of so much trouble could be settled to the satisfaction of both parties. The separation of Rose Goldblum and Chrissie Daniels had to be decisive and, to prevent reconciliation, Daniels had to be dealt with in a manner which would be both final for Rose and ignominious for Daniels.

'Sid, I believe I can help you,' said Warriner. 'But the only thing is, it's going to cost you.'

'When you say that you can help me, Mr Warriner,' eagerly replied Goldblum, 'is that for definite?'

Warriner nodded. 'Absolutely.'

This was exactly what Goldblum wanted to hear. 'Right – so what's it going to cost? I can stick a nice, safe drink into you, no problem.'

Warriner smiled and shook his head. 'Sid, I'm not talking about a drink.' Then he told him what he had in mind for recompense. Goldblum sat back and drained his glass of Scotch and smiled for the first time that evening; for the first time, in fact for several days. 'That is definitely not a problem, Mr Warriner; and thank you. Thank you very much. Another drink?'

The following day, Warriner paid a visit to the station's uniform superintendent, Jim Alloway. He had joined the Metropolitan Police in 1933 and, after a brief sojourn as an aid to CID (the details of his demise are not recorded), he had sought advancement through the uniform branch and in so doing had attracted the admiration of both uniform and CID alike. After some desultory chit-chat, Warriner asked, 'Guv'nor, I'm looking for some likely candidates for coming out as aid to CID. Anyone in mind?'

Alloway smiled. 'There's one or two, Ted, but I've got to say there's one who's head and shoulders above the rest. Dick Higgins. PC 254. If you saw him in the street, you'd miss him, even if the little fucker was in full uniform. And believe me, I know what I'm talking about.' He did. Alloway had aided with Matthew Brinnand who had gone on to be a leading light of the Ghost Squad, whom a contemporary described as being able to 'pluck a result out of the air'.

'Thanks, Guv'nor,' replied Warriner. '254 Higgins. I'll have a word with him.' And he did.

Next, Warriner spoke to the first class detective sergeant, who was traditionally in charge of the aids to CID. 'Who are the liveliest aids? Those who could be confidently recommended for permanent appointment to the CID?' The first class sergeant told him and, Warriner spoke to them, one at a time. What he said delighted them. Then he telephoned Sid Goldblum and told him he expected two telephone calls. The first of these phone calls happened the following morning, after Goldblum had told Chrissie Daniels that he needed him to pick up a package at a certain address, at a certain time, adding that there would be a good drink in it for him. Daniels eagerly agreed. 'He's on his way in fifteen minutes,' was Goldblum's cryptic message to Warriner.

In those days, each division in the Metropolitan Police was issued with a nondescript van. This unmarked vehicle was used for observation purposes by the CID and also for uses not strictly recognized as desirable or necessary. This particular van drove out of Plaistow police station with four aids to CID in the back. The departure had not been noted in the Book 66, used to record the departure or return of police vehicles, nor was any entry made of the mileage in the vehicle's log book. This discrepancy would be – er – adjusted later. And the duties in the aids' diaries would reveal that all of them were engaged in an observation, several miles hence.

The observation van came to a halt in the street where they had been instructed to stop. They did not have long to wait. Suddenly, Chrissie Daniels hove into view. The aids in the back of the van tensed. Every one of them had accounts to settle with that bastard. There was time for one last quick look round, through the van's spyholes. Nobody else was in the street. And as Chrissie Daniels swaggered past the van, the back doors burst open, he was grabbed, dragged into the van and a hood was pulled over his head. The doors slammed shut and the van roared off. It was inevitable that Daniels would struggle and he did. He sustained a welter of vengeful punches before his clothing was pulled off him and the van ground to a halt. Daniels, completely naked, save for his shoes and socks, was pushed out of the van and landed in some roadside bushes. The hood was pulled from his head, the doors slammed and the van tore off. Daniels scrambled from the bushes, ran into the roadway and started to chase after the van. 'YOU SLAGS!' he screamed. 'I'LL FUCKING HAVE THE LOT OF YOU!'

This, not surprisingly, had an effect on the twenty-three thirteen-year-old schoolgirls who were in the school playground across the road. They fled, screaming with terror, to the sanctuary of their classroom, given the terrifying sight of the naked man who appeared to be screeching at them from a few yards away. It is a fact of life that when matters start to go cataclysmically wrong, as indeed things had in the case of Chrissie Daniels, fate intervenes and adds to the misery. The schools' games mistress had been supervizing the girls' recess and had seen the emergence of Daniels from the bushes and heard everything.

For a five-foot-two woman, weighing twelve stone, Miss Phyllis Botomley moved across the road towards Chrissie Daniels with remarkable speed. At that time, few women had been awarded a second Dan black belt at judo, but Miss Botomley had. It is difficult to execute a *Seoi-Nage* (or shoulder throw) when one's opponent is stark naked, but not impossible, as Miss Botomley demonstrated and Daniels flew screaming over her shoulder. As his back hit the pavement with a dull thud, it coincided with the arrival of Police Constable 254K Higgins. 'Thank you, Madam,' he said, quietly, as though he had expected to walk round the corner and be confronted by the sight of a naked man outside a girls' school (as indeed he had). 'I'll deal with this.' With that, he pulled Daniels to his feet, performed a dextrous 'snap' and his rolled-up cape flew open and encircled Daniels' nakedness. (This public spirited action in the cause of common decency would later earn him a commendation from the trial judge.)

'Are you sure you can handle him, Officer?' asked Miss Botomley, anxiously. She thought the delicious officer looked very smart in his uniform, although a little on the small side.

'Quite sure, Madam,' replied PC Higgins. 'If you'll just be kind enough to phone 999 and ask for the van to come.'

At the very mention of the word 'van', Daniels went berserk, screaming and struggling violently. 'I knew it,' said Miss Botomley, grimly. 'Take that!' and using a *Hiji-Ate-Waza* (an Atemi blow with the elbow) struck him an atrocious blow to the jaw. 'Nasty customer!' she commented as Daniels once more slumped to the ground.

A search of the area where Daniels had been arrested revealed his neatly-folded clothing; a search of his lodgings revealed a sickening collection of indecent photographs of small children. Instead of being charged with flashing (or indecent exposure) for which the maximum penalty was three months' imprisonment, Daniels was charged under the recent legislation which had been passed to protect children, namely the Indecency with Children Act, 1960, for which the penalty was two years' imprisonment.

Daniels, true to form, defended himself at the North East London Quarter Sessions. This time, it did him no good at all. First, there was the compelling evidence of Miss Botomley whose calm testimony and resolute action at the scene brought a strong commendation from the trial judge. Then there was the evidence from PC Higgins, who, after Miss Botomley had left the scene, had cautioned Daniels who had allegedly replied, 'I can't help it, mate. I can't help taking my clothes off when little girls are around.' This brought screeching denials from Daniels in the dock but, as the judge remarked in his summing up, could one place any credence on such denials, coupled with what the jury might consider to be ludicrous assertions that he had been kidnapped and stripped, particularly when one balanced these denials with the revolting photographs of children discovered in Daniels' flat (similarly refuted) which had caused physical nausea from one of the jury members?

The jury returned its verdict after fourteen minutes. It would have been sooner had not several members demanded a much-needed smoke break. The judge decided that the most unappealable sentence he could impose, given all of the circumstances, was one of fifteen months' imprisonment.

The second telephone call of the day that Sid Goldblum made to Ted Warriner was in respect of a lorry-load of cigarettes which had been diverted from its prescribed route. It was a case that should have been dealt with by the Flying Squad or, rather, the recently-formed Regional Crime Squad but Warriner felt such a case was well within the capabilities of the CID and the aids to CID at Plaistow. Strictly speaking, the A127 is not a road within the boundaries of Plaistow police station but, nevertheless, it was there in a lay-by that the lorry, its cargo of cigarettes, the thieves who hijacked it, the driver who was fully implicated in the theft and the receiver who was waiting to redistribute the load, were all arrested. It was Sid Goldblum's delivery of his trade-off.

The coverage by the *Stratford Express* of Chrissie Daniels' case was highly impressive; it had something to do with the paper's crime reporter being informed by the detective inspector at the local police station that there were plenty more stories like that. Rose Goldblum was suitably disgusted. Who, she demanded to know, would want to marry such a pervert? She felt it unnecessary to mention to her father that this had been a course of action which she had once considered but, of course, he was not to know that and he merely shrugged his shoulders helplessly and sighed.

And for those of you who like happy endings to stories, let me oblige you. Sid Goldblum got his wish. Rose met and married a nice Jewish chartered accountant and in the fullness of time, before Sid went to that great market stall in the sky, she produced twin boys, whom Sid spoiled shamelessly.

Ted Warriner stayed only a short time at Plaistow Police Station, to the CID office's infinite regret; he had improved morale out of all recognition and there being a lack of detective chief inspectors at the time, he was swiftly promoted and eventually retired having achieved very high rank and being recognized in the honours lists.

Phyllis Botomley was so taken with the calm efficiency of PC Higgins that she forswore the pressing attentions of her university friend Clare, made up her mind on her own, slightly confused sexuality and embarked upon a passionate and adulterous affair with Higgins which lasted several years. Higgins rid himself of the uniform which had so entranced

Miss Botomley and became one of the Yard's top undercover men.

And Chrissie Daniels? Within minutes of entering the penal system, he discovered that nobody loves a nonce. At the conclusion of his sentence, he discovered that not only was his sphincter in tatters, so was his reputation. He moved away from Canning Town and, whatever he did and wherever he went thereafter, he never again made the mistake of making a fallacious complaint, or even a justifiable one against police.

A Round of Applause

Benny the Barber is the traditional type of hairdresser who is seldom visited by men under the age of fifty. He dresses immaculately. He is calm and courteous, a professional right to his fingertips and knows his trade inside out. There is no reason why he shouldn't; his father was a barber and it was in his father's shop that Benny learnt his trade. Later, he worked in some of the salubrious hairdressing salons in the West End of London; Austin Reed's and Trumper's.

Now, at the age when most men are considering retirement or, indeed, have already retired, Benny still keeps his hand in. One look at a client's cranium is sufficient for Benny; he knows instinctively to the nearest millimetre how long the client wants his hair. And all the time, Benny's voice is murmuring polite, soothing conversation. He keeps off controversial subjects which might offend; years of experience, from dealing with dustmen to dukes have instilled in him the gift of sticking to middle of the road conversations which do not give offence.

He would not, for example, expound on the characters of Reginald and Ronald Kray; he would not wish to enter into a lively discussion as to whether the Twins were once collectively described as being 'the Scum of the Earth' or individually referred to as 'diamond geezers'. But if he wished, he could, because Benny was born in Bethnal Green, in the heart of Kray territory so it was inescapable that he would know of them, and know the fearsome stories that surrounded them. Of course, being a straight person, involved in a respectable business, there was no reason why he should have anything to do with them, although that was a close-run thing. Ronnie Kray had decided that he should be shaved and have his hair cut at home, in Vallance Road. A barber was summoned from his shop in the Whitechapel Road and for this Benny was truly thankful; his father's shop was in the Bethnal Green Road.

So, well over fifty years ago, the clientele was as diverse as the area; cunning coppers, customers with razor scars across their faces – 'Try not to cut me', as one client jocularly instructed Benny – and always there was talk about Jack Spot (even though he had long since moved from the area), dodgy gear and where commodities might be found that could be purchased 'off-ration'.

One of these assorted customers was Ollie, a huge, heavy-weight wrestler, who used to frequent Benny's father's shop on a regular basis and the three men were very chummy. One day, Ollie, in the midst of having his head carefully shaved – he believed, with some justification, that his bald appearance made him appear more menacing in the ring – told them that he would acquire complimentary tickets for them to attend a boxing evening at the famous York Hall Public Baths and father and son were delighted. For many years the name of York Hall had been synonymous with first-rate boxing and wrestling bouts.

One of the more spectacular wrestling turns was billed as 'Mad Max – the Butcher of Bavaria', who could be relied upon to transport the audience into a frenzy when he screamed, 'Schweinhund!' at them. After one such thrilling exhibition, during which the Teutonic monster was well and truly trounced by a good, East End boy, Ollie asked Benny if he would care to meet him. ''E's a really nice bloke,' added Ollie.

Given Benny's Jewish background, he was understandably reticent about meeting anybody from a country which had carried out such appalling war-time crimes against his race but, by the same token, he did not wish to offend Ollie, who was such a good friend, so with considerable misgivings, he agreed.

In the dressing room, Ollie performed the introductions and the enormous Butcher of Bavaria held out a ham-like hand. 'Wotcher, mate,' he said. 'Pleased ter meecher!'

An astonished Benny gingerly shook the huge hand. 'You're – er – not actually from Bavaria, then?' he asked, timorously.

'Me? Nah – Dalston, mate,' cheerfully replied the giant.

It was in this fashion, courtesy of Ollie, that Benny made the acquaintance of the Swedish Axeman who came from Hoxton, Paddy O'Flynn, the Fighting Tiger of Donnegal who had been born and raised in Hackney and the Masked Maniac from Chicago who had lived all his life in a house two streets away from where Benny lived. The mask, of course, was an absolute necessity, to prevent local recognition.

Benny and his father turned up at the hall at the appointed time and Ollie, tickets in hand, greeted them with news which was both good and bad. The good news was that he had acquired ringside tickets for them; the bad news was that seated on Benny's left were none other than Reggie and Ronnie Kray. Benny trembled at the news. Like the rest of the inhabitants of Bethnal Green, he was aware that the Twins fighting ability extended beyond sixteen ounce gloves and usually involved cutlasses, hatchets, sheath knives and automatic pistols.

'I'll give you two bits of advice,' Ollie told Benny. 'First, if they talk to you, just answer back; be polite but brief. Under no circumstances try to start a conversation, understand?'

Benny, who had started to perspire freely, dutifully nodded his head. 'And the second?'

'The second thing,' intoned Ollie, grimly, 'is when the bouts have finished and you get up to leave, for Gawd's sake move to your right. If you go to the left, in front of the Twins and you accidentally tread on their shoes, that'll be your bleedin' lot – you got that?'

Yes, Benny had indeed 'got that' and he nervously made his way down to his seat. There, already in place, were the fearsome Twins; the only thing they had in common with Benny and his father was that none of them had paid for their tickets. Benny slid into his seat, noticing as he did so the Twins sharp suits, their tightly knotted ties and, worst of all, the gleaming toe-caps on their shoes. But, after a while, Benny started to relax whilst he waited for the bouts to begin. Neither of the Twins, who were quite content to murmur between themselves, had attempted to engage him in conversation.

Just prior to the night's first bout, the management decided, as was quite normal, that it would be a good idea for a celebrity to say a few words to the audience. The personality who was introduced was a former middleweight European champion who was long past his sell-by date and, due to some of the ferocious batterings he had received in later years, was what is colloquially known as 'punchy'. In consequence, as he rose to his feet to address the audience, the words which he uttered were almost unintelligible and the former champion went on and on. Finally, he finished and sat down. Unlike nowadays, perhaps, no one heckled him but, by the same token (and because everybody was impatient for the boxing to commence), nobody said anything, either.

No one that is, except Ronnie Kray who lumbered to his feet, turned to the audience and growled, 'Clap, fuck yer!'

The hall reverberated to the sound of sustained applause, whistles and admiring shouts, as the audience leapt to their feet and gave the ex-boxer due reverence for being the former

European champion. It was irrelevant that this had occurred so long ago that most of them hadn't then been born.

The lights went down and the first of several splendid bouts commenced. Benny really enjoyed that evening and had been amazed at Ronnie's rough and ready compassion, although, at the conclusion, he was *very* careful to make his exit to the right!

Blind Justice

The usage of the term 'villains' is a fairly pejorative one and I use it in this book to describe all kinds of wrong-doing. But the description of a person as being a villain is carefully categorized amongst the criminal classes. Someone who was a villain was Timmy Hayes. He would smash up pubs and billiard halls in order to impress upon the terrified owners that they really needed his services to prevent others from behaving in a similar fashion. In 1926, he received a sentence of four years' penal servitude, plus a few more years on top for being a habitual criminal.

Wayne Crispin did not behave in such an audacious fashion but one would be hard-pressed not to apply the title of villain to him. Crispin was a thin-shouldered, rat-faced creature who had been spawned in a council sink estate in London's East End. He progressed smoothly through Juvenile Courts to Magistrates' Courts and served several periods of incarceration but as he progressed into his middle twenties, he was convicted less and less. Not because he had turned over a new leaf, nor because he had come to a sudden halt on the road to Damascus, but because he simply wasn't being caught.

Crispin had turned his hand to what is now known as 'distraction burglaries' and these offences were usually only carried out if he had discovered that the back door of the premises which he intended to screw was locked.

In that eventuality, posing as a gas, electricity or water board official, he would get his victim to turn off the water or check the cellar lighting whilst he relieved them of the contents of their handbags, screwed their gas or electricity meters, nicked their life's savings or filched just about anything else of resaleable value. But, as unpalatable as these offences were, Crispin added a cherry to top the cake. By some devious means, he managed to ensure that his victims were either blind or partially sighted, as well as being elderly, of course. With identification an issue, Crispin was getting away with this type of offence scot-free. Crispin a villain? I'd say so, although put him in the same room as Timmy Hayes and he would have lasted all of two seconds before Hayes had knifed his face open. Crispin was once described by a detective as having less charm and personality than the cheese under his foreskin, a sentiment with which everybody agreed, although one which few would have cared to investigate.

Matters came to a head after four reports of this type of offence were recorded in two days. The *Stratford Express* was making much of this and the local detective inspector copped it right in the neck from the area commander for being made to look a fool by the newspaper. Everybody had a pretty good idea that Crispin was responsible but ideas are not evidence and therefore, given the inability of the victims to identify him, he would have to be caught right in the act.

The detective inspector brought in four of his aids to CID and borrowed two more from a neighbouring division. 'Right, get out there, use the nondescript, use your loaf, just nick this fucker,' he growled. 'Don't give me any excuses and don't come back without him. And if you can't nick him,' he added threateningly, 'I'll get someone who can – while you lot are back in uniform, taking turns to direct traffic at Stratford Broadway!'

The threat was sufficient to stiffen the resolve of the most recalcitrant of aids and they set to work with a will. They set up observation posts on the tops of buildings around Crispin's home so that, when they spotted him, they would have to race downstairs to get to the nondescript van to point them in his general direction. In those days, personal radios did not exist and, although portable radio sets were in use, they were difficult to acquire, weighed a ton and simply could not be left on the roof of a block of flats. Added to this, the weather was extremely inclement and it was certainly no fun being exposed to the elements when only a certifiable lunatic would go out screwing in the pissing rain. However, the aids would have been deemed to be certifiable lunatics themselves if they had deserted their posts and Crispin had gone to work; the threat of 'the big hat' was not one to be taken lightly.

But on the third day, the aids' luck changed. Crispin was spotted leaving his home, the aids rushed down from their observation posts, jumped into the nondescript van and headed off towards him. The van had already parked up when Crispin started darting looks up and down a street and then – whoosh! – he vanished. It was clear that he was round the back of one of the houses. But which one? Two of the aids were dropped off; they walked down to more or less the area where Crispin had last been seen and hid themselves in the bushes in the neat frontages of the adjoining houses. Two more were dropped off further down the street and they similarly hid themselves; the nondescript van, together with the one remaining aid, drove around the block, in case Crispin should endeavour to escape through the back gardens.

Unseen by them Crispin emerged through the front door of one of the houses. As he walked into the street, he was grabbed, searched and found to be in possession of £80 cash, some jewellery and a pension book, the property of the occupier of the house he had just left. 'Found these on the pavement, didn't I?' he said, coolly. 'Just on me way down to the nick to hand 'em in, weren't I?'

A little investigation revealed that the occupier of the house – by sheer coincidence, she suffered from glaucoma – was absent at the time of the burglary. Entry had been made via the unlocked back door. It was clear that Crispin was not going to make any admissions to the aids about this job, nor any of the other offences he had committed. It was also clear that a little pressure would have to be exerted.

Crispin was brought into the CID office of the grimy, Edwardian North Woolwich police station and was seated in front of the desk of Detective Sergeant (Second Class) Dennis 'Knuckles' Docherty, who looked at him impassively.* 'Won't keep you a moment, son,' he said. He then picked up a thick A–D telephone directory and holding its spine in between just his thumbs and forefingers, he effortlessly ripped it in two and then, without turning, threw the torn sections over his shoulder. They both landed neatly in a wastepaper basket behind him.

'Sorry about that, lad,' said Knuckles. 'Every time I get really pissed off with something or somebody who won't do what they're told, I find that doing that sort of relieves the tension. Calms me down, so to speak. If I don't, I go a bit mental. Know what I mean?'

Crispin looked into his eyes which did indeed display traits of insanity. He was as unnerved with the way that Knuckles had smoothly torn the directory in two as much as he had

---

* For a further disturbing account of Knuckles Docherty, see *The Real Sweeney* (Constable & Robinson, 2005)

been concerned in the almost supernatural way in which both sections of the book had gone sailing over Knuckles shoulder, straight into the bin.

'Anyway, I'm all right now, I think,' he continued. 'I'm not upset with anything or anybody. No one's telling me lies, which is something that *really* pisses me off.' Again, there was the same mad glare from his eyes which had begun to thoroughly unnerve Crispin. 'There's just one thing . . .'

'What's that?' enquired Crispin, nervously.

'I just happen to have run out of telephone directories,' replied Knuckles, mildly. 'Now, I think there's some things that you want to clear up, lad, starting with today's little caper . . . ?'

Wayne Crispin confessed everything confessable and the judge at the North-East London Quarter Sessions described his catalogue of crimes as 'despicable'. Telling him that had he used violence towards his blind and partially sighted victims, he would have doubled the sentence, Crispin was sentenced to five years' imprisonment.

A couple of months into his sentence, Crispin started to develop a rather abnormal thirst, so much so, that he nocturnally used his chamber pot to such an extent that in the mornings, his slopping out required a very steady hand indeed. He also felt excessively tired, noticed that his never over-large physique was looking even scrawnier than usual and that from time to time, his vision was getting blurred. Eventually, he visited the prison doctor who quickly established that most unusually for someone who is not over forty, overweight or of Afro-Caribbean or Asian origin, Crispin was suffering from Type 2, or mature onset diabetes.

The doctor prescribed tablets and suggested a healthy, low sugar diet and regular exercise, with no smoking but Crispin ignored much of the advice. When he collapsed, having suffered a hyperglycaemic attack (as he did on several occasions), he was taken to the hospital wing where the doctor administered insulin but, for this type of diabetes, insulin is not normally administered on a regular basis and Crispin was referred, once again, to his tablets and the necessity of a proper diet.

Towards the end of his sentence, Crispin's blurred vision grew worse and the doctor sat him down and firmly informed him that, upon his release, he should see an eye-care specialist with a proven track record for treating patients suffering from diabetes and, in addition, he should have a dilated pupil examination, at least annually. Diabetic retinopathy is treatable, providing that the patient follows his doctor's orders to the letter. Predictably, Crispin did nothing of the sort.

Having served just over three years of his sentence, Crispin was released and returned to the family home. Every copper on the beat knew that Crispin was out and about but, surprisingly, nothing happened. Things were unusually quiet in and around the Crispin household. One of the newly formed Crime Prevention Officers issued leaflets aimed at the blind and partially sighted residents of the area, warning them against bogus officials. And still nothing happened.

One day, Police Constable 915K 'Tommy' Cooper, a local beat officer, had come on duty at two o' clock and was strolling through his beat where, of course, he knew everybody when he saw a familiar face walking towards him. It was Terry Crispin, a former cat burglar (now retired) and father of Wayne.

'Hello, Terry,' said PC Cooper. 'Long time no see.'

'No, well, been spending me time at Moorfields, Mr Cooper, ain't I?'

PC Cooper raised his eyebrows at the mention of the well-known eye hospital, but said nothing.

'It's our Wayne, ain't it? Only gone blind, ain't he?'

Here was a case of the biter, bit. Someone who had made

it his business to prey on the weak, the elderly, the blind and the partially sighted. And now . . . ? When PC Cooper merely said, 'Oh!' this was clearly insufficient. It was a time when an outpouring of emotion was required. He bade farewell to Wayne's grieving father and turning the corner, continued on his beat.

The following telephone call was received at North Woolwich Police Station, ten minutes later.

'Hello? Please put me through to Inspector Bradshaw. Tell him that it's The Reverent Mr. Duckwood and the matter is urgent. Thank you. Inspector? I am afraid it is my unpleasant duty to report one of your constables for misconduct. Yes. I'm referring to Police Constable Cooper for using blasphemous language and being drunk on duty. Yes. I was looking out of the window of the vicarage, when PC Cooper walked around the corner. He was laughing and then – and then he stopped, flung his arms up in the air and – may God forgive me! – he shouted, "I knew it! There is a fucking God! Whoopee!" And with that, inspector, he turned a perfect cartwheel and wandered off, still chuckling to himself! He must be drunk – there can be no other rationale explanation! Do something, inspector – do something!'

The Chopper Man

Queensbridge Road, Hackney, stretches from Hackney Road in the south to Dalston Lane in the north. It is a fairly unprepossessing area but, then again, it always has been. During the 1960s, it was in this thoroughfare that Dr Christopher Michael Swan took over a general practitioner's surgery, a practice which had 2,500 National Health patients on its books, plus 998 private patients. Outside, iron railings protected the unwary from falling into the 'area' or basement; a dozen stone steps led up to the grim-looking entrance.

Swan, who had been born in 1935, had qualified as a doctor in 1961. Later, it would be said that, even before his qualification, his superiors suspected that he was schizophrenic, which does not say a great deal for the General Medical Council. Smooth, dark haired, charismatic, and married with a young daughter, Swan lived in the very smart area of Forest Hill. He also possessed two expensive cars, one of them a Mercedes Benz sports model. Swan could afford to; he worked for several large companies, as well as receiving the income from his practice. But when the Dangerous Drugs Act came into force in April 1967, it prevented him from prescribing heroin and cocaine to his clients, four of whom had died as the result of overdoses.

Drug addiction was becoming a problem in London. In 1958, there were 442 addicts known to the Home Office. In 1963, the number had risen by half as much again, to 635. By 1968, the figure had shot up to 2,624. What follows explains, in part, why.

Following the introduction of the new legislation, Swan renamed his surgery, The East London Drug Addiction Centre and soon Swan, who had called a press conference to mark the opening of the centre, was regarded as a pioneer, helping drug addicts. But not everything was as it seemed. Dr Swan was a wrong 'un. He was a villain. Dangerous enough to start with, he would later be exposed as someone who had murder – or even several murders – on his mind.

In the first nine months of his practice, Swan prescribed drugs for 273 of his National Health patients. But fifty-four of the chemists in that area grew somewhat alarmed at the sudden rise of prescriptions that Swan was issuing. In September 1967, Swan prescribed 168 Drinamyl tablets. Within just two months, this had snowballed to 7,000 tablets. Two months after that, the number of tablets had increased to 23,000, three months later, to 44,000 and two months after that, to a staggering 64,000. In a three to four month period, Swan had netted something like £15,000 – and that wasn't all. An associate, John Joseph White, had carried out an illegal abortion; Swan assisted him. He was one of a number of people whom Swan had assisted in many ways, and *vice versa*; people who might well prove to be an embarrassment, later on.

Another of them was Stephen Hartford, then in his early twenties, a former drug addict, who had apparently been cured following a drug rehabilitation scheme at a hospital and had joined the National Association of Drug Addicts. There, he performed some sterling work, rehabilitating addicts until, as a result of his work, he met Swan and became his medical secretary. It was not too long before Hartford was drawn into

Swan's web. Swan and Hartford supplied addicts with prescriptions, issued in the names of other patients. These were usually sold by Hartford, who picked up around £4 per prescription. Because such large quantities of drugs were issued, often surplus to the addict's requirements, they sold them on to other addicts.

The *Daily Express* picked up the story and carried out a thorough investigation, which they published. Swan and three hoodlums turned up at the offices of the *Daily Express* to voice their displeasure.

The newspaper's disclosures were now taken up by the police, with Detective Superintendent John Cass of City Road police station in charge of the enquiry. His investigations revealed that Swan had issued 5,279 prescriptions to private patients for 530,000 Drinamyl tablets and 41,000 methadrine tablets. Swan and Hartford were charged and bailed but, believing that they had been initially betrayed to the newspaper by John Wall, who had formerly been one of the centre's staff, the two men decided that he should be appropriately punished. Another of Swan's associates was David Gordon, who was the proud possessor of sixteen previous convictions. He had been responsible for pushing drugs at the Limbo Club, Soho. Now he was given the job of stabbing Wall, which he did.

Swan's bail was promptly rescinded and he was remanded in custody at Brixton prison, to await his trial at the Old Bailey.

Swan decided that the only way to stop other co-defendants from compromising him was to silence them – permanently. He approached a fellow remand prisoner, Brian Stevens, and told him that he was willing to pay £4,000 each for someone on the outside to eliminate White and Hartford, both of whom were on bail.Stevens (who had not been told the identities of the intended victims), seeing that he might be able to do himself some good, told Swan that he might indeed know such a person: he contacted Superintendent Cass.

John Vaughan, who was then aged forty-three, had seen active service during World War Two, serving with the Argyll and Sutherland Highlanders. He was later commissioned and seconded to the Royal Military Police, and served as Deputy Assistant Provost Marshal in Egypt, Palestine and Transjordan, returning to the United Kingdom in 1947. Within ten days of resigning his commission in 1948, Vaughan joined the Metropolitan Police. Appointed to the CID as soon as possible, Vaughan served all over central London before spending three-and-a-half years with the Flying Squad, partnering the legendary Jack Slipper. In 1966, he was posted to G Division, as a detective sergeant, which was where he was under the command of Superintendent Cass. Because Vaughan had taken no part in the initial Swan investigation and because of his Flying Squad experience, Cass asked him if he would be willing to take the part of 'Sid Green' – the chopper man – and Vaughan leapt at the chance.

Vaughan's brief was to discover who these victims actually were, so that they could be protected. On 30 August 1968, Vaughan entered Brixton Prison as a visitor and as he sat down at the table with Swan, Vaughan looked nothing like the excellent copper that he was. Dressed in a fashionable mohair suit, a coloured shirt, a yellow spotted tie and suede shoes, he looked much more like Sid Green except that Sid Green would not have been issued with a miniature tape recorder, with the microphone threaded through his wristwatch strap.

'I have been approached in case you want a bit of business done,' murmured Vaughan.

'Do you know about the business already?' asked Swan.

'I've been told you want a chopper man,' replied Vaughan.

'That's right,' nodded Swan and then provided Vaughan with the names of two of the men he wanted killed – Hartford, his secretary, and White, the abortionist – together with their addresses and their descriptions.

Vaughan looked round apprehensively. 'It's a bit dodgy writing stuff in here.'

'Listen, remember it's Hartford, Stephen Hartford,' replied Swan.

'He's the finger who was nicked with you, wasn't he?' asked Vaughan.

'That's right,' replied Swan, adding, 'I only wish I could do it myself, mate. I tell you, they're absolute bastards those two. I don't want no kids on this. I want a professional. Okay?'

Vaughan nodded. 'That's why they have brought me in.'

'Stevens has given me his word that you are absolutely reliable,' said Swan.

'I've had a figure given of four grand apiece,' said Vaughan. 'When do I get the money?'

'This is where I have to plead for trust,' replied Swan. 'I will guarantee you this money and more, because it means so much to me.'

'I've got to take care of one or two other people,' said Vaughan.

'You've got to wait until I get out of here to get the full whack,' replied Swan. 'Do you understand? I can do fuck all while I'm in here. If you can get these two people, I am going to get out of these charges, okay? Then I will be able to pay you.'

'Have you any preference how you would like them done away with?' asked Vaughan.

'I want it done completely and permanently,' replied Swan, decisively. 'I have no preference.'

'Well, just with a shooter?' asked Vaughan.

'Just with a shooter,' agreed Swan. 'But you've got to get

rid of them down the river or something like that. Down the river or down the sea.'

'Down the sea you'd like them?' asked Vaughan.

'Anywhere that would be permanent,' replied Swan, adding, 'and they'll never be seen again.'

'When do you want it done?' said Vaughan, flatly.

'This is very important,' replied Swan. 'When you have studied the set-up and are poised to go, let me know by sending me a card saying: "I hope the day is right. Happy birthday. Sid Green." That will let me know you are ready and then I will tell you when to go ahead. I don't want anything done in under three weeks because I have another firm dealing with two other people. Do you understand? Doing the same job.'

'What, knocking them off completely?' asked Vaughan.

'Yes,' replied Swan.

'Can't I do all the business?' enquired Vaughan.

'It's a question of money,' replied Swan. 'These other people want £500 apiece because they know me. I would rather you do the lot, but I can't afford it.'

Vaughan then asked, and was given, the names of the two further victims whom Swan wanted murdered; both were crucial witnesses in the case.

'I'll do the whole lot for you, for ten grand,' said Vaughan and, referring to the two most recent additions to the list, he added, 'I'll throw the other two mugs in for that.'

So it was agreed. After Vaughan had sent the 'birthday' card, Prisoner No. 059842 Swan C.M. sent the following letter to Sidney Green Esq., c/o King's Arms, Cheyne Walk, Chelsea on 21 September 1969.

The pub was one where John Vaughan went for a glass when he was off duty and the publican agreed to accept delivery of it. However, this most important document almost went astray; the envelope was marked-up by the Post Office 'Not SW3 – Try SW10'.

But when it did arrive and the envelope was opened, the letter read as follows:

Dear Sid,

It is now three weeks since you said you would get all those parts right and if you remember I promised to get in touch about this time. From what I've heard, things are A1. It certainly is good of you to go to all the trouble necessary – one sure gets to know one's friends when the back is to the wall! and as you realize I am extremely grateful to you.

Believe it or not I haven't yet had a visit from my solicitor; if the blasted man doesn't come next week I'll give him the push – even though it's a late stage and I'll have to ask for an adjournment; so although I thought he'd advise you to decide where it would be best to advertise I have decided to give you complete freedom of your discretion as to when you do it. Another reason for not relying on him is that unfortunately you'd have to do a bit more work (which I know he should do but what the devil can I do if he persists in not coming to see me!) & as I don't know your movements & commitments I have decided to let you do it in your own time as you think fit – obviously this is more convenient all round – especially as I would not wish to cramp your style!!! But I think, if I may say so, it should all be done by the end of this month. As I don't have the garage any longer & I don't want it in the open it's best to get rid of the whole thing as soon as you can manage it. Incidentally, it is reasonable to reckon my case will be not up before November – but I'll need the money for approaching, at least initially, a top class criminal solicitor.

(Swan then provides details of two people, both witnesses for the prosecution whom he wants Sid Green to 'deal with'.) The letter then continues:

My wife is still not very well so I'm going to have to land you with this extra work (that's why she hasn't been able to go & put her foot down with the solicitor.) Anyhow you'll be pleased to know that when this extra is done & the car is sold I'll be in a much happier state of mind because I'm not going to let the police court choose the solicitors, and I'm sure I'll get my freedom from the independently chosen solicitors: I'm amazed really I've had the patience to wait so long already: of course I'm reporting the blasted man to the law society.

So Sid please see to these two extra jobs, don't worry your expenses will be gratefully met: if for any reason you have to come to see me give FOR 3011 a ring the day before then none of the neighbours will visit me on the day you come so you'll be able to definitely see me * Visiting is 10.30 – 12 & 1.30 – 3.30 ex Sun * but I can't see any reason why you should have to because I give you full authority to go ahead. Cheers Chris.

P.S. When you've done it drop me a card just to confirm the price you got! – £15000 at least

When Superintendent Cass informed Swan that his chopper man had in fact been a police officer, Swan simply refused to believe him. It was only when Vaughan walked into the committal court that Swan's jaw dropped. It was sufficient for him to plead guilty to a total of thirteen charges at the Old Bailey.

On 10 January 1969, Sir Carl Aarvold, OBE, TD, the Recorder of London told Swan, 'You used your position as a doctor, not to spread health and happiness, but to spread misery and illness. In your hands were the powers of healing and health but you used them instead to degrade and destroy.'

He then sentenced Swan to seven years for incitement to murder four witnesses, five years for contravening the Drugs Act, two years for conspiracy to assault a former attendant at his clinic and one year for being an accessory to two abortions. All the sentences were to run consecutively to each other: fifteen years' imprisonment.

Stephen Hartford, who came perilously close to being one of the victims, had already been sentenced to two years' imprisonment for illegally obtaining drugs and conspiracy to assault a man.

David Gordon who was convicted of obtaining drugs by false pretences, conspiracy to assault and wounding a man was sentenced to a total of four and a half years' imprisonment.

The Recorder gave Detective Superintendent Cass a fulsome commendation, saying that, 'The community owes you all a great debt of admiration and gratitude.' Thanking the Recorder, Superintendent Cass added, 'I had admirable support.'

This comment led the Recorder straight into commending John Vaughan and in part, he remarked, 'It was a piece of acting, I am bound to say, that would deserve an Oscar in any other sphere.' Sir Norman Skelhorn, the Director of Public Prosecutions sent a transcript of the Recorder's remarks to the commissioner of the Metropolitan Police adding at the same time his own congratulations. When the commissioner added his own commendation, it brought to total no less than twenty-five commissioner's commendations during John Vaughan's distinguished twenty-five year career.

In December that year, the Court of Appeal (Criminal Division) dismissed Swan's appeal that he had been unfit to plead at his trial and the following February, at a hearing of the General Medical Council, Swan was struck off the medical register. He was not present. His legal representative informed the committee that it had been thought inadvisable for Swan to attend the hearing, 'in the interests of his mental health'. He probably had a point.

By now, Swan had been transferred to Broadmoor. Although he had pleaded guilty, he was utterly convinced that he had been wrongly charged. It was a view not widely accepted, especially by Lord Justice Fenton Atkinson, who was one of the three appeal court judges. Referring to Swan, he said, 'He is a very dangerous and very evil man. It is very dangerous for him to be at large.'

These were sentiments with which 'Sid Green' wholeheartedly agreed.

The Visitor from Above

Since time immemorial, criminals have befriended gullible serving girls from grand houses in order to obtain information regarding the whereabouts of their employers' valuables. This was not without its risks, because during the course of the police investigation, there was always a chance that the susceptible girl, realizing that the family silver had vanished at just about the same time as her *inamorato*, might put two and two together and blurt out the identity of the perpetrator. A variation on the theme was when a West End masseur used to milk the secrets of the whereabouts of his clients' goodies and then pass them on to the likes of George 'Taters' Chatum, one of the greatest cat burglars of all time, who was still out screwing in his seventies and eighties.

But time moves on and now the young woman who became the screwsman's dupe was Marion Bettingham who provided a top-class catering service for the homes of the great and the good. Marion was a plump, pretty girl and she was completely taken in by Ian Jamieson who appeared to display a genuine interest in her and her work. He encouraged her to tell him every detail of the dishes she had prepared for the houses she had visited and he was so fascinated with her work that he insisted on knowing every detail about the house and what jewellery the hostess was wearing. Jamieson, needless to say, was a screwsman and a good one, and his line of patter was so convincing that, implausible as it seems, not once did Marion realize that she was his unwitting accomplice.

However, Marion came back to her flat unexpectedly and she found Jamieson sitting on the floor in the middle of her lounge, surrounded by a large quantity of silver. 'Ian, what on earth is all this? Where did it all come from?' she gasped.

'Oh, don't worry, Babe,' smoothly replied Jamieson, giving her one of his easy-going grins. 'I did a deal with a guy I know. I was with him when he got it cheap at an auction a couple of weeks ago; didn't really know what it was worth. I've got a buyer all lined up – I should make a nice few bob on the deal.' He stood up and kissed her fondly on the cheek. 'Might even take you out to dinner,' he added, lightly.

'Oh,' replied Marion and then she stopped, stock still. She was looking at a silver photo frame. She stooped and picked it up and stared. In the frame was a photograph of General and Mrs McPherson, for whom she had provided the catering at their house in Stapleford Abbotts just two nights previously. And that photograph had been displayed on the mantelpiece in the dining room. But Ian had said . . . it simply *couldn't* have been obtained from an auction by Ian's friend a couple of weeks ago.

'Ian,' she said, slowly, as a dreadful doubt began to form in her head. 'What's the name of your friend?'

'Who? Oh – er – John. Yeah, John.'

Marion's mind was racing. All those questions over the past weeks and months. Now, this silver. It was all starting to fit into place.

'Liar!' she shouted. 'You bloody stole this!'

Jamieson accepted the accusation quite calmly. 'Yeah, well, if you insist on leaving your appointment book about where anyone can see it, that's your look-out.'

More than anything, Marion was shocked by his calm acceptance of the situation. 'You bastard!' she screamed. 'Get out!'

Jamieson shrugged his shoulders philosophically and Marion covered her face with her hands and burst into tears. When she had gained control of her emotions and had stopped sobbing, Jamieson had gone. So had the silver.

Marion made herself a cup of tea and sat down. She was furious at the way Jamieson had duped and used her. Finally, she made up her mind, got up and made her way to her local police station. She reported the matter to Detective Constable Jim Evans, who photocopied her appointments book and quickly discovered that a large percentage of the houses she had catered for during her liaison with Jamieson had been the subject of burglaries.

Evans started making himself busy in his search for Jamieson, but without success. Unfortunately, when enquiries are made in an effort to trace somebody, it is often inescapable that that person will get to hear of it. Jamieson did. And Marion was about to discover that quite apart from being a parasitic burglar, Jamieson was also a vicious sadist, bordering on the psychotic.

A week later, just as Marion Bettingham was about to enter her flat, late at night, she was suddenly seized by a steely hand gripping the nape of her neck. 'You fucking little grass!' snarled Jamieson.

'Ian – I didn't – I never—!' she gasped.

'Shut up – I'll show you what happens to grasses' replied Jamieson and with that, he punched her hard in the face. Her head spinning, she was dimly aware of being pulled down the steps, across the pavement and into the back of a car, before being driven off, very fast indeed. The rest of the night was a nightmare. Jamieson took her to Epping Forest where he subjected to a long, slow, painful and humiliating beating, repeatedly telling her that this would be just a sample of the treatment she could expect unless she retracted her accusations about him. Eventually she lost consciousness and it was not until early the following morning that she staggered on to the Woodford New Road. The motorist who was on his way to work, almost ran her down and he was appalled at the sight of the bloodied and bruised young woman whose clothes were in tatters. Helping her into his car, he hurriedly drove to Woodford police station.

Detective Constable Jim Evans was contacted and was furious when he saw the state that Marion was in. He redoubled his efforts to find Jamieson and, within a week, a snout informed him that he could be found living at his ex-wife's address.

Very early the following morning, Evans arrived at the council house on the Broadmead Estate where the tenant was Jamieson's former wife. Accompanying Evans was Alan Barker, a tall, slim, good-looking fellow detective constable. Evans bent down and peered through the letter-box. It was not yet light, but he felt there was something – well, not wrong, but not quite right. He squinted into the letter-box again. First, there was a peculiar smell. Then there was – well, it was rather like a pumping sound, as though someone was running a generator. And then – what in God's name was it? It was something pink that kept on waggling up and down.

Evans slowly stood up. 'Alan,' he said quietly. 'I think there's a fucking dog in there!'

He was right. As they had approached the front door, so a giant German shepherd dog had risen from its somnolent position in the hallway and, as the letter-box had been pushed inwards, the dog had opened its mouth so wide that, as Evans peered inside, all he could see was its tongue, all he could smell was its foetid breath and what he had thought was a generator was the dog's panting.

Evans was not particularly happy around large dogs. 'Go on, Alan,' he said. 'Kick the door in.'

Barker was equally apprehensive. 'You kick the fucking door in!' he retorted.

The loud exchange caused the dog to start barking and it took several minutes for the former Mrs Jamieson to answer the door; time enough for her errant husband to hide.

Glenda Jamieson (née Walker) was a thin, emaciated, bleached blonde who was no stranger to the police. As well as having a few convictions of her own, her aura of criminality was strengthened due to the fact that she was also related to Ted Marchant, a good-looking blagger and fighting man from Upton Park. In fact, she was still in mourning for him, since his early and unexpected demise, following a fatal encounter with the business end of a sawn-off. She instinctively identified the profession of Evans and Barker and extended the type of cordial welcome that the detectives had fully anticipated: 'If you ain't got a warrant, fuck off!'

She was to be disappointed because the officers were in possession of a search warrant; they also demanded to know the whereabouts of her former spouse. 'Ain't seen 'im for months,' she replied. 'Wouldn't 'ave 'im in the house, mate, tell yer that fer nothin', dirty no good slag.'

The German shepherd, grumbling at being cheated of biting off one detective's nose and the general mauling of another, was locked in the kitchen and as Glenda Jamieson trailed after the officers, she added, 'Look all yer like, mate, you won't find nuffin' 'ere,' and it appeared she was quite correct. Not one single item of stolen property could be found; nor was there any trace of Jamieson. Not until Barker climbed into the loft and found him there, covered in dust.

CID offices were traditionally situated on the first floor of the police station, in the interests of security. Access to the office, where suspects were interviewed, was gained by a flight of stairs, which were also handy for recalcitrant suspects to fall down. However, Jamieson admitted absolutely nothing. In fact, the case against him was pretty thin. There was the circumstantial evidence that Marion Bettingham's appointments book, to which he had access, had contained the addresses of the burgled premises but not one scrap of stolen property had been found and Jamieson had left no traces at the various scenes which could be detected by a forensic examination. But, on the plus side, Marion had provided an impressive statement regarding the finding of Jamieson with the stolen property and was quite resolute regarding giving evidence about that aspect of the case, in addition to her later mistreatment by him.

So Jamieson was charged with kidnap, grievous bodily harm and the most recent burglary and was remanded in custody, to await his trial at the Old Bailey. Since at that time no Victims' Support Units existed, Detective Constable Alan Barker frequently visited Marion Bettingham to ensure her well-being whilst his counterpart, Jim Evans, ensured that every possible scrap of evidence was meticulously collated.

Even without his already impressive amount of form, Jamieson knew that if he was convicted, even the most benign judge would ensure that he would be locked up and the key thrown away. Therefore, what was required was a result. Apart from concocting a defence for him, Jamieson's weasel solicitors had instructed a former police officer, who now ran an investigation agency, to dig the dirt on Marion. Derek Jimson liked to describe himself as being 'formerly of Scotland Yard' and given that he had spent a considerable time as a uniform constable in the Yard's Information Room, this description was factually correct. But as a uniform station sergeant, he had been called upon to be a 'bag carrier' to chief inspectors carrying out internal investigations. Seeing his colleagues squirming as they were questioned about possible breaches of the discipline code was very much to Jimson's liking. So now, he spent much of his time snooping around the contents of other people's dustbins (his former contemporaries unkindly commented that not much had changed *there*, then) and he had managed to discover that Marion, a reasonably highly sexed young woman, had had several lovers before Jamieson came on the scene. Next, Jamieson's solicitors sought the services of Sir Lionel Thompson as his defence counsel, a barrister well-known for his blustering, bellowing attack on witnesses and also any prosecuting counsel or judge who might be obstreperous enough to challenge his authority. Sir Lionel did not let his client down; he tore into the wretched Marion, accusing her of completely fabricating her evidence since it was she who had masterminded the entire series of burglaries. When Sir Lionel brayed that since she had been so free with her sexual favours it could be (and probably had been) any of her erstwhile lovers who had perpetrated the burglaries; providing, he added with a sneer, that they could be persuaded to vacate her bed, Marion was reduced to tears.

The jury did not take very long at all to acquit Jamieson of all charges. They probably would not have acquitted him any quicker had they known that Detective Constable Alan Barker had been enthusiastically shagging Marion during his benevolent visits ever since Jamieson's arrest, although knowledge of Barker's nocturnal calls might well have resulted in his advancement in the CID being severely curtailed. But of course, neither Jamieson nor anybody else was aware of this and such was his pleasure at being so providentially released, had he known of those circumstances at that moment, Jamieson could not have cared less. As he trudged up the steps from the cell block, holding his plastic bag of possessions, he encountered

Detective Constable Jim Evans. 'No hard feelings, eh, mate?' he grinned, holding out his hand. 'I mean, who'd believe a slag like that?'

'Shut up, Ian,' replied Evans equably, ignoring the outstretched hand. 'Just mind how you go. I assure you, I will.' With that he turned on his heel and walked off. Jamieson smirked at his retreating back.

Within weeks, Jamieson brutally raped Marion; well, she was nothing more than a slut – Sir Lionel had said so – and with his sociopath's twisted logic, decided she deserved it for telling those lies to Old Bill, lies which had been utterly rejected by the jury. Marion tearfully reported the rape to Jim Evans but before he could even call the Divisional Surgeon to carry out a medical examination, she retracted the allegation. She simply could not face the thought of attending the Old Bailey once again to be utterly humiliated by the likes of Sir Lionel Thompson. So used and abused, poor Marion, feeling irredeemably worthless, left the Greater London Area and moved far away. Jamieson now felt that he could practically walk on water. He returned to his profession of screwsman but now he was so confident that he left significant clues behind at two of the burglaries. Evans nabbed him and saw him sentenced to four years' imprisonment; a fraction of what he should have received but, as Evans would later philosophically comment, better than a kick in the arse.

But of course, all that was in the future. Now, Jamieson stepped out on to the pavement outside the Old Bailey and blinked at the sunshine which had been denied him during the last four months. He grinned and winked at a pretty girl who walked by. And then, Jamieson started to chuckle and next, he laughed out loud. Passers-by turned and stared at the young man clutching the plastic bag who was laughing uproariously. He couldn't help it. He was thinking back to the time of his arrest, when he was grabbed by Alan Barker in the loft and lowered to the ground. Glenda, his estranged wife, who had been vociferously informing the officers that she hadn't seen him in months, looked up. ''Ere!' she exclaimed in outraged tones. 'What're you doing in my loft, you slag?'

Petermen

There has always been something irresistible about petermen, those who unlawfully open safes, with or without the use of explosives. The public warmed to safebreakers, perhaps because there seemed to be something daring about the crime, something perhaps reminiscent of E.W. Hornung's Raffles or Leslie Charteris' Simon Templar, aka the Saint. Perhaps it was because the public thought that even if the owners of the money couldn't afford the loss, at least it would be covered by insurance, and perhaps it was because usually nobody was hurt. Except the night watchman, of course, who got a crack over the head.

Now, of course, safe jobs rarely occur. The safe manufacturers constructed safes that jammed if attempts were made to blow them, alarms got better and more sophisticated and when petermen started using thermic lances, they discovered that these did open the safes but also incinerated any money that was inside. But, at one time, petermen were regarded as rather glamorous characters. Men, for instance, like Johnny Ramensky.

Born in 1905, Ramensky was the son of a Lithuanian immigrant who became a coal miner. After his father died, young Ramensky also went to work in the pits and it was there that he developed his skill with handling dynamite. Together with his widowed mother and two sisters, Ramensky moved to the tough Gorbals district of Glasgow during the depression. A thief from the age of eleven, Ramensky developed tremendous physical strength and agility and these attributes, together with his skill with explosives, were put to good use cracking safes.

He served a considerable amount of time in Barlinnie and Peterhead prisons. In fact, he spent over forty of his sixty-seven years behind bars and made his first escape in 1934, after the prison authorities refused him permission to attend his wife's funeral.

But it was in 1942, when he was serving a further prison sentence that he was given an irresistible offer by the Army – blow open safes in the service of his country. After commando training, he was infiltrated into enemy-held territory where he blew open safes in order to steal German documents. When he entered Rome, he managed to blow open the safes of no less than fourteen foreign embassies, all within the space of one day. In recognition of his wartime service, Ramensky was awarded the Military Medal and a free pardon. Unfortunately, his war service had honed his already outstanding safeblowing skills and before long, he was back to his old occupation where recognition was not in the form of decorations but long periods of incarceration. In 1955, he was sentenced to ten years' preventative detention. To highlight his lack of privileges, he escaped, was recaptured and escaped again – on five occasions.

He sustained severe injuries at the age of sixty-five when he fell, attempting to break into the County Buildings in Stirling and was serving what would be his last sentence in Perth Prison in 1972 when he collapsed and died.

The Scots loved Ramensky. *The Ballad of Johnny Ramensky* (with quite incredible lyrics) was composed and his obituary appeared in the Scottish press.

Another character who caught the public's imagination was Eddie Chapman, mainly because of a film, *Triple Cross* (1967) starring Christopher Plummer and Yul Brynner, which allegedly depicted his wartime exploits.

Edward Arnold Chapman was born in 1914 in County Durham. Enlisting with, and then deserting from, the Coldstream Guards, Chapman commenced his career as a safebreaker by prising the back off a very old riveted safe in the Fyffes banana factory. But he soon formed a gang of safeblowers and, using gelignite stolen from quarries, he concentrated on the rather basic safes which were used by the Odeon Cinema chain, all over the country. Chapman's method was this: he would tie the office typewriter to the handle of the safe. Using just a few grammes of gelignite with a detonator, inserted into a condom, he pushed this into the keyhole, then tamped it in place with chewing gum. The very small explosion which followed pushed everything momentarily outwards and it was sufficient to lift the levers restraining the bolt mechanism. The weight of the typewriter was enough to turn the mechanism, thereby opening the safe. Using this simple, foolproof method, Chapman was responsible for approximately forty successful safeblowings. It was not too long before Detective Inspector Ted Greeno of the Yard's Flying Squad was on his trail. That enormously tough and highly unorthodox detective was looking to pin about ten years' preventative detention on Chapman, who promptly skipped to the Channel Island of Jersey. There, he was caught blowing a safe, sentenced to two years' imprisonment and when war was declared and the Germans marched in, Chapman took very little time in offering his services to them. It was an offer that was accepted by the *Abwehr* (German Military Intelligence), who flew him to Germany where he was codenamed 'Fritz' and trained in radio transmissions and sabotage. Parachuted into Cambridgeshire with instructions to blow up the De Havilland factory, the home of the Mosquito aircraft, Chapman walked into the nearest police station and demanded to surrender to Detective Superintendent Len Burt from whom he could expect 'fair treatment'. It is difficult to say whether or not this was the true reason, or because he had a shrewd idea that Greeno would award him a punch in the face if he expressed recalcitrance at confessing his misdeeds or – and this is far more likely – because he knew that Burt had been seconded to MI5 as a lieutenant-colonel. In any event, it was MI5 who recruited him as a double agent (code-named 'Zig-Zag') and when the conjuror Jasper Maskelyne camouflaged the De Havilland factory so convincingly that German reconnaissance planes were able to report the factory had been totally destroyed, upon his return to Germany, he was awarded the Iron Cross and given 110,000 *Reichmarks*. He was sent to teach at a spy school in Oslo but after the allied landings, the *Abwehr* returned him to England to report on the effect of the V1 and V2 weapons.

Chapman had had enough. He disingenuously told his MI5 handlers that he had confessed to his Norwegian girlfriend that he was working as a double-agent and, not being able to prove or disprove this, they considered that if he had been compromised, it would have been too dangerous to allow him to return. After the war, Chapman was granted a bounty of £6,000, permitted to keep £1,000 of the money given to him by the Germans and given a free pardon for his pre-war crimes.

After the war, Chapman was involved in a cigarette smuggling operation with Billy Hill and others in Tangiers. He was fined for breaching the Official Secrets Act, after his wartime exploits, *Ma Fantastique Histoire* was serialized in a French newspaper and although the authorities attempted to stop him from doing so, *The Real Eddie Chapman Story* was published, followed by his post-war experiences, *Free Agent – Being the Further Adventures of Eddie Chapman*. The first book led to the production of the film, *Triple Cross* and with the fee he received for his assistance with the film, Chapman set up a health farm. He died in 1997.

But Chapman was a user, a manipulator. Before his war service, he had a number of affairs with London's society women, had compromising photographs taken by an accomplice and then blackmailed them. On one occasion he passed on a venereal disease to a young woman and then blackmailed her, telling her that unless she paid up, he would inform her parents that it was *her* who had infected *him*.

The MI5 officer probably had it about right when he wrote, 'Chapman loved himself, loved adventure and loved his country; probably in that order.'

At round about the time that Eddie Chapman was putting the finishing touches to *The Real Eddie Chapman Story*, another peterman had been industriously at work. The man I shall refer to as Derek Hallam was, like Ramensky and Chapman before him, an expert in his field. Much of his work was carried out in the north of England. Rather than insert gelignite in the safe's lock, Hallam would tip the safe on its front and blow out the back and achieved a remarkable amount of success using this method. Being exceptionally good looking, he also attracted the same degree of success in catching the attention of beautiful women. And last, but by no means least, he was also exceptionally violent.

On one occasion, Hallam had forsworn his usual trade or calling and had opted for common or garden smash and grab. His companion, a stunningly attractive top fashion model, Audrey Ward, looked at Hallam with barely controlled excitement as he got out of his estate car, and smashed a pickaxe handle into the window of a large electrical store. Helping himself to a selection of televisions and other expensive electrical goods, Hallam packed the boot of the car with the goods and drove off at high speed. By a deeply unfortunate coincidence, the whole episode was witnessed by Billy Turner and his girlfriend, Mavis, who rushed to the nearest police station to tell the desk sergeant exactly what they had seen, together with the registration number of the car; best of all they had recognized the perpetrator as Derek Hallam, and they knew his current address.

Police Constable Roger Simon and his companion found the car, loaded up with stolen property, right outside Hallam's address. Rather than crash into his address there and then, and risk Hallam later alleging in court that someone had obviously nicked his car to do the shopbreaking and then left it outside his house to thoroughly compromise him, PC Simon decided to keep watch on the car instead.

'I don't care if it takes three fucking days,' he whispered to his companion. 'We're going to catch this bastard bang to rights.'

In fact, it took less than an hour for Hallam and the fashion model to emerge from the house and head for the car. As Hallam got into the car, PC Simon rushed forward.

'Hallam, I'm arresting you for breaking and entering—' and that was as far as he got.

'Get in the car and lock the door!' Hallam shouted to his companion, who did just that. PC Simon made a spirited attempt to snatch the keys from the ignition, without success. As the engine roared into life, PC Simon stood in front of the car, his arms raised, secure in the knowledge that, vicious though he was, not even Hallam would be stupid enough to drive straight at a uniformed constable. Of course, he was wrong. The front bumper smashed into his legs, just below the knees and as he crashed to the roadway, Hallam drove straight over the constable. Incredibly, Simon was not seriously hurt, although Hallam was not to know this. Stopping the car, he reversed at Simon, now on his hands and knees and smashed into him before driving off at speed. The car was found abandoned, still with the stolen load intact, some distance away.

Police officers tend to get a little uncharitable towards those who try to kill their colleagues and the balloon went up. A city-wide search was carried out and Hallam was arrested the following day in Nottingham as he tried to board a bus bound for Birmingham. It is difficult to fully comprehend what happened next. Charged with the most serious of offences, plus the shopbreaking, Hallam, who had just finished a ten year sentence for almost killing a night-watchman with a shovel, appeared before the local Magistrates' Court and was promptly given bail. Although that might cause you some astonishment, it will come as no surprise at all to learn that Hallam promptly went on the run.

Seven months went by before he was caught. Hallam had not been idle, having ventured down to London where he committed a whole string of robberies and safeblowings before he was caught by a couple of aids to CID. PC Simon, his colleague and his two witnesses went to Bow Street Magistrates' Court, from where Hallam was committed, this time in custody, to stand his trial at the Old Bailey.

Hallam admitted nothing; not the attempted murder of PC Simon, nor one of the twelve robberies and safeblowings with which he had been charged. The evidence was overwhelming, so much so that the jury refused to retire and found Hallam guilty of everything, there and then. After complimenting PC Simon for his courage and fortitude, the judge sentenced Hallam to another ten-year stretch.

PC Simon went down into the cell area to restore some personal property belonging to Hallam. Apparently unfazed at the thought of doing another ten, back-to-back, Hallam said softly, 'I'll do my ten years and, after that, you'll spend the rest of your life looking over your shoulder. One day, I'll be standing behind you and on that day, you'll be dead. I failed to kill you last time. Next time, I'll finish the job.'

'That is,' replied PC Simon, 'if I don't see you first.'

So Hallam went off to Dartmoor and PC Simon collected a gallantry award and ten years passed before they met again. As Detective Sergeant Simon, as he now was, walked into his local police station in Nottingham, he saw a man speaking at the counter whose voice he recognized. As the man finished his conversation and stepped away from the counter, so Sergeant Simon grasped him warmly by the throat. 'Time to settle up, Derek,' said Simon, genially. 'I think we've got some unfinished business.'

And then Simon released his grip. Although he and Hallam were the same age, he was looking into the face of an old, old man. Hallam, his good looks gone, his hair greasy and grey, was now devoid of menace. Two, almost consecutive, ten-year sentences had broken him.

'Leave it out, Guv,' muttered Hallam. 'That was just said in the spur of the moment. I've finished with all that now. Fancy a drink?'

Simon's reply was extremely rude and dismissive and Hallam shuffled out of the station. His remarks had been over-heard by the uniform sergeant to whom Hallam had been speaking.

'Bit rude, weren't you?' he said, reprovingly. 'Know him, do you? Didn't seem a bad bloke to me. Just came in to see if we had a list of bed and breakfast places. Seemed fairly friendly to me.'

Simon privately thought that the sergeant was a drip and far too young to hold such a responsible rank. He was unaware that in time to come, the injuries which Hallam had inflicted would turn into osteo-arthritis which would result in him being discharged from the service prematurely. But, just then, he felt hugely disinclined to explain to the twerp of a sergeant the full circumstances of his and Hallam's last encounter.

'Yeah, he's quite an amusing bloke,' he commented, briefly. 'He pulled my leg, once.'

A Family Affair

In the East End of London, before World War Two, it was quite common for families to live in close proximity to each other. Sometimes, they all lived in the same rented accommodation or, if not, certainly in the same street. Children of the East End grew up, addressing neighbours, who were quite unrelated to them by marriage, as 'Uncle' and 'Auntie' and, in the fullness of time, the children who had formed friendships when they were at school, grew up and were married. And when this happened where the children were members of criminal families, the ties between the two families could often grow stronger through this alliance. Or not, as the case might be.

Two such families were the Arnolds and the Levetts. The heads of each of the respective families had been born in the 1930s. Harry Arnold had been trouble from the start and very soon found himself completing his education at Approved School. From there, a miserable series of appearances at Juvenile Court followed, mainly for malicious damage, assault and larceny from telephone kiosks until he progressed to warehousebreaking, which brought him into the first division of juvenile delinquency with a sentence of Borstal Training. Following his release, he managed to get a job as a van driver and also get Ann Levett, a year his junior, pregnant. When Ann's parents discovered her delicate condition, it was only the fact that Harry Arnold expressed a willingness to marry her, plus the fact that he had a steady job with which to support his young family, that saved him from harm and certain long-term animosity between the two families.

Bill Levett had a few juvenile convictions to his credit, mainly for fighting, before being called up for National Service with the Royal Engineers. But he enjoyed Army life so much he signed on for a nine-year engagement and decided to channel his aggression by volunteering for selection with the newly reconstituted Special Air Service. He saw active service in Malaya and Aden and, after demobilization, Levett, by now a very tough customer indeed, was employed as a Ford worker, and got married. This was after his sister, Ann was found to be 'in the family way' and Harry Arnold's agreement to 'do the right thing' was considered by everybody to be an exceptionally sensible course of action.

Twenty-three years later, the first of the fruits of the loins of Harry and Ann Arnold was a thorough-going pain in the arse to the law. Stephen Arnold's speciality was stealing cars, ringing them and selling them for a handsome profit. Not that this had been an easy road he'd travelled; he had been nicked time and again and on the last occasion that he had been caught with stolen car parts in his workshop, he had copped fifteen months for it. But now, in an eighteen-month period, he had had his workshop turned over no less than five times and on each occasion the law had gone away empty-handed, Arnold's jeering laughter ringing in their ears. This was nothing less than reckless behaviour because the police are as human as anybody else and they do not like to be mocked.

Stephen Arnold pushed his luck a little further. He would drive around Chigwell in his gleaming 3 Series BMW, one which was completely straight and paid for. He particularly liked driving past the entrance of the Metropolitan Police Sports

Club. It was his way of showing his contempt for the law; that, and signing on for his unemployment giro every other Tuesday.

Years before, Stephen Arnold would have admiringly been referred to as a 'wide boy' by his peers; now, he was known as a 'diamond geezer'. He had a smart, detached house in Chigwell and a pretty, if fairly scatty, young wife. And his income, although the tax and VAT man were both unaware of it, was around £20,000 per month; fairly healthy money for the 1980s.

His business was, of course, dealing in stolen cars. At this time, the public could not get enough of certain of the Ford range; XR2s and XR3is, especially the Cabriolet model, all of which were selling over book price. Arnold made it his business to satisfy the need. This is how he did it.

Arnold would visit the scrap yards which are many and various all around east London and he would buy up scrap XR3is. Some of these had been sold as salvage or as vehicles capable of being rebuilt. Others had been sold as scrap where the bodywork and the mechanics had been so badly damaged that it would not be viable to rebuild the vehicle but where the component parts could be used to repair other similar vehicles.

But it was scrap that Arnold wanted for three reasons and three reasons only; the registration number, the VIN (Vehicle Identification Number) which was riveted inside the engine compartment and the chassis number which was stamped into the driver's footwell, underneath the carpet. The scrap would then be delivered on a low-loader to his lock-up garage, close to Barking Creek, where Arnold would carefully remove the VIN plate and cut out the chassis number. Once that was done, Arnold would break up the rest of the scrap and sell it on as spare parts to various second-hand spares outlets at knock-down prices; the remaining scrap would be sold on to another salvage yard and, due to its condition, was usually crushed for scrap metal.

What Arnold was doing was not dishonest. Certainly, it was suspect but not, at this stage, illegal. That was about to change.

Arnold next got his younger sister, Angie, to send off the log book to the DVLA, saying that she had purchased the car, was going to use it on the road and pay for six months' Road Fund Licence. In fairness, he filled the form in for her and simply said, 'Sign there.'

And that was the first part of the operation completed.

Stephen Arnold's associate, Mick Walker, was an expert car thief; the vehicle did not exist that he was unable to gain entry to and start up within seconds. Apart from being of enormous assistance to Arnold, he was also much in demand by teams of blaggers. Walker's instructions were to go out and nick a Ford Escort XR3i and, having done so, drop it off at a lock-up, quite separate from Arnold's other lock-up and one which, to all intents and purposes, was quite unconnected with him. Then it was the job of Stuart Grinham to spend the next few days in the lock-up, carefully removing the stolen car's engine number with a grinder, as well as the VIN plate and the chassis number. Next, it was a simple matter for Grinham to re-stamp the scrap car's engine number in the appropriate place, for which Arnold had handed him a set of genuine Ford number and letter stamps. With the techniques available in those days, it was impossible to trace the original engine number underneath the new number and once some gritty grease was rubbed in, this would certainly pass basic inspection. Next, the VIN plate would be super-glued into place, with the original rivets intact, so as to give the plate an 'original' appearance. Last, the cut-out chassis number would be secured into the donor hole using a combination of packing material, body filler and a 'blow-over' of matching body paint.

If a police officer from the Metropolitan Police Stolen Vehicle Unit had inspected this vehicle, given the scientific techniques which they possessed at that time (matters are somewhat different now), he would have come to the conclusion that yes, the vehicle was probably stolen. However, if he could not prove the original identity of the vehicle, he could not prove theft. It would appear that Arnold & Co. had the perfect car-ringing business.

So now the car could be removed from the lock-up and brought to Arnold's sister's house in Woodford, just down the road from him. She had recently broken up with her worthless husband and she needed some money. She got it. Angie placed advertisements for these cars in the local newspaper. The price would be pitched slightly lower than the trade price, which made the car almost irresistible to the prospective buyers. When Angie sighed and mentioned that she was forced to sell because her husband had run off with another woman – or that her husband had just been made redundant and one of their cars had to go – or that her husband had just got a new job which came with a company car – the punters could hardly wait to thrust a banker's draft into her hand.

Angie was selling approximately four cars per month, at £5,000 per time, although, given her persuasive skills, she could, had it been possible, have sold ten cars per night. So the banker's draft would be paid into her bank, it would be cleared by special arrangement and the money would be withdrawn in cash. This, minus her cut, would be handed to her brother who had set up an off-shore shell company with a bank account in the name of the company.

However, the police, as I have said, do not care to be mocked by cocky little yobs. One of Angie's neighbours, fed up with the number of cars coming and going to and from her house complained to the local police. As luck would have it, an officer who had previously served at the station and was now attached to the Stolen Vehicle Unit was in the station when the call came in and immediately took an interest when the telephonist mentioned that he was aware that the person complained of was none other than Stephen Arnold's sister.

Every vehicle that Angie had sold was traced and was called in for an inspection. The police were looking, of course, for evidence that the vehicle was stolen but that was not all. Before the insurance companies had written-off the vehicles, they had photographed them and the police investigators were now comparing the damage from the accident with the condition of the vehicle bearing that identification. Not one of the vehicles examined revealed any sign of the repairs which would have been needed on the original car. It was high time for Stephen Arnold and Angie to receive a 'six o'clock knock'.

Both were brought into separate police stations and interviewed. Stephen Arnold, due to his pedigree said nothing at all; Angie, not so worldly wise, burst into tears and said she'd, 'only been selling cars for Steve, as a favour.' Both were bailed whilst further enquiries were carried out.

There was enormous consternation in the Arnold household and Ann Arnold tearfully sought solace from her brother, Bill Levett. He and his wife had been childless but Bill had always been particularly fond of his niece, Angie. He regarded Stephen as a thoroughgoing little shit and he made no attempt to disguise it. The Special Air Service had instilled in Levett a strong sense of physical fitness, and although he was almost fifty he was a formidable personality. Absolutely no nonsense was tolerated at the boys' boxing club which he ran in his spare time and he worked-out at every possible opportunity. He had been half-listening to the account given by his obnoxious nephew when his head suddenly jerked-up.

'Yeah, that DS Streeton, he don't know nothin'' Stephen Arnold had sneered. ''Im and his daft questions—'

'Streeton?' interrupted Levett. 'Not Bob Streeton?'

Arnold was surprised at Levett's contribution to the discourse. 'Er – I dunno, Uncle Bill,' he replied. 'Big bloke, like you. About your age, an' all. A bit of his ear missing. Why?'

Levett ignored him. 'I want a word with you, Ann,' he said to his sister and he pushed her wheelchair into the hallway. She was suffering from multiple sclerosis which had advanced at an astonishing rate. 'Not you,' he added, as her husband started to follow them. 'I dunno if I can do anything,' he said to her, quietly. 'If I can, I'll only be able to do something for Angie. Not him.' He jerked his head contemptuously in the direction of the lounge and Ann Arnold needed no interpretation as to 'him' might be. 'He gets whatever's coming to him. Right?'

Ann Arnold nodded her head, dumbly. The last time she had seen her brother like this was when he had come home from Aden, all those years ago. It would not have been advisable for her or anybody else to have crossed him just then.

Two nights later, Levett and Detective Sergeant Bob Streeton were having a glass in a pub in Epping. 'Well, I'll tell you what the score is, Bill; it won't do any harm, because it's going to happen anyway,' said Streeton. 'Your nephew is sewn-up, tight. Because we can't strictly prove those cars are stolen, he and your niece will be charged with conspiracy to cheat and defraud. All the evidence is there. I don't suppose they'll say a word when they're brought back in and they don't have to. The evidence is all there, bank accounts, everything. You've got to look at both of them going away for this. Him longer than her, of course, but in my experience, both of them going away.'

Bill Levett nodded his battered head, slowly. 'Can anything – anything – be done, Bob?'

'Nothing.'

Levett expected nothing less, but it had to be tried. 'Another Scotch, Bob?'

'Please,' replied Streeton, 'and then I'll have to be on my way.'

With two fresh glasses on the table, Levett looked shrewdly at Streeton. 'Bob, that fucking Stephen's got to go for this, that's obvious. He's been taking the piss for too long and he's well overdue, I know that. But if you could drop the girl – Angie – out, I'd appreciate it.'

Streeton sighed. 'I don't see as how I can, Bill.'

'It's just that I thought that if you could see her as a bit of a dupe, you know, just helping her brother out, sort of thing, she could be dropped out.'

As Streeton drew in his breath to reject the offer, Levett continued, 'Of course, you couldn't do that for nothing. I thought perhaps that things would be different if that Stephen stuck his hands up to everything and named the rest of the team.'

'Well . . .' replied Streeton.

'Plus, of course,' interjected Levett, 'they'd have to stick their hands up as well. Naturally.'

'If you could arrange all that, so that we could charge them all with theft,' replied Streeton, 'I think we could regard the girl as a prosecution witness. A prosecution witness who, of course, would never be called as a witness. Not if you were right, of course. Not if everyone else pleaded at court.'

'When do they come back to the nick?' asked Levett.

'This Friday morning,' answered Streeton.

Levett stood up and shook hands with Streeton. 'Take care, Bob.'

On the Thursday night, the night before Stephen Arnold and his sister were due to answer bail, Mick Walker and Stuart

Grinham received a peremptory summons, via Arnold, for the three of them to go to Bill Levett's boys' boxing club. The last of the boys had finished their training and had just left before their arrival.

'Right, listen up you lot,' said Levett. 'You three have been taking the piss, big time. Not that I particularly object but now my niece is involved and I ain't going to see her dragged down by you cunts. So tomorrow, the three of you are going to Woodford nick together, and you're going to stick your hands up to what you've been up to. Is that clear? Good, right, fuck off, then.'

Stephen Arnold knew, from what his mother had hinted about what happened with his uncle in Aden, that it would be a prudent move to do exactly as he said. The other two were not quite so easily convinced.

'You, what?' scoffed Walker.

'I think you must 'ave lost it, mate,' sighed Grinham and of the two comments Grinham's was the most inflammatory. Levett hit him right in the solar plexus so hard and so fast that he went skidding across the floor, on his arse, before being stopped by the wall. Even before he was halfway en route to the wall, Levett had seized hold of Walker in a crippling wrist-lock and dragged him with very little effort over to where Grinham was gasping for breath. Levett forced Walker down to the ground so that he was sitting next to his accomplice, keeping the excruciating pressure on his wrist.

'I don't think you quite understand what I've been saying,' he said quietly. 'But first, I'm going to tell you what I did to a whole Arab village once. And when you've heard me out, just think what it'd be like if that happened to your mums and dads, your brothers and sisters, even your fucking pet hamster. Because unless you see a little sense, that's exactly what's going to happen.'

In 1964, 3 Troop of the Special Air Service's A Squadron, on patrol in Aden, was ambushed. The patrol's leader, Captain Edwards and Trooper Warburton were both killed by rebels, beheaded and their heads were exultantly paraded on poles. A few weeks later, the remainder of A Squadron returned to the United Kingdom. What was not generally known was that a suitable revenge was extracted.

Over twenty years later, in a dingy, rather damp-smelling boys' boxing club, one of those soldiers from A Squadron told two little shits, named Stuart Grinham and Mick Walker terrible things that had happened all those years ago, in a country far away. He recounted matters so graphically that Walker imagined he could hear the howls of the dogs, the screams of the dying, the mothers begging for mercy for their children and Grinham imagined he could smell the smoke before the tents, the flames licking around them, crashed to the flinty soil in a shower of sparks.

'So have we got an understanding, lads?' Levett asked, as he pulled the two white-faced car thieves to their feet. They nodded, fiercely. 'Good. I don't expect to see you again, then.' He paused. 'If I have to, things'll be . . .' He paused, as though he was searching for the right word. Finally, he said, 'Unpleasant.'

He pushed Walker and Grisham towards the door. 'Stephen,' he called. 'Come here.' Arnold, his cockiness evaporated, shuffled over to his uncle. 'Right, I've never liked you and I'm not having your mum upset anymore than's necessary. You're going to stick your hands up to this, do your bird and then you get out of the area. And whatever you do in the future, I couldn't care less about, but whatever it is, you don't involve your sister in it. Understand?'

'Yes, Uncle Bill.'

The judge at Snaresbrook Crown Court told the three that

he was giving them credit for admitting their guilt to the police at the earliest opportunity and for pleading guilty and asking for a substantial number of offences to be taken into consideration, but Stephen Arnold, as the ringleader, had to go to prison for three years. Walker, the car thief, received thirty months and Grinham, two years.

Although East End families could grow stronger through marriage, this was not the case between the Levetts and the Arnolds. Ann Arnold died shortly after her son was released from prison and, after the funeral, the families never met or even spoke, again.

Some things are sometimes stronger than families. The Special Air Service Regimental Association, for instance, of which Bill Levett and Bob Streeton were both members. After the conversation in the pub and the subsequent somewhat surprising triple confessions, Streeton reckoned that he could afford a little leeway when it came to Bill Levett's niece – such as dropping her right out of the frame as the fourth defendant. After all, when he'd passed out after a bullet from a rebel's rifle had shot away part of his ear, all those years ago in Aden, it had been Bill Levett who'd carried him back from that blazing village to their own lines.

Last Orders, Gents, Please!

In the early 1980s, two heavily built and thuggish-looking gentlemen descended on the rural Kent countryside and before too much comment could be made as to their somewhat distinctive appearance – because shaven heads, dark shades, black suits and an excess of gold around the neck, wrists and fingers were not the norm in the picturesque village of Hever – they made their way to a local, quaint-looking pub. One of them placed a carrier bag full of used notes on the counter, together with a contract of sale, and the other informed the landlord that it would be in his best interests if he picked up the former and signed the latter.

The landlord did so. He was then informed that, as a sign of good faith, he should pack up and vacate the premises within forty-eight hours. That too was complied with. The pub then closed for two weeks whilst certain alterations were carried out. When it re-opened the bar and the restaurant had been redecorated in a way not really in keeping with a rural, English village. That was not all that had changed. Some new rules had been introduced.

Within a very short time of the pub's re-opening, the first customer stepped through the door. He had lived in the village all his life and had recently sold his ironmongery store. Since this pub was his local, he decided to introduce himself to the new landlord, gracefully accept a courtesy drink and have a brief chat about the village and its occupants. He did not even get to first base.

'Oi, you – fuck off – you're barred.'

The former ironmonger stopped in his tracks and looked behind him, to see who the bulky, menacing person in front of him was talking to. There was no one behind him. The stocky figure actually was addressing him.

'I said, fuck off out of here,' said the man with the south London accent. 'You, mate, are fucking barred, so go and tell the rest of them Swedes they're fucking barred as well. I ain't having you in here – understand?'

Yes, the prospective customer did understand. He turned on his heel and left and lost no time in passing the pronouncement on to his fellow villagers.

The name of the new landlord was George Francis. Behind the acquisition of the pub was a syndicate of south London gangsters, who wanted a smart place to wine and dine their wives and girlfriends, away from the sharp ears of Flying Squad narks – or those belonging to the locals. Francis had a chequered history behind him and was due to experience an interesting future.

He had been born in 1940 and had a series of convictions for theft and violence. He claimed acquaintance with the Krays (but didn't everybody?), some regarded him as an enthusiastic receiver of stolen lorry-loads and others as a grass. Just about everyone accepted that he had a finger in any number of dishonest pies but he next came to notice following the events of 20 October 1979.

'Operation Wrecker' was a Customs and Excise operation, regarding the importation of two-and-a-half million pounds' worth of cannabis resin from Pakistan. Specially converted containers had been sent to a shoe factory in Pakistan where the cannabis was shipped back to the United Kingdom; a scheme which had worked perfectly on four occasions. But on the fifth occasion, when the surveillance team was spotted by the gang, customs officers moved in and one of them, Peter Bennett, was shot in the stomach and died. The man responsible, Lenny 'Teddy Bear' Watkins was later sentenced to life imprisonment for the murder and committed suicide whilst serving his sentence at Long Lartin Prison. George Francis was one of those who stood trial for the cannabis plot and, feeling hugely disinclined to stand the risk of copping a not insubstantial amount of bird, spoke to a certain, notorious north London family. As a result, it has been suggested that £100,000 was promised to ensure that the jury at the Old Bailey was nobbled. Well, whether they were straightened out or not, at any event the jury was unable to agree and a re-trial was ordered. This time, Francis was acquitted. Others of the team pleaded guilty. One of them was the Krays' henchman, Freddie Foreman, who was sentenced to two years' imprisonment.

Following the success of the previous four cannabis runs, the team had celebrated in south London pubs, where they lit their cigars with £20 notes. Working on the dictum that one cannot expect to blush unseen, it could well be that this was the reason for the acquisition of the pub in Hever, where the ostentatious lighting of cigars could be carried out in comparative safety.

The next time that Francis came to the attention of the police was after half a dozen armed men entered the Brink's-Mat depot at Hounslow on 26 November 1982. They overpowered and handcuffed the guards, poured petrol over the genitals of two of them, to help them remember the combination for the vault and then grabbed three and a half tonnes of gold, valued at £26,369,778. The company had been betrayed by Tony Black, an inside agent, who was later sentenced to six years' imprisonment in recognition for identifying members of the gang and, later, giving evidence against them. Within weeks, Mickey McAvoy, Brian Robinson and others were arrested and charged with the robbery but little of the gold was found. McAvoy and Robinson were the only two, out of the six men involved, to be convicted of the robbery and they were both sentenced to twenty-five years' imprisonment.

One of the people suspected of handling the gold was Kenneth Noye. His comings and goings were noted and he was arrested after he stabbed an undercover police officer to death when he was keeping observation on Noye at his home. Noye was acquitted after he claimed that stabbing Detective Constable John Fordham five times in the front, three times in the back and once each in his armpit and head was self-defence. However, eleven gold bars were found at his home, he was later convicted of dishonestly handling the Brink's-Mat gold and was sentenced to a total of fourteen years' imprisonment.

It was believed that Francis had extensively laundered the proceeds of the robbery but although his garden was dug up and he was questioned by police, he gave away nothing. Not only that, he had also been slow in paying a large amount of his jury-nobbling fee.

In May 1985 an unwelcome visitor burst into Francis' pub in Hever, and before Francis had a chance to tell him that he, too, was barred, the hooded man shot him at close range in the shoulder, using a 9mm pistol. It was a lesson learnt; Francis duly settled the debt.

However, the nobblers decided not to assist Francis again; in August 1990, he was found guilty of smuggling one million pounds' worth of cocaine and was sentenced to sixteen years' imprisonment.

It was widely held that Francis – who was released after ten years – had held on to the money which represented the proceeds of the Brinks Mat robbery, together with another man, named Brian Perry. The police believed that Perry had been one of the six Brinks Mat robbers, but there had been insufficient evidence to charge him. There had also been insufficient evidence to bring charges against Perry after it was strongly suspected that he had endeavoured to intimidate witnesses at McAvoy's trial. And when police received information that both Perry and Francis were arranging a helicopter to spring McAvoy from prison, no action was taken since to do so would have thoroughly compromised their sources.

There was, however, sufficient evidence to arrest and charge Perry with conspiracy to handle the stolen gold, an offence for which, in 1992, he was sentenced to nine years' imprisonment.

What had happened to the Brink's-Mat gold? Some of it was smelted at a company named Scadlynn who sold it back to Johnson Matthey, from whom it had been originally obtained. Scadlynn's director, Garth Chappell was sentenced to ten years' imprisonment for conspiracy to handle the gold, and Brian Reader, described by the trial judge as Noye's 'vigorous right hand man', received nine years. It was strongly suspected that quite a lot of it had been smelted by one Saul 'Solly' Nahome, a Hatton Garden jeweller who had emigrated to England from Burma in 1961. He was regarded by the police as a specialist in fraud and money laundering but, if this was true, Nahome took the secrets to the grave with him. As the forty-eight-year-old jeweller got out of his car on 27 November 1998 and walked towards his house in Arden Road, Finchley, he was shot four times. His killer escaped on a motorcycle.

Nick Whiting, a close associate of Noye was another who was suspected of laundering the proceeds of the robbery. He was abducted in June 1990; his body was later found dumped on Rainham Marshes. He had been stabbed nine times and shot twice, with a 9mm pistol.

Over the years, recovery for the gold has vigorously been pursued through the civil courts where the burden of proof is lower than that demanded by the criminal courts. To date, twenty-five people have been obliged to repay nearly £17 million, including Noye, who repaid almost £3 million. It leaves approximately £10 million still outstanding.

There has been a smell of death hanging over the whole case; some of the victims have already been mentioned. Another was twenty-one year-old Stephen Cameron, who was in a van driven by his fiancée, nineteen-year-old Danielle Cable. There was an altercation with a man driving a Land Rover Discovery, who forced her to stop. When Cameron got out of the van, the driver of the Land Rover punched him in the face, then stabbed him in the heart and liver. He died at the scene; the Land Rover roared away. Two years later, the man responsible was arrested in Spain; in April 2000, he was convicted of murder and sentenced to life imprisonment. His name is Kenneth Noye.

Still the killing goes on. Hanging on to the proceeds from the robbery was a matter that Francis and Perry both denied to McAvoy, who was released in 2000. They were not believed. Following his release from prison for the conspiracy offence, Brian Perry had started to rebuild Blue Cars, his taxi business. On 16 November 2001, outside his offices, a gunman shot him three times in the back of his head.

On 14 May 2003, at 5 o'clock in the morning, as Francis arrived in his green Rover 75 at his couriers business, Signed, Sealed & Delivered, in Lynton Road, SE1, he was shot four times in the head and chest and died instantly. The method of execution was practically identical to that used on Brian Perry, who had been killed just a couple of hundred yards away.

But sometimes, the truth can be obscured by coincidence. Four years later, three men stood trial at the Old Bailey for the murder of Francis. The case for the prosecution was that Francis was owed £70,000 on a business deal by Harry 'Big H' Richardson, who refused to discharge the debt. This alleged liability, together with any knowledge of the murder was denied by Richardson and he was acquitted by the jury.

But Terence Conaghan, aged 54 from Springburn, Glasgow and John O'Flynn, aged 53 from Cheshunt, Hertfordshire had left their DNA traces at the scene. With 120 previous convictions between them, they were convicted of the murder and on 3 August 2007, the trial judge sentenced each of them to life imprisonment, with the recommendation that they serve at least twenty years behind bars.

During the trial, Francis' widow admitted, with masterly understatement, that her late husband was 'no angel'. Sentiments which, I feel sure would be accepted without reservation by a disgruntled former ironmonger from Hever.

Safe as Houses

The Church Elm pub, situated at the corner of Church Elm Lane and the Heathway, Dagenham, has closed. It's just as well. Not by any stretch of the imagination could it have been considered to be a place where the beautiful people of Dagenham would come to strut their stuff, and to see and be seen in all their finery. During its heyday, it provided a temporary home to charmless strippers, including some who had not been hired by the management. The latter group represented a cross-section of the inebriated old slappers from the flotsam and jetsam of the streets who had decided to provide an *ad hoc* performance. The Church Elm was a place where deadbeats went. On one occasion, the clientele spotted someone pouring a liquid on to the counter and the thought of cleanliness permeating into the grubby surroundings generated interest and a buzz of conversation. It was only when the drenching of the counter was complete and the person concerned flicked a lighted match to it and with a roar the bar went up in flames, that the customers realized that something a little more volatile than Flash All Purpose had been used and fled for their lives. It later appeared that the person responsible had approached the management for a slice of the action; it was accurately considered that he was mentally ill.

So when Curtis Patterson and Leroy Beamish decided to meet there a man known only to them as 'Sean', who was, they hoped, going to arrange a safeblowing for them, none of them looked especially out of place, especially Sean. He was short and thin, aged about thirty-five with ginger hair, which was already starting to thin, and pale blue, almost washed-out eyes. It was his eyes more than anything else which unnerved the two street-wise young men. Just from the way he looked and spoke, both Patterson and Beamish had rapidly come to the conclusion that Sean was capable of any villainy. That was the impression which had also been reached by Patterson's friend, 'Pea-wee' who had effected the introduction. 'Just watch 'im,' he had said to Patterson. ''Im one tasty geezer.'

'What exactly is it you're looking for, boys?' asked Sean quietly.

'We want somefin' blown open, innit?' replied Patterson.

Sean permitted himself a thin smile. 'Something or somebody?'

'It's a safe,' whispered Beamish urgently. 'A safe we want blown open. We heard you Irish army people can do fings like that.'

Sean looked at them, from one to the other. His pale blue eyes never seemed to blink. When he spoke, his words were mild but there was more than a hint of menace in them. 'Now, who's been filling yer heads with that nonsense? Me and my associates are businessmen, that's all. We carry out business here and over the water – back home. Everything comes with a price. We're businessmen, as I say – just looking for a profit.'

Patterson shifted uncomfortably. 'We'll pay ya, won't we?'

Sean provided another thin smile which was devoid of mirth. 'I know yer will.' He put both hands flat on the table. 'Right. What's the job, what's in the safe and what's in it for me and my associates?'

'It's loads of benefit books,' replied Patterson. 'Course, you

267

wouldn't be interested in them, so we was finking about twenty-five grand.'

Sean leant forward without a hint of a smile on his face. 'So yer a fockin' mind reader as well, are yez? As it happens, yeah, I am interested in benefit books – as well as twenty-five grand.'

'How much ya lookin' at then?' asked Beamish.

'Half,' replied Sean, flatly.

'Wot – half the books – and twenty-five grand? Fuckin' 'ell, man!' gasped Beamish.

'We fort you'd do the job for wages,' muttered Patterson.

'Sure, wages,' agreed Sean, 'plus just a wee bit of commission.'

Patterson and Beamish glanced apprehensively at each other. Eventually, Patterson said, 'We got to fink about this.'

'Sure, you do that,' replied Sean who drained his glass and stood up. 'Ye've found me once and if yer interested in doing business, ye'll find me again. But boys, just one thing. If we're going to do business, we don't meet in a fockin' shite place like this, understand? Find a place that serves Bushmills.' With that, he was gone.

Two days later, a further meeting had been arranged, this time outside the Bull public house, at the junction of Rainham Road South and Ballards Road, Dagenham. Patterson and Beamish were sitting in Patterson's red BMW 5 series, on the pub's forecourt when, in his wing mirror, he saw Sean approaching, in company with another man, slightly taller than him and fair-haired. Both men went to either side of the car and got into the rear seats.

'This is me man, Michael,' said Sean shortly, by way of introduction. 'Just pull round the corner, will yer?' Patterson duly drove into Sandown Avenue and parked up.

'Right,' said Sean. 'Michael knows more about this sort of thing than I do, so just go through the story for us.'

'There's this geezer, right? 'E's a nigger,' said Patterson. When Sean and Michael looked at each other uncomprehendingly, Patterson added, ''E's African, right? 'E ain't like us.'

'Ah,' replied Sean, whilst Michael simply nodded.

'Anyway, this geezer, 'e's a security guard at the Civic Centre, just down the road. And 'e's been 'aving benefit books away, right? The other week, 'e found out there's thousands of these blank books in the safe there. You jus' fill 'em in an' cash 'em up. 'E's 'ad some blank books 'e found on a desk but 'e's got to get the book they write the book numbers down in. See, they keep it in the safe. Wiv that book and all the blank ones, no one knows oo's got what.'

'What sort of a safe is it?' This from Michael.

Patterson shook his head. 'Dunno. Just a big one, 'e said, full of blank books. Look – go and see the geezer yourself. I've squared it with him. All I got to do is call 'im, 'e'll turn the cameras round so no one'll see you go in and he can show you round tonight.'

'OK,' said Sean. 'This is what we'll do. Drop us off back at the pub forecourt. Make yer call to yer man. We'll get our own motor; it's a Merc. Then we'll follow yer down to this Civic Centre.'

Fifteen minutes later, the two cars were travelling in convoy, north along Rainham Road North. As they approached the Wood Lane roundabout, with the Civic Centre on the eastern side, Patterson indicated a left turn into Bradwell Avenue and Sean followed him in. He and Patterson got out of their cars.

'I've had a word with the geezer. 'E wants me to go in, tell 'im what's going on and then your mate can come in and 'ave a look at the safe.'

'Right,' said Sean, curtly. 'Do it.'

Ten minutes later, Patterson returned. Everything was clear. Michael got out of the car and walked across to the Civic Centre where, under the security light, he saw a tall, thin figure beckoning to him. This was Jonah Okonjo-Guba, the night duty security guard. He had been stringently vetted by Barking and Dagenham Council, which meant that they had simply accepted his word that he was who he said he was and hired him.

Entering the building by a side entrance brought Michael into a small room banked with security cameras. As he stared at them, he heard a chuckle behind him. 'Do not worry, my friend. The cameras have been turned round to the front; nobody will know that you came in here.'

Michael nodded. 'Good. Right – show me the safe.'

As the six foot six security guard set off, Michael practically broke into a trot to keep up with him. After a long walk through sets of governmental double doors, they entered a large room, which was crammed with desks and chairs.

'There,' said Okonjo-Guba, pointing. 'There, in the corner.'

Michael looked. It was an old Chubb, about four feet high and two and a half feet wide. It was a key-operated lock with a large brass handle. He nodded. He had seen this type of safe before. Michael turned to the guard.

'When d'yer work here?'

'Every night during the week,' replied Okonjo-Guba, adding, 'and some weekends.'

'What time are your shifts?'

'I start from six in the evening until six the following morning,' replied the guard. 'So you could come anytime between those hours. However, you will have to tie me up with rope to make it seem that you have robbed me.'

'Yeah, that's no problem,' nodded Michael. 'Now – what's in this safe?'

Okonjo-Guba frowned. 'You know this; there are blank books for all the benefits.'

'Sure, but how much?'

'I think they are worth millions of pounds,' confidently replied the venal security guard.

'I'm going to get some tools to help me work out the plan,' said Michael. 'When can I come back?'

'Anytime – that is no problem,' replied Okonjo-Guba. 'Any evening this week, if you wish. Just call me first and make sure you approach the building exactly the same way as you did tonight. Then I can remove the camera which would have picked you up.'

They walked back to the security office and, before he opened the exit door, the guard took down a rota from the wall. 'See – I am working this weekend in two weeks' time. That is when you could do it.'

'Yeah, that sounds good,' remarked Michael. 'When I come back later on this week, I'll know how much stuff'll be needed to open it.'

Back in Bradwell Avenue, Michael explained the situation to Sean, Patterson and Beamish and a few moments later the four men left in their respective vehicles.

Two days later, Michael was back; he was carrying a small grip and his companion, a six foot, thin-faced man in his late thirties named Liam, was carrying a laptop bag. Michael tapped on the side door, which was wrenched open by a wide-eyed Jonah Okonjo-Guba.

'You should have let me known you were coming!' he gasped. 'You will have been caught on camera! And who is this?'

That evening, Michael was in an irascible mood. 'Don't worry about him; he's with me,' he snapped. 'Now, get me the tape.'

'I can't!' stammered the guard. 'They are all numbered; they will know one is missing!'

Both Michael and Liam stepped inside the lobby. 'I don't care,' he growled. 'Just give me the fucking tape!'

With great reluctance, Okonjo-Guba removed the tape from the machine and handed it over. 'Right,' grunted Michael. 'Let's see that safe again. I need to do some tests.'

The three men walked through the darkened building in silence. As they reached the room containing the safe, so Michael took out the laptop and told Liam to get out the scanner. The guard was watching intently.

'Right,' said Michael. 'Now, has anybody been asking any questions?'

'No, everything's fine,' replied the guard, still intently looking at the laptop. 'No one is interested in the security here; they haven't even missed the books I've been taking home.'

'Books?'

'The benefit books,' patiently explained Okonjo-Guba. 'I've taken loads of them. They just leave them out at night. I just take them and cash them up – it's easy.'

'And what about that weekend?' asked Michael. 'Is that still on to blow the safe?'

'Of course. Just remember to bring the rope to tie me up with.'

Michael nodded. 'What's the fire system, here?'

'The alarm goes straight through to the fire station,' replied the guard, 'and there are sprinklers in every office.'

'Jaysus,' muttered Michael. The fire station was just yards away, almost opposite the junction with Bradwell Avenue. He walked around the office and counted six sprinkler heads and four fire sensors. 'We'll need to cover those sensor heads,' he murmured to Liam, who nodded his head in agreement. 'Remember to bring some of those tubes of silicone to cover them up,' added Michael as an afterthought. 'Tell you what, Liam – we'll leave the water on. That way if we pop the alarm when we bang the box, we'll know it's fucked and we can get out, quick.' He frowned, deep in thought. 'Right, that's it then. Now, let's get going with this.'

Within minutes, Michael was running a scanner, which was connected to the laptop by a lead over the front of the safe by the lock area. The scanner's head glowed with a low, ultra violet light and from time to time, it would emit a 'beep!'

Whilst this was going on, Liam was giving a running commentary. 'Yeah, just there. Back a bit. To the right – yeah, that's dead on.'

Okonjo-Guba was mesmerized by the whole business. 'What is this?' he asked, pointing to the laptop.

'It's a computer,' muttered Michael, concentrating on his work.

'Yes, I know that,' persisted the guard, 'but what does it do?'

Michael sighed and straightened himself up. 'It works this scanner,' he replied. 'Look, I know this type of safe. It's old. It was made in the 1950s. Round about that time, there was a lot of guys going round blowing safes. So the manufacturers fitted a steel cable around the door, connected to a lever which released the bolts. Along the cable were small plates of toughened glass. The explosion to open the safe would normally shatter the glass – that released the cable and it jammed the lever which opened the door. So I'm checking with the scanner so that I can—'

'Holy Mother of Christ, Michael,' muttered Liam. 'Will yer catch yerself on? I've got somewhere to go, tonight. Let's get on with it, shall we? Yer wasting yer fockin' time, trying to explain this to an ignorant fockin' darkie.'

Michael completely missed the look of outrage from the guard and nodded, absent-mindedly. 'Yeah, dead on.'

A few minutes later, Michael looked up and said, 'OK, I

think we're done here,' and both men packed their equipment away, before Michael turned, once more to the guard.

'Right, we need to sort out the money. We need it when we come here on the night – that's before we blow the safe.'

'You'll have to sort out the money with the other guys,' replied Okonjo-Guba, sullenly. He was still smarting from the 'darkie' remark. 'And anyway,' he added, 'they said we were sharing the money from the books.'

Michael looked up at him. 'The deal is that we get paid first. Twenty-five grand, up front. We have an agreement from the others about payment of the money but on the night, they're not going to be here – you are. So twenty-five grand up front – or no bangs. You understand?'

'I don't know,' muttered Okonjo-Guba. 'I will have to speak to them first. I am not happy about this arrangement.'

Michael shrugged his shoulders. 'You suit yourself, but I'm telling you now – no pay, no bangs. It's as simple as that.'

The following evening, just as Jonah Okonjo-Guba booked on duty, he was surprised to be greeted by a reception committee from the investigation department of the Department of Health and Social Security. He was taken into a side office where he was introduced to two other men. Both of them were detective sergeants from the Regional Crime Squad and they were in possession of a warrant to search his home address. There they found seventeen assorted benefit books. They were made out in both male and female names, which suggested African origins and which had been encashed. In addition, there were a number of other documents which would assist as forms of identification and which tallied with the names in the benefit book. The detectives, who then conveyed Okonjo-Guba to Dagenham police station, decided that some sort of explanation was called for.

'I shall tell you everything I know, Sergeant,' said Okonjo-Guba. 'A few weeks ago, I was approached by police officers in plain clothes. They told me that an unscrupulous gang of Irishmen were planning to blow open the safe at the Civic Centre and they asked my help in bringing them to justice. Of course, I was delighted to assist the authorities. These policemen said the Irishmen would contact me and do you know, Sergeant, they did! I pretended to go along with them. I even took the books which you found at my house to help create a cover. But of course, there is no need for me to tell you this; you must already know it! Why have you not contacted your colleagues already, Sergeant, to verify my – good heavens! A thought has just occurred to me! Could it be, Sergeant, could it possibly be, that those men were not police officers at all? Could that be the case? Tell me, what do you think, Sergeant?'

'I think you're a lying fucker,' equably replied the officer.

Okonjo-Guba leapt to his feet. 'There is something you must know, Sergeant,' he snapped, furiously. 'My father is the chief of our village and the people, they treat me as a god. It may sound foolish to you westerners, I know, but they are just children. But if they were to hear your words to me, I could not control them. There would be a bloodbath. Thank God we are here, instead of there.' He gained control of himself and sat down. 'Now, not withstanding your insults, if I can help you to catch these dangerous men, I shall.'

The second sergeant nodded. 'Will you? Good. Come in here.' With that, they all went into another office where there was a television and a VCR player. The television was switched on and a tape was inserted into the machine. As the tape started, so two men could be seen, walking towards the camera. It was Michael and Liam, on their way into the Civic Centre.

'That's them!' shouted Okonjo-Guba. 'The two Irishmen! I'd know them anywhere!'

'Good,' said the sergeant, who had previously been so disbelieving. 'Come back in the other office, would you?'

But as the former security guard walked back to the office, he was thinking, 'But that must have been the tape that I gave to Michael. There wasn't another copy, just that one. And if the police have got it, that means . . .'

Back in the office, one of the officers pressed a switch on a tape recorder. And there was Okonjo-Guba's voice. 'The benefit books . . . I've taken loads of them . . . they just leave them out at night . . . I just take them and cash them up – it's easy . . .'

It is, of course, quite easy to conceal a tape recorder in a laptop which has no other use than to covertly tape conversations, in company with a scanner which doesn't scan at all, even if it does give off a nice comforting glow and a reassuring 'beep!' from time to time.

At Okonjo-Guba's trial, ten months later, the court heard that had this been a genuine safeblowing, the contents of the safe would have yielded as much as £7 million depending on how much the gang could obtain before all the books were identified and cancelled. But, of course, a genuine safeblowing had never been intended. Michael and Liam were both undercover police officers. Michael's convincing Irish accent came from his mother, who had been born off the Antrim Road in North Belfast. Liam's parents, on the other hand, had both been born in Hammersmith. However, before joining the Metropolitan Police, he had been a leading light in a local amateur dramatic society, which often staged plays by Sean O'Casey. Liam's performance in *The Plough and the Stars* had been regarded as 'outstanding'.

It is seldom that informants, participating or otherwise, are paid by cheque. However, there are exceptions to every rule and the Yard has set up a number of pretty convincing bogus companies. One such company posted a cheque, which represented the goodwill of both the Metropolitan Police's Informants Fund and that of the Department of Health and Social Security to the address of Sean, who lives in a terraced house, in the Cavehill Road in North Belfast. He is the legitimate owner of a builders' merchants. The cheque, which was really quite a generous one, was drawn on a firm to whom a company such as Sean's had allegedly been supplying goods. It caused no dissent at all when he paid it into his account at the Shankill Road branch of the Ulster Bank.

The police were reasonably ambivalent regarding the prosecution of Curtis Patterson and Leroy Beamish. Both of them were separately hoiked off the streets and spoken to, in a friendly, albeit forceful, fashion. They were told that they could go into the system and cop about five years with the crooked security guard or start informing, big-time, in which case they would be looked after. Following a certain amount of navel-searching, both opted for the latter option. In fact one was less successful that his contemporary in their new careers. Leroy Beamish was found shot to death in South Esk Road, Forest Gate, and it was rumoured that his demise was something to do with a drugs deal which went slightly boss-eyed, although that has never been satisfactorily resolved. The internal investigation, conducted by a fat little chief inspector, who was variously described as a nonce and a pimp, concluded that the mysterious disappearance of Beamish's contact sheets, which outlined his progress and had been submitted by his handler, was the result of those sheets being shredded and the fragments reduced to ashes and submitted to the four winds for dissemination. It was nonsense, of course.

Curtis Patterson, at the last count, was bringing in resounding successes, not only for the Metropolitan Police but also for constabularies in the Home Counties, as well as becoming quite outstandingly well off.

And Jonah Okonjo-Guba? He was eventually found guilty of a variety of offences, including incitement and conspiracy to steal, as well as obtaining twenty-two thousand pounds' worth of benefits from the Department of Health and Social Security. He was sentenced to a total of six years' imprisonment and recommended for deportation. It is not entirely clear if that recommendation was actually implemented. Okonjo-Guba appealed, stating that he faced certain death if he were to be returned to his home country; then again, according to his interview, an entire village, children though they might be, were waiting to elevate him to deity-like status.

So it begs the question, at the conclusion of his sentence, was he deported or not? Unfortunately, not even the Home Office can answer that one.

Chatting to the Fishes

By the end of World War Two, the British government began looking for immigrants to address the labour shortages. People arrived from many countries, including the West Indies and in June 1948, with smoke billowing from its twin funnels, the *Empire Windrush* docked at Tilbury where hundreds of West Indians disembarked. In the years that followed, the black immigrants settled in Nottingham, Birmingham and west and south London.

What is not known by the British public, is that, following this lawful influx of immigrants, there was a stealthy insertion of the scum contained in the main prison in Kingston, Jamaica. As soon as their sentences were completed, many of the inmates (whose offences filled the criminal calendar from murder downwards) were shipped out on the first available boat for England. With the likes of such luminaries as Noël Coward and Ian Fleming purchasing properties on the island, the Jamaican authorities were understandably delighted to see the back of the crims.

These criminals carried on with their illegal enterprises just where they'd left them off. In many cases their targets were the decent, elderly and conscientious, hard-working fellow West Indians. One such low-life was ex-convict Wesley Sylvester Bailey.

Bailey had been fortunate indeed to have avoided the

hangman's rope in Kingston; a certain paucity of evidence resulted in him being acquitted of murder but convicted of manslaughter and, in consequence, he was sentenced to eight years' imprisonment. He was tall, tough and exceedingly mean. One of his first actions after entering Britain was to acquire the services of one Marlene Clutterbuck. She had been named, as were many girls of that era – often quite inappropriately – after the famous German film actress. Poor Marlene was a thin, awkward, blonde nineteen-year-old from Skipton, North Yorkshire who had travelled south to London, in the hope of finding fame, fortune and adventure. She believed she would encounter all of these desirable virtues when she met Wesley Sylvester Bailey but, of course, she was quite wrong. Her lot would be degradation, poverty, the acquisition of a number of deeply unpleasant anti-social diseases, several prison sentences and, ultimately, heroin addiction and an untimely death.

Having persuaded Marlene to enter the world's oldest profession – it was colloquially referred to as being 'on the bash' – Bailey lived off her immoral earnings and thrashed her whenever she expressed reluctance at having to service in excess of twenty-five customers during an evening, or whenever such a belting was necessary. He also encouraged her to go shoplifting and fraudulently encash stolen cheques. Marlene handed over every penny she acquired to Bailey, received a further beating if he suspected that she was holding monies back from him (although she never did) and he grudgingly paid her fines whenever she was caught. Marlene's presence is mentioned, purely because she plays an important part in the drama which unfolds.

Marlene's contribution to the budget was an important consideration for Bailey but it was not his sole income. He continued robbing and burgling, to the prejudice of black people in the area of Brixton, south London. He made no secret of it; he felt it added to his persona for his victims to know who was responsible. And to his catalogue of crimes, he now added running protection rackets amongst the black cafe proprietors of the area. Bailey was in danger of getting far too big for his oversize boots. Quite a lot of Brixton's population thought so. And some of them were getting seriously pissed-off with Mr High and Bloody Mighty Bailey.

One such person was Elijah Sigismund Frazer. He was in his fifties, and he lived by himself, in a rented flat, off Coldharbour Lane, Brixton. Frazer was not excessively tall, but he was exceptionally broad-shouldered, with a barrel of a chest. The reason for his impressive physique was because, years before, he had earned a respectable living by wrestling alligators in the Negril Swamps in his native Jamaica. Since there was a distinct lack of these reptiles to be utilized for grappling purposes in England, Frazer contented himself by working for London Transport. He was liked in the community but he was quiet and kept himself to himself. His passion was music and he had a large quantity of hi-fi equipment, together with records and tapes of calypso music.

Arriving home from the early work shift, he saw that the front door of his flat had been kicked in. Horrified, he rushed inside to discover that his expensive hi-fi, his tapes and his records had all been stolen. In fact, one or two records had been left behind. They had been smashed underfoot. Frazer made enquiries of the occupants of all the other flats in that large, dilapidated Victorian house but, although there was plenty of eye-rolling and sighing from his neighbours, nobody professed to have heard or seen anything. The other occupants, all of whom had been at home during the entry into Frazer's flat and who, of course, had heard and, in some cases, seen everything, expressed noises of compassion for Frazer's misfortune but, with a great deal of head shaking, firmly shut their front doors. They knew better than to get involved with a police investigation, which would inevitably result in becoming entangled with the likes of Wesley Sylvester Bailey. In this, they were wrong. Elijah Sigismund Frazer had no intention of involving the police.

But nevertheless, the police did get to hear of it. Police Constable 448 L Dave Burgess had joined the Metropolitan Police after seeing wartime service with the Royal Armoured Corps and all of his service had been spent at Brixton. A very tough character, he was well respected by the locals, the more so because of his uncomplicated ways of dealing with problems, the way, in fact, that they were dealt with back in their native West Indies. This was demonstrated during his one and only encounter with Bailey. Something had happened in Effra Road, a quarrel between two shopkeepers perhaps, that had resulted in a gathering of youths on the pavement and which had caused pedestrians to walk into the roadway to avoid them. PC Burgess strolled up. 'All right, boys, just move along now.' The words were easy-going enough but the authority behind them was absolute and the youths started to drift away, all except Wesley Sylvester Bailey, who saw this as a heaven-sent opportunity to exert his own, not inconsiderable authority.

'Boy!' he bellowed. 'Oo you call "boy" mon? You 'ear 'im? 'Im call me "boy"!'

PC Burgess had not administered a racial slur; he was merely addressing Bailey and his hangers-on in the same way that he would have addressed any group of youths, whether they were black or white. In fact, it would have made little difference if PC Burgess had addressed Bailey as 'Monsignor'; the effect would have been the same.

'Right, you, shut up and push off,' replied Burgess, adding, 'before you find yourself bang in trouble.'

''Ark at 'im,' sneered Bailey. '"Bang in trouble." Yo no be so tough wivout your uniform, Mr Po-lice-man.'

Several of the youths who had initially decided to depart, stopped and turned. One of them nodded his head. 'Yeah, 'im right.'

This, PC Burgess decided, was a situation that had to be defused there and then, before things spiralled out of control. He took off his helmet. 'Here, hold that,' he said, passing it to one of the shopkeepers. Another shopkeeper, who was sick and tired of Bailey and his attendant riff-raff, eagerly stepped forward. 'I'll hold yer jacket, Mr Burgess.'

Bailey was big and hard, but no matter how finely honed a man may be, he has little chance against someone who has experienced a number of victories in the ring. The fight, such as it was, lasted, in the way that most fights do, less than thirty seconds. Bailey simply rushed at PC Burgess who, with consummate ease, kept him at arm's length with a series of left jabs before, with one mighty right hook, he knocked him clean off his feet. Bailey struggled to his feet. 'Right, push off and don't come back,' said PC Burgess, who was not even out of breath and Bailey slouched away. That evening, Marlene received the hiding of her life from Bailey. Since, the previous day, she had serviced the needs of a record-breaking thirty-eight punters and had thought she'd done rather well, she was somewhat disconcerted at the unexpected thrashing.

PC Burgess often picked up bits and pieces of interesting information, usually by the process of just chatting to people in the street, and even if the section sergeant spotted him, he was hugely disinclined to report him for 'idling and gossiping' because he knew that PC Burgess had brought in some very fine arrests as a result.

So although Elijah Frazer never officially reported the theft of his beloved hi-fi to the police, nevertheless, PC Burgess got to hear of it. He heard about the theft and, from a number of different sources, that it had been Bailey who had been responsible. Out on his beat one morning, he spotted Frazer, whom he knew by sight, on his way to commence duty at the bus terminal, strolling along the street, his Public Service Vehicle badge swinging on his broad chest.

Stopping and then commiserating with him, PC Burgess was surprised at Frazer's reaction. 'It nuffin' to do wit' you. Min' yer hoan business. It ain't nothin' for the Government to fret themselves about.'

With that, he walked away. PC Burgess stared after him for a moment, then shrugged and continued on his beat.

Outwardly, Elijah Frazer was his usual quiet, courteous self, polite to work colleagues and neighbours alike. Inwardly, he was seething. He, too, had heard that it had been Bailey who had been responsible for the ransacking of his flat and the theft of his precious calypso music and he was determined to retrieve them if he could and, at the same time, extract a suitable revenge. The problem was the girl. He knew that Bailey had got a whore living with him. In fact, he had seen her, a sad but pleasant little thing, tottering along on her skinny legs, wearing those ridiculous high heels. For what he had in mind for Bailey he wanted her neither present nor to be in a position to come home and make a fuss. But when the ideal opening presented itself, it came, as such opportunities tend to do, right out of the blue.

Frazer was sitting in a local cafe one afternoon, enjoying a post-work cup of tea before returning home when he became aware of a conversation between two local women behind him. At first, he took no notice, since women's conversations were of no interest to him, at least, not until he heard the magical name 'Bailey'.

'Pore littl' bitch,' one of the women was saying. 'She get eighteen munfs fer doin' nuttin'.'

'Yeah,' agreed her neighbour. 'Wonder what that dog Bailey goin' to do now?' and both women collapsed in shrieks of laughter. Frazer started listening to the rest of the conversation with great interest.

What he later discovered was that Marlene Clutterbuck had set off for the Inner London Quarter Sessions that morning. She had been committed there for sentence, following her most recent conviction for shoplifting, but she had a great deal more to contend with than that single episode of hoisting. Apart from her previous convictions, she had also breached a couple of conditional discharges. She had also been placed on probation, had committed further offences during the period of that probation order and a fresh probation order had been substituted. Now, in addition to everything else, not only had the latest shoplifting conviction been committed whilst she was still subject to the fresh probation order, she had not attended the probation officer's office on one single, solitary occasion. The reason for her reluctance was that she had a long-term commission with Wesley Sylvester Bailey to bang her brains out with a never-ending stream of indifferent punters but her 'dock brief' thought it inadvisable to offer this as mitigation to the stern-faced judge. Telling her that she had been given 'chance after chance, which she had recklessly thrown away' the judge, re-sentencing Marlene for all of the original offences, whose orders she had breached, as well as the current shoplifting offence, topped the weeping girl up with a total of eighteen months' imprisonment.

Bailey, of course, was completely unaware of his trollop's fate, so later that afternoon, as he lazed in an armchair and heard the knock on the door of his Railton Road flat, he screamed, 'Forget ya key, bitch?'

When no key was inserted in the lock and the knock was repeated, Bailey got up and tore the door open. There stood Elijah Frazer. Bailey stared at the grey haired, elderly fat man who was facing him, with a rather resolute expression in his face. He had never seen him before. 'Wot you want, hole mon?'

Frazer stepped into the flat and shut the door behind him. 'Yo took a liberty wit' me record collection,' he said simply. 'I want 'im back.'

Suddenly, recognition dawned and Bailey roared with laughter. 'Wot, them shit records, mon? They not worf nuttin' – me mash 'em, innit? Now, fuck orf.'

They were the last words he spoke. Frazer darted forward, flung his arms around Bailey and squeezed. The last things that Bailey heard before he lost consciousness was the sound of the air whistling out of his lungs and an ominous cracking sound.

As PC Burgess patrolled his beat in the days, then weeks, that followed, he was aware that both Frazer and Bailey were missing. Had Frazer, more upset than had previously been thought at the loss of his beloved calypso music, returned to the Caribbean, a broken man? He didn't know, nor did he enquire at the bus depot where Frazer worked, which was miles off his beat. And as for that arrogant shit, Bailey, well, who knew where he'd gone and who cared? Marlene Clutterbuck, banged up in HM Prison Holloway cared, in fact, she cared very much indeed but in some ways she was a realist and quickly came to the conclusion that her beloved Wesley would never visit, or write to her in prison and indeed would undoubtedly find a Marlene-type substitute to provide him with his main means of income. She shrank from the idea of returning to Skipton after her release. Perhaps she'd stay in London, make a new start and meet somebody *really* nice.

Right.

And then, PC Burgess started hearing rumours. To start off with, it was that 'that rass-claat, Bailey, 'im never comin' back, mon.' Amen to that, thought Burgess, but then as the weeks went by the rumours were getting stronger. 'Im in thuh river, innit? In thuh Thames, right? In a sack.'

There was nothing for PC Burgess to trouble the CID about, just rumour and innuendo about a worthless piece of shit that nobody (with the possible exception of Marlene) gave a toss about.

One evening, off duty, PC Burgess walked into a shebeen. The proprietor nodded at him but he knew that Burgess would not report him for running an illegal drinker. Burgess knew that he could often pick up remarkable bits of information about his community, simply by sitting down and having a chat with the locals. As it was on this occasion. There in the corner, a half empty bottle of Three Daggers rum in front of him, sat Elijah Sigismund Frazer who was splendidly pissed. Burgess sat down and the two men chatted about inconsequential matters, made more difficult given Frazer's inebriated state, until suddenly, he said, 'Yo' bin lookin' for Bailey, I hear?'

PC Burgess nodded.

Frazer poured out two more generous tots of the cheap rum and chuckled. ''Im took a liberty wit' me record collection. You doan 'ave to look for 'im no more, me friend.'

Burgess took a sip of the fiery rum. 'Well, I would like to have a word with him.'

Frazer stared at him for a moment, before bursting into laughter, as though PC Burgess had said the funniest thing he'd ever heard. He tried to choke back his laughter as the tears of mirth ran down his face. 'Yo can't,' he wheezed. 'Bailey's too busy to talk to yo', mon – 'im chattin' to the fishes!'

The next afternoon as he came on duty, PC Burgess made for the canteen, where, as he hoped, he saw Police Constable Hubert Casson-Clarke MA. His contemporaries usually referred to him as 'The Professor' or 'Prof', because he was one of the first post-war university educated men to join the Metropolitan Police. His upper-crust voice had caused much derision when he first arrived at Brixton but, after a while, his colleagues came to like the strange bloke with the drawling voice, who could give as good as he got. He was soon held in very high esteem after he had arrived at the scene of a fellow constable who was being badly beaten up by a gang of youths in Atlantic Avenue and PC Casson-Clarke had tossed the ringleader through a plate glass window. It was not generally known, but he had been awarded a brown belt in the then little known sport of judo. 'There's more to Oxford than just reading books, y'know!' PC Casson-Clarke nonchalantly replied, following being applauded for his actions.

'Ah, Professor, just the bloke I want to see,' said PC Burgess, sitting down at Casson-Clarke's table. 'Now look – you know everything, don't you?'

The Professor sighed and put down a copy of Rostand's *L'aiglon*, which he was reading, naturally, in the original French, and which made fairly incongruous reading material in the canteen, where copies of the *Sketch* and the *Mirror* predominated. 'More than you, I feel sure, m'dear fellow,' he murmured. 'What is it?'

PC Burgess tried to pick his words carefully. 'Well . . . in the Thames . . . y'know, in the river, I mean . . . well, are there fish in there that could eat a human being?'

'My dear chap, must you parade your abysmal ignorance

like a flag?' sighed Casson-Clarke. 'Have you never heard of "The Great Stink"?' Seeing the look of total incomprehension on his colleague's face, he continued, 'It was in 1858. The pong of the raw sewage in the Thames was so atrocious that Parliament had to be dissolved. Twenty years after that, the pleasure steamship, *The Princess Alice* went down and the six hundred-odd passengers perished, not simply because they drowned but because they were overcome by the human and industrial filth which saturated the Thames.' He laughed. 'What I'm endeavouring to impart to you, you dear old ignoramus, is that there are no fucking fish in the Thames. The whole stretch of water is a bloody karsy!'

The Professor was absolutely right. In 1957, the Natural History Museum declared the Thames biologically dead.

PC Burgess sat bolt upright. Bailey was missing, but there wasn't a body. Frazer said that he was 'chatting to the fishes' but he'd been pissed and there weren't any fishes in the Thames – Prof had said so. Burgess clapped him on the shoulder.

'Thanks, Prof – that's a load off my mind – I owe you a drink!'

As he hurried out of the canteen, Casson-Clarke picked up his neglected Rostand and called after him, 'Make mine a Campari!' but Burgess didn't hear him. He was too busy thinking, 'No body, no fishes and no need to bother the CID!'

PC Burgess retired just before the Brixton riots of 1981 and realized every copper's dream of owning a pub in the country. Privately he felt the riots could have been avoided with some of his old-fashioned style of coppering.

Elijah Frazer eventually returned home to Jamaica, where he succumbed to a massive heart attack. He was buried in the little hamlet of Green Island, not a million miles away from the Negril Swamps where very old twenty foot reptiles trembled

289

at the memories of the squat young man in bathing trunks who so many years ago had cruelly mistreated them.

And the Thames has really cleaned up its act. The water quality has improved to such an extent that, now, one hundred and twenty different species of fish, including Bottlenose Dolphins, and hundreds of thousands of birds populate the Thames. One day perhaps, one of the herons which dive for the fish will come across a water-logged sack and its probing bill will worry open the stitching. If somebody looks inside that sack, it might well be that they will discover the skeleton of what was once a rather large man.

If that were the case and the discovery were to be published in the newspapers, perhaps it might have rung a bell in the memory of ex-PC Burgess. But this is all speculation of course. Such a sack has never been found and, in any event, Burgess died a long time ago.

But if it were to be found . . . just supposing . . . what conclusion would be reached about the skeleton's ribs? Because it might be felt that considerable force must have been used to crush them.

When Things Aren't
What They Seem . . .

There are few sounds as alarming as the sound of one's front door being smashed in at five o'clock in the morning. It tends to show that something is well and truly up. This feeling of unease is somewhat intensified when the owner of the front door is a middle-ranking drugs dealer. Tony O'Neill was such a dealer and, as his front door gave up the last vestiges of providing a secure barrier between him and a cruel, outside world, he heard the sound of feet running up the stairs towards him. With mounting apprehension, he realized that the drugs squad officers who were about to seriously invade his privacy would not take too long before they discovered the four ounces of whizz – amphetamine sulphate to the uninitiated – which was stashed under the bed. *His* bed.

O'Neill's wife, Gloria, who was a seasoned campaigner of early-morning police raids was ready to launch her customary broadside; her screeching verbal abuse of the officers would not help the situation one jot, but at least it would make her feel so much better. So as the bedroom door crashed open, she screeched, 'Woss yor fuckin' – 'and then she stopped. For one thing, police officers do not arrive in drug dealers' bedrooms at five o'clock in the morning wearing ski masks. Next, although they are often equipped with truncheons, pickaxe helves or, on occasion, firearms, it is not generally known for drugs squad operatives to be in possession of baseball bats. And lastly, although it is sometimes suggested that police officers might use intemperate language, it is not usual for one of them to backhand the lady of the house across the face, to the accompaniment of the words, 'Shut it, you fat cunt!' nor for the other to press the said baseball bat across the throat of the gentleman of the house, at the same time saying, 'Give us your stash or I'll fuckin' kill yer!'

So, in those few short seconds, Mrs O'Neill came to the irrevocable conclusion that any further insolence should definitely be abandoned there and then, and that her husband would be well advised to offer up his supply of whizz, because the intruders were not the police officers that had been supposed, but were common or garden thugs who were intent on 'taxing' Tony O'Neill.

'Taxing' was a craze which started in the 1980s and still continues to this day. Quite simply, criminals, usually drug dealers, get to hear that another dealer is in possession of drugs or money (or both) and, like some modern-day highwayman, they relieve him of it. They do so, safe in the knowledge that the victim of this unofficial excise is hardly likely to report the matter to the police since to do so would incriminate him.

The offending whizz was offered up, O'Neill received a couple of admonitory slaps and the invaders left as suddenly as they had arrived. Gloria O'Neill was in a state of shock and when the eldest of their three children put his head round the bedroom door to enquire as to what had occurred, she simply muttered, 'Fuck off, Jason – just – fuck off!'

There we must leave Gloria O'Neill, with her obvious lack of parenting skills, because she makes no further contributions to this story. Instead, we shall concentrate on Tony O'Neill, who in due course will make a significant input into the way this tale pans out. He sat on the edge of his bed and tenderly rubbed his throat where the baseball bat had been used to telling effect. He was short and rather weedy looking, not a physical sort of person at all. Certainly no match for that pair of bastards. The bigger of the two must have been over six feet tall and broad with it, just about Roy's size. He paused. Roy. His mind in turmoil, O'Neill went downstairs, past the shattered front door and into the kitchen and put the kettle on. As he thoughtfully poured the hot water over the teabag in the mug, he thought about the situation more and more.

Although O'Neill could not be considered to be a wholesale dealer of drugs, he was nevertheless a dealer of some note in his Yorkshire neighbourhood. Through his connections in London, he could be relied upon (for the right sort of client, naturally) to pull up half a kilo of puff (cannabis) or whizz. These commodities would be securely kept in the lock-up garage that nobody knew about and from where he would take out sufficient for an agreed sale at his home; hence the four ounces of whizz being secreted under his bed for a quick sale later that morning. To Roy.

As he sipped at his tea, he turned the situation over in his mind. Why would Roy Adams want four ounces of whizz? Trading with that amount was way out of Roy's league. He'd want it for his own use, certainly, but how could he afford four ounces? Some addicts would add the granular-type powder to beer, others would shoot it up, very much like heroin, and some could be relied upon to dab it on the end of their tongues, much in the same way as a child deals with a sherbet dip. But Roy Adams practised none of these pursuits. He would simply stick his face in the bag of amphetamine sulphate and slurp it up, in the same way that a thirsty dog laps at a bowl of water.

In fact, Adams had form for this type of 'taxing' offence. Several years previously, he had been carrying out this lucrative occupation with one Tim Welsh. The two men had just relieved a dealer of a few ounces of puff and, with Adams driving, they were making their getaway when they were spotted by a police patrol car. In those days, police officers did not agonize over decisions as to whether or not to 'stop and search' a low-life. They recognized Adams as being one such creature and, executing a screeching U-turn, the officers set off in pursuit.

Police drivers have to observe stringent rules concerning the safety of other road users when participating in the pursuit of a felon, but the likes of Roy Adams, who at the time was completely out of his head on drugs, was unfettered by such a strict code of conduct and, in his desire to escape, took risks that few other drivers – and definitely not police drivers – would take. In this, he was successful, because he lost the pursuing patrol car but his drug-induced state was such that he kept going at full speed until entering a sharp bend at a less than prudent speed, he lost control of the car which slewed sideways, passenger side first, into a very thick and immovable oak tree which brought the car, and Tim Welsh's life to an abrupt halt.

Roy Adams was unaware of his accomplice's demise but, had he known, he would not have particularly cared; he was out of the car and away. His dash to the sanctuary of his girlfriend's house was somewhat hampered by the fact that his left leg was shattered in two places but his pain threshold was held back by the amount of whizz which he had ingested and he was able to drag himself over the half-mile journey. But when the effects of the drugs had worn off, Adams accepted with gratitude his girlfriend's offer to call an ambulance, an appreciation matched by those police officers who were waiting at the hospital for his arrival. Adams was well looked after in the prison hospital which was where he was remanded and, in due course, he received three years' imprisonment for the manslaughter of Tim Welsh.

Back now to Tony O'Neill, who was busy making arrangements for both a new front door and extracting a suitable revenge on Roy Adams, who, he was certain, had set him up to be robbed – an assumption which was quite correct.

Over the past few weeks, Adams had mentioned to O'Neill the bare bones of a job which, he was convinced, would set him up for life. He asked O'Neill if he knew of anyone who could assist in the dispersal of four lorry-loads of stolen whisky. This was not O'Neill's bag of tricks at all, but he muttered that he'd bear it in mind, rather than offer an uncompromising 'No'. And now he was glad that he had . . .

Because he was a survivor, O'Neill, who had spent several short terms in prison for dealing drugs and had no desire to repeat the process, was an informant for a detective sergeant, attached to the Regional Crime Squad. Over the years, he had passed on information to his handler which had resulted in the arrest of a number of well-known villains for possession of both drugs and firearms. Because of his successes, he worked on the assumption that the RCS would rather nick the villains that he was offering up, than scratch around trying to nick *him* and, to a certain degree, he was right.

However, the dictum that he should be left alone had not filtered through from the RCS to the local drugs squad, and O'Neill was currently on bail to them for possession of drugs, with intent to supply. It had not been a huge amount of drugs for which he had had his collar felt but, nevertheless, it was sufficient, as his solicitor gloomily predicted, to send him away for a couple of years. If he could come up with something – something to enable the police to send a letter to the judge at his forthcoming trial and to pay that bastard Adams back for setting him up to the 'taxers', he would be well pleased. Something, for instance to do with stolen whisky . . .

O'Neill's friendly detective sergeant thought this was an excellent idea. He told him exactly what to do.

Two weeks later, Roy Adams stepped off the train at King's Cross Station. He had made the journey in response to a telephone call which he had received from O'Neill the previous day, who told him that he was down in London and had been introduced to one Brian Kelly who had become very interested indeed when he had mentioned the four lorry-loads of stolen whisky.

Tony O'Neill was there to greet him but, as they shook hands, Adams' attention was drawn to the man standing just to the right of and slightly behind O'Neill. At six feet tall, Adams was big enough but O'Neill's companion was much taller, broader, too. He was aged about thirty-five, with long, dark, curly hair, and the leather jacket he was wearing must have cost a small fortune. Under his open-necked shirt, Adams could see a thick belcher chain, matched by the solid gold identity bracelet on his right wrist and the solid gold Rolex Oyster Perpetual on his left. He dripped money; more important, he exuded menace. This, thought Adams, is a fucking gangster, no error.

O'Neill introduced his companion to Adams as Brian Kelly, who permitted himself a thin smile as he shook hands with Adams.

'Nice to meet you, Roy,' grunted Kelly, and they walked outside the station. Kelly nodded towards a gleaming Mercedes. parked in Cheney Road. 'Come on, jump in the motor.'

He suddenly stopped and turned as O'Neill walked towards the car. 'Where the fuck're you going?' He jerked his head in dismissal. 'Fuck off – this is my and Roy's bit of work – not yours. Wait for me in the bar; I'll be back for you, later. Go on – push off.'

As O'Neill scuttled away, back towards the main line station, Kelly slid into the driver seat and Roy Adams, who got into the front passenger seat, was thoroughly bemused. 'What's happening, Brian?'

'You wait.' With that, Kelly turned the key in the ignition, the engine roared into life and they were off, down Cheney Road, left into Battle Bridge Road and, before reaching the junction with Pancras Road, screeching right into Goods Way. The car came to an abrupt halt by the Grand Union Canal and Brian Kelly, with a look of sheer malevolence on his face, turned to Adams.

'"What's happening, Brian?"' he mimicked. 'First of all, pal, you tell me who you are?'

'I'm Roy!' gasped a very unhappy Roy Adams.

'Yeah? Well, that little scrawny cunt back there is on bail – did you know that?'

Adams furiously shook his head. It was a lie, he did know that O'Neill was on bail but a denial seemed the most sensible course of action, in the circumstances.

Kelly looked at him, half disbelievingly. 'I don't do nuffin' with people on bail – got it? You know the old saying: "You won't go to jail if you keep away from people on bail." So I don't work with people on bail. But what I really fuckin' hate are grasses – understand?'

'I ain't no grass, Brian,' whispered Adams, the sweat starting to form on his forehead. 'I ain't on bail, either!'

'Ain't yer?' responded Kelly grimly. 'Let's make sure – lift your arms up. I want to see if you're wearing a wire.' With that, Kelly patted his hands down Adams' body until he appeared satisfied. 'All right, then. But let's get things straight. If you're a grass, a wrong 'un in any way, I'll find out and I'll cut your bollocks off and stick them, one after another, up your arsehole before sticking you in there.' At that, he gestured towards the Grand Union Canal. 'Understand?'

Adams squeezed his eyes shut as he visualized his fate, should he be found to be a 'wrong 'un' but, nevertheless, nodded his head, vigorously.

Kelly, too, nodded his head, although not quite as force-fully. 'Right. If you're proper, then you're OK. But just be warned, pal. I've got more than enough Old Bill straightened out and if you're on bail, I'll find out even before you get off your train back home.'

Adams swallowed, grateful to hear that he was going to be even permitted to board the train back to Yorkshire. 'That's fine, Brian.'

Apparently satisfied, Kelly said, 'Right, what's this bit of work? Four prizes, I hear?'

Adams explained that his girlfriend's father was a night watchman at a lorry compound, just off the A1 in Yorkshire. Whilst it was used by many lorry drivers as a stopping-off place and rest area, one particular company of hauliers had a contract to transport whisky from a Scottish distillery to a distribution centre in the south. The reason for this was because drivers of heavy goods vehicles cannot legally drive for more than four and a half hours at one time without having a statu-tory break. Therefore, the company had identified various secure compounds on the route south, no more than a four-and-a-half hours drive from the distillery so it was at one of these compounds, rather than at an insecure motorway service area, that the driver would end his journey. The added bonus was that upon his arrival, the driver would uncouple his trailer. A driver from the south would arrive at the compound, pulling an empty trailer, the two drivers would swap trailers and, after the appropriate period of rest, the driver from the south would return to the south, together with the trailer-load of whisky and the driver from Scotland would return to the north, pulling an empty trailer, all ready to be replenished at the distillery. The system is known as 'corralling'.

The father of Adams' girlfriend had identified the one night during the week when four trailer-loads of whisky would be left in the compound. No further vehicles were permitted to enter the compound after eleven o'clock at night; no vehicles were allowed to leave before six o'clock in the morning. Therefore, if could be as long as seven hours before the loss would be discovered. It was Adams' plan that he would cut through the wire in the perimeter fence and tie-up the night watchman in his hut. And that was as far as his plan had progressed. What was needed were four tractor units and drivers, to drive out the trailers, have somewhere to hide them thereafter and, most importantly, the means to organize distribution of the stolen whisky; hence Brian Kelly's involvement. And now, for Adams' all-important question. 'What'll you pay me, Brian?'

Kelly shrugged his shoulders. 'Dunno what it is yet, do I?'

Adams squinted at Kelly, as though he was simple. 'I told you, Brian,' he replied, patiently. 'Four container loads of Scotch, mate.'

Kelly returned the look, which made Adams feel as though *he* was the one who was simple, with good reason. 'Yeah – but are they pints or litres? Are they forty-footers or twenties? Fully loaded or part loads?'

Adams, who was a child when it came to the composition of lorry-loads, scratched his head. 'Well, how much a bottle, then?'

Kelly gave the sort of disgusted look that would result if someone broke wind at the vicar's tea-party. 'I don't deal in bottles.' There was a silence and Kelly sighed. 'Look,' he said, more reasonably, 'if it's a forty-footer – double loaded – that's forty to forty-eight pallets. Say nine cases on a pallet, that's twelve bottles a case; so, four hundred cases of Scotch. I can knock them out wholesale for about fifteen, twenty quid a case. Say seven-and-a-half large per motor – thirty large for the four – you want me to bring the motors up and go on the plot as well?' He paused while he worked out some tricky calculations in his head. 'I reckon, on a good day, you'll get a drink of five or six grand.'

'Five grand!' echoed Adams. He had been looking for the Holy Grail and here he was, ending up with hardly a pot to piss in.

Kelly was disinterested. 'Yeah, about that. Take it or leave it, pal, but that's your corner, provided everything's A1 at Lloyds.'

'I dunno, Brian.' Adams shook his head. 'I'll have to think about it.'

Kelly patted him on the shoulder with one ham-like hand. 'You do that. If you do want to go to work, here's my number. Come on, I'll drop you back at the Cross.'

Several days passed and Adams did give the matter a great deal of thought. Certainly his cut was not the sort of El Dorado he had anticipated but he could munch his way through an awful lot of whizz with five or six grand. So he telephoned Kelly, told him the job was on and arranged to meet him at a service station on the A1 a few days later, so that Kelly could see the compound.

Adams got into Kelly's Mercedes at the service station. 'Just direct me to the compound, Roy,' said Kelly, as he started the engine. 'I've got to work out where the motors are going to be laid down, before we get grafting.' After they had parked up, they skirted the perimeter fence.

'Where you going in, then?' asked Kelly.

Adams pointed. 'Over there, by them trees. I came down here the other day and tested the fence to see if I could cut it. No problem.'

'Yeah?' Kelly raised his eyebrows. 'And what happens if they find the wire's been cut?'

'No worries, Brian,' replied Adams, confidently. 'The security here's bollocks, mate. It's just for show. I told you; my bird's old man worked here.'

Kelly stiffened as he noted the change of tense. 'What d'you mean *worked*? I thought he was giving you the word on the four lorry loads?'

'Yeah, he told me about the night just before he packed the job in. He told me they come in every Thursday between nine and ten.'

'But you were supposed to wrap up the night watchman in his hut – I thought it was your bird's old man?'

'No, Brian,' replied Adams. 'See, it's some old geezer; fuck me, he won't be no trouble! If he plays up, I'll fucking belt him, like – fuck me, he's only an old geezer.'

Kelly grunted. 'Right.'

'Anyway, Brian, there is another thing,' said Adams, nervously. 'I'm going to need a hand in there to help tie him up.' There was a slightly longer pause. 'See, well, Tony was going to give me a hand, but he's bottled it.'

Kelly spun round as though he'd been stung. 'You – *WHAT!* You told that little cunt O'Neill about the job? You must want your fucking head tested!'

'Tony's OK, Brian,' replied Adams, desperately. 'He's sweet – he's just bottled it, that's all!'

'Tony's not fucking sweet!' roared Kelly. 'He's on fucking bail! The moment we go in that compound, the fucking filth will be all over us!'

'No, Brian, honest!' pleaded Adams. 'It's sweet, mate!'

301

Kelly shook his head. 'It stinks to me, pal.'

'Honest, Brian, stand by me,' wailed Adams, seeing five grand disappearing right in front of his eyes. 'It's fine!'

Kelly sighed, expelling the air in his lungs with a hiss. Again, he shook his head. Quieter now, he said, 'I must need my fuckin' head examined for even talking to you. Right – this is what you do. Don't tell O'Neill we met today. Tell him I phoned you up and fucked you on the price and you're still looking for a buyer; then we'll have to get the job done quick.'

'Right, Brian,' replied Adams, excitedly. 'This Thursday, then!'

'Thursday it is,' agreed Kelly. 'But Roy – you took a fucking liberty telling O'Neill. That was plain fucking stupid. And I meant what I told you to say to him on the phone. I *am* fucking you on the price. Your corner is down to four and a half. Got it?'

Adams bent his head, penitently. 'Yes, Brian.'

The following Thursday, the plan was fully operational. They met at the same service station and Kelly had brought with him a man, whom he briefly introduced as 'Steve'. It was his job, explained Kelly to drop them off near to the compound. From there, Kelly and Adams would walk the half-mile across the fields until they reached the cover of the woods, from where they would force entry to the compound. Steve would go on to where the four tractor units and drivers were waiting, ready to receive Kelly's signal that they had overcome the night watchman and had opened up the compound's gates. After Kelly and Adams had used the service station's toilets to change into boiler suits for the raid, they checked that they both had ski masks and Adams displayed bolt croppers to cut through the fence, a large sheath knife to frighten the night watchman into docility and a length of rope with which to bind him.

The tail lights of Steve's car disappeared into the distance and the two men trudged across the fields, stopping every so often to ensure that they were not being followed. It was a moonless, November night, bitterly cold, and their breath blew white plumes into the air.

They reached the perimeter fence without incident. Adams pulled out a half-bottle of Scotch. 'Want a nip, Brian?' He giggled, momentarily. 'Be more of that soon, mate!'

Kelly shivered. 'It's fucking cold up here,' he muttered and pulled on his ski mask.

'You soft southerners can't take it, Brian,' chuckled Adams and giggled again. It felt so good to be working with a professional, although the giggling could have been attributable to the fact that it had been five or six hours since he had stuffed his face in a bag of whizz and the effect was wearing off. He pulled on his ski mask and then cut through the perimeter fence.

Within an hour, in the distance, they saw four sets of lorry headlights approaching the compound from the direction of the A1. Kelly checked his watch. 'It's nine fifteen.'

'That's them, Brian,' replied Adams, excitedly. 'It's on, mate!'

It took just over an hour for the switch to take place, followed by the statutory break period. Two of the drivers sat in the hut with the night watchman, warming themselves by his gas heater and sipping his tea. Just before ten thirty, the last lorry pulled out of the compound. 'Give it an hour, Roy,' said Kelly, 'just to make sure that no more come in and that them other ones don't come back, neither.'

'Right, Brian,' replied Adams, adding, 'I'm fucking buzzing, mate!'

Kelly had spent nearly three hours scanning the area, looking for any hint whatsoever of police activity. There were no cars cruising past the compound, nothing. He was satisfied. It was midnight when he turned to Adams and said, 'Well, Roy – what d'you reckon?'

'Yeah!' breathed Adams. 'Let's do it!'

'Right, I'll ring Steve and tell him to get the motors moved up closer – they're about ten minutes away.' He picked up his mobile phone – they were in their infancy then, and this one was the size of a house brick – and dialled a number. 'Steve, it's me. Them fings'll be available in about fifteen minutes, mate; get the air up.'

(This was a reference to the fact that heavy goods vehicles need to have their engines running to produce air in the brakes. Depending on the age of the vehicle it can take a few minutes to reach the right pressure and permit the vehicle to move.)

Pulling back the fence wire, Kelly and Adams crept into the compound, and up to the parked lorries, stopping at each to see if they could detect movement either from the night watchman or the drivers of the vehicles. There was none.

They were ten yards from the watchman's hut; then seven; then five. They crept nearer. The dim glow of light from the hut came from the watchman's portable television; he was slumped in his armchair. Adams slowly drew out the sheath knife. The watchman was oblivious to their presence. He didn't stand a chance. And neither did the intruders.

'*ARMED POLICE, STAND STILL!*' suddenly screamed a very authoritative voice and, at the same instant, police flood lamps, which had been rigged to the compound's security lighting, instantly illuminated the entire area.

Men in uniform dashed from the rear of the four lorries towards them and someone roared, '*ON THE GROUND – N-O-O-W!*'

Kelly dropped flat to the ground, where he was handcuffed, dragged to his feet and led away. Adams simply froze and four or five police officers leapt on him, dragging him to the ground where he was similarly handcuffed.

Between then and the resultant trial, two things happened.

Firstly, Tony O'Neill went to court and pleaded guilty to the offence of possessing drugs with intent to supply. Before passing sentence, the judge was very interested in the content of a letter which the officer in the case handed to him. In all the circumstances, the judge felt that justice would be best served by sentencing O'Neill to two years' imprisonment – the sentence being suspended for two years.

And secondly, just before packing up, selling his house and moving with his family to an unknown destination, he sent Adams' girlfriend a message. It said, simply, 'Tell Roy we're even.'

Adams pleaded not guilty to incitement to commit robbery and, deprived of his normal, vast amounts of whizz, became more and more unglued as the trial progressed. He had a fairly eminent Queen's Counsel representing him, one who was doing quite a creditable job, but Adams declared that he was a wanker and sacked him. It was a mistake. Wanker or not, eminent QCs can pull things out of hats, undreamed of by their clients, but by defending himself and stating publicly that the judge was bent, Adams confidently thought he would secure victory. He thought wrong. As he was dragged down to the cell passageway, having just been sentenced to six years' imprisonment, he screamed to the judge, 'You fucking wanker! You're all cunts! I hope you get cancer and die!'

In a voice nowhere near as bellicose as Adams', the judge demanded that the dock officers return the prisoner before him.

'For that outburst, I shall add twelve months' imprisonment to your sentence for your flagrant contempt of court,' he said quietly, but firmly. 'You have no counsel to speak for you or mitigate on your behalf and frankly, even if you had, it would be a pointless exercise, as I can bear witness to your complete contempt of this court. The twelve months will run consecutively to your sentence, making a total of seven years' imprisonment. However, I shall spare you the ordeal of listening to what I have to say next; take him down.'

In the silence which followed, the judge addressed the senior police officer who was in overall charge of the case, asking him to pass on his commendation in respect of the officer who had done so much to bring about Adams' downfall.

He was referring to the police officer who, during the trial had used a different entrance and exit from everybody else in the proceedings and who had given evidence from behind a screen, where he was visible only to the judge, barristers, jury and the defendant.

In fact, the judge (plus everybody else in the proceedings) was unaware of the officer's true particulars; throughout the trial, they had referred to him as Brian Kelly.

Bibliography

BALL John, CHESTER Lewis and PERROTT Roy	*Cops and Robbers*	André Deutsch 1978
BEVERIDGE Peter	*Inside the CID*	Evans Bros Ltd 1957
CLARKSON Wensley	*Public Enemy Number 1: The Life and Crimes of Kenneth Noye*	Blake Publishing 1997
CLARKSON Wensley	*Killing Charlie*	Mainstream Publishing 2004
FABIAN Robert	*Fabian of the Yard*	Naldrett Press 1950
FABIAN Robert	*London After Dark*	Naldrett Press 1954
FORBES Ian	*Squadman*	WH Allen 1973
FRASER Frank and MORTON James	*Mad Frank – Memoirs of a Life of Crime*	Warner Books 1995
GERAGHTY Tony	*Who Dares Wins*	Little, Brown 1992

Bibliography

GOSLING John	*The Ghost Squad*	WH Allen 1959
GREENO Edward	*War on the Underworld*	John Long 1960
HIGGINS Robert	*In the Name of the Law*	John Long 1958
HILL Billy	*Boss of Britain's Underworld*	Naldrett Press 1955
HINDS Alfred	*Contempt of Court*	Bodley Head 1966
HOGG Andrew, McDOUGALL Jim and MORGAN Robin	*Bullion: Brinks-Mat: The Story of Britain's Biggest Gold Robbery*	Penguin Books 1988
KIRBY Dick	*The Squad – A History of the Men and Vehicles of the Flying Squad at New Scotland Yard 1919-1983*	Unpublished manuscript 1993
KIRBY Dick	*The Real Sweeney*	Constable & Robinson 2005
KIRBY Dick	*You're Nicked!*	Constable & Robinson 2007
KRAY Reg	*Villains We Have Known*	Arrow Books Ltd 1996
LINNANE Fergus	*The Encyclopedia of London Crime and Vice*	Sutton Publishing 2003

Bibliography

LUCAS Norman	*Britain's Gangland*	WH Allen 1969
MASSINGBERD Hugh (Editor)	*The Daily Telegraph Fourth Book of Obituaries – Rogues*	Pan Books 1999
MILLEN Ernest	*Specialist in Crime*	George G Harrap & Co. Ltd 1972
MORTON James	*Gangland Today*	Time Warner Books 2002
MORTON James and PARKER Gerry	*Gangland Bosses – The Lives of Jack Spot and Billy Hill*	Time Warner Books 2005
MURPHY Robert	*Smash & Grab*	Faber & Faber 1993
PEARSON John	*The Profession of Violence*	Panther Books 1977
PROGL Zoe	*Woman of the Underworld*	Arthur Barker 1964
READ Piers Paul	*The Train Robbers*	WH Allen & Co. 1978
SPARKS Ruby and PRICE Norman	*Burglar to the Nobility*	Arthur Barker 1961
WICKSTEAD Bert	*Gangbuster*	Futura Publications 1985
YOUNG Winifred	*Obsessive Poisoner*	Robert Hale 1973

DICK KIRBY

has also written

Rough Justice

'He treats criminals the only way they understand. His language is often shocking, his methods unorthodox.' NATIONAL ASSOCIATION OF RETIRED POLICE OFFICERS MAGAZINE.

'His style of writing pulls no punches and he tells it like it is. Highly recommended.' POLICE HISTORY SOCIETY JOURNAL.

'Real *Boys' Own* stuff, this. Tinged with a wry sense of humour makes this an excellent read.' METROPOLITAN POLICE HISTORY SOCIETY.

'*Rough Justice* is a fast-paced, amusing and enjoyable read, full of absorbing crime stories.' SUFFOLK JOURNAL.

The Real Sweeney

'Everyone's talking about *The Real Sweeney* . . . Tough, fast-paced and funny, this one's a must.' LONDON POLICE PENSIONER.

'His reflections on the political aspect of law enforcement will ring true for cops, everywhere.' AMERICAN POLICE BEAT.

'Its no-nonsense portrayal of life in the police will give readers a memorable literary experience.' SUFFOLK JOURNAL.

'. . . these are the real-life accounts of a tough London cop.' DAILY EXPRESS.

You're Nicked!

'Dick Kirby . . . gives a gruelling, gritty, yet funny look at life on the front line against crime.' ROMFORD RECORDER.

'It's full of dark humour, tense busts and stand-offs. As crime rates rocket, this book will go down well.' DAILY SPORT.

'A great read with fascinating stories and amusing anecdotes from a man who experienced it all.' SUFFOLK NORFOLK LIFE MAGAZINE.

'*You're Nicked!* is a gritty series of episodes from his time in the Met – laced with black humour and humanity.' EAST ANGLIAN DAILY TIMES.